1992

Wild Animals and American Environmental Ethics

Early days in Yellowstone. Courtesy, Yellowstone National Park Photo Archives.

Wild Animals and

American

Environmental Ethics

Lisa Mighetto

The University of Arizona Press
TUCSON

The University of Arizona Press
Copyright © 1991
The Arizona Board of Regents
All Rights Reserved
♾ This book is printed on acid-free,
archival-quality paper.
Designed by Amy Evans
Manufactured in the United States of America.

96 95 94 93 92 91   6 5 4 3 2 1

Library of Congress Cataloging-in-Publication Data
Mighetto, Lisa, 1955–
    Wild animals and American environmental
ethics / Lisa Mighetto.
        p.   cm.
    Includes bibliographical references and index.
    ISBN 0-8165-1160-8. — ISBN 0-8165-1266-3 (pbk.)
    1. Human-animal relationships—United
States—Philosophy.   2. Animal rights—United
States.   3. Wildlife conservation—United
States—Moral and ethical aspects.   I. Title.
QL85.M54   1991
179'.3—dc20   91-16910
                                        CIP

To Frank

I think I could turn and live with animals, they are so
    placid and self-contain'd,
I stand and look at them long and long.

WALT WHITMAN, "SONG OF MYSELF"

CONTENTS

Preface   xi

Acknowledgments   xiii

Prologue   1

1. Science and Sentiment: *Animals in the "New School" of Nature Writing*   9

2. Wilderness Hunters and Bird Lovers: *Early Motivations for Wildlife Protection*   27

3. The New Humanitarianism   42

4. The Barbarisms of Civilization: *An Analysis of Humanitarian Protests*   53

5. Working Out the Beast: *American Perceptions of Predators*   75

6. Biocentrism: *A New Ethic for Wildlife*   94

7. New Directions for Protection   107

Epilogue   119

Notes   123

Select Bibliography   147

Index   167

Photographic Essay   following page 74
*Nature Writers · Hunters · Market and Pot
Hunting · Humanitarians and the Treatment
of Animals · Wildlife in the National
Parks · Predator Control · Illustrations
of Predators*

PREFACE

For over a century, American conservationists have been working to protect animals. This book concerns their motivations. From the beginning of the conservation movement, Americans have had different incentives for saving wild creatures. Today, as in the nineteenth century, many conservationists argue that animals should be protected because humans find them useful. Others claim that animals have intrinsic worth apart from their usefulness to people. This book emphasizes the development of the latter view.

Because most of the ideas examined here are new to the Western world, they have only a small number of advocates. The notion that animals have rights, for instance, is not widely accepted, even by conservationists. Still, mere numbers of advocates cannot measure the significance or effectiveness of an idea. There were only fifty-six signers of the Declaration of Independence, yet they started a nation. Although the abolitionists of the 1830s and 1840s were also few in number, they became an especially visible, vocal force that contributed to the onset of the Civil War. Similarly, most of the animal lovers discussed in this book represented a minority—and sometimes eccentric—position. Even so, they were among the first Americans to reject the human centeredness that has pervaded Western thought. By encouraging people to view animals as something more than conveniences or objects for amusement, they helped forge a revolutionary way of looking at the natural world—one on which the modern environmental movement is based.

The sources used for this book, then, convey a strong message. Much of my evidence is drawn from the writings of animal lovers who hoped to convince Americans that wild creatures should be saved from abuse, slaughter, or extinction. Written for a general audience, these publications were often lively, humorous, and entertaining. They can also appear proselytizing, even strident in tone—and some readers might find them to be wrongheaded or offensive. In any case, my intention here is to place the ideas discussed in this book in historical context; the views examined do not always coincide with my own.

Moreover, my sources cannot always be accepted as scientifically accurate. The portrayals of animals examined in this book often appear romantic or unrealistic—but that is not the point. I am more interested in how Americans have *perceived* wild creatures than in the actual habits and behaviors of animals. Like the writer Edward Abbey, who once claimed that the only birds he could identify were the turkey vulture and the fried chicken, I am not a wildlife biologist. How animals have affected the American imagination is of greater concern here. My subject is the development of values and ethics, which are human constructs. This book, then, is more about people than it is about animals.

What follows is not a study of the depletion of wildlife populations. Nor is this book devoted to the construction of policies or organizations to save them. Instead, I am interested primarily in the *arguments* used to protect animals. The word "conservation" is used in its most general sense here, to indicate the desire to defend wild creatures—as individuals or as species. This is a history of how attitudes toward wildlife have changed over the last hundred years, and, more importantly, of how new values and ethics regarding the animal world have emerged.

ACKNOWLEDGMENTS

Moving around the West by degrees, I incurred many debts. During my undergraduate years at the University of California, Santa Barbara, Roderick Nash encouraged my interest in environmental ethics. In the master's program at Arizona State University, L. Christian Smith offered further support. At the University of Washington, George K. Behlmer, John Findlay, William J. Rorabaugh, and Lewis O. Saum read initial drafts of the manuscript and provided valuable advice. Morgan Sherwood of the University of California, Davis, also read a chapter. I am especially indebted to Alfred Runte, who has extended many kindnesses to me during my years in Seattle. After guiding me through my Ph.D., he continued to urge me to write and publish. He and his wife Christine have included me in several train trips; they helped me see the environment of the West from a new perspective.

Recently, my colleagues in the Department of History at the University of Puget Sound have encouraged me. On the topic of wildlife, Thomas R. Dunlap of Texas A&M University has shared his ideas and research with me in a generous spirit. Tom has provided more than historical guidance; he is also a good hiking and birding companion.

For this project, I have consulted a variety of archives. These include the state historical libraries of Alaska, California, and Washington, the Rare Books and Manuscripts Collection at the Boston Public Library, the Library of Congress, the Newberry Library in Chicago, the Library of the California Historical Society in San Francisco, the Bancroft Library and Museum of Vertebrate Zoology at the University of California, Berkeley, the Huntington Library in San Marino, and the John Muir National Historic Site in Martinez. I have appreciated the efforts of their staffs.

For my research on John Muir, the Holt-Atherton Center for Western Studies at the University of the Pacific in Stockton was particularly valuable. Stephen Zimmer, Director of Museums at the Philmont Scout Ranch in Cimarron, New Mexico, provided information concerning Ernest Thompson Seton. On the subject of Jack London, Sara S. Hodson of the Huntington Library and Russ Kingman of Glen Ellen were helpful. Mary Vocelka, formerly of the Yosemite Research Library, provided *Yosemite Nature Notes* as well as aid in locating numerous photographs of animals. Similarly, Jim Peaco guided me through the wildlife illustrations in the Yellowstone National Park Photo Archives. Bob Ardren of the John and Mable Ringling Museum of Art in Sarasota, Florida, helped me obtain circus posters. My brother, George Hawkins, also assisted me in locating photographs.

Portions of three chapters have appeared in the *Pacific Historical Review*, *The Pacific Historian*, the *Environmental Review*, *Sierra*, and *The Alaska Journal*. My thanks to the editors of these journals for allowing me to reprint my ideas here.

Most importantly, I owe a special debt of gratitude to my husband, Frank L. Mighetto, whose enthusiasm for the outdoors and interest in environmental issues have inspired me throughout my adult life. He has taken me on wilderness excursions all over the world, continually reminding me how I became interested in environmental history in the first place. I will always be grateful.

PROLOGUE

Appreciation of animals is nothing new. Celebrated thinkers ranging from Pythagoras to Leonardo da Vinci to Montaigne expressed not only an interest in wild creatures but also a concern for their welfare. In the United States, however, it was not until the last hundred years that an urban population, far removed from the processes of the natural world, could afford to romanticize and cherish wildlife. Moreover, the late nineteenth century was unlike previous eras both in the larger number of people who devoted considerable energy to this topic and in the content of their arguments, most of which drew from science. When Charles Darwin published *The Origin of Species* in 1859, the link between humans and animals became difficult to deny. During the decades that followed, numerous American writers explored how this revelation would change the nation's treatment of other creatures.

These writers were well aware of the uniqueness of their time. The popular journals of the late nineteenth and early twentieth centuries abounded with articles concerning the need for an expansion of ethics to include the animal world. A contributor to *Harper's Weekly*, for example, explained that the "scientific research" of his era had prompted a "changed attitude of civilized man toward the non-human species." Another commentator agreed that knowledge of evolution "lowered our pride of exclusiveness," while an article in the *Arena* claimed that "what science reveals of our common relationship and origin" has required humans to revise their conduct toward "the entire animal creation."[1] On both sides of the Atlantic, the word "new" was often evoked: one Victorian detected the emergence of a "comparatively modern social manifestation," which he labeled "the New Humanitarianism." Similarly, advocates of "The New Ethics" adopted "The New Charter."[2] Although there was confusion regarding the meaning of these terms, subscribers to the new ethics agreed that humans should exercise restraint in their use of animals.

This sympathy would have seemed strange indeed to the first white settlers in the New World. For the most part, colonists had little regard for other creatures. From New England to Georgia, they especially abhorred wild animals. According to one description of colonial Virginia, the land had been "possessed and wrongfully usurped by wild beasts, and unreasonable creatures."[3] Puritans, too, found the "howling wilderness" to be "hideous and desolate"; the inhabitants of the New England woods were thought to be "hellish fiends."[4] Unfamiliar animals, particularly predators, were bound to frighten colonists who were struggling for their very survival. But the Puritan fear of wild beasts went far beyond mere concern for physical safety. To them, wilderness represented an amoral void that harbored the agents of the devil. Because they associated order with godliness, Puritans viewed the wilderness—which was chaotic and uncontrolled—as a place of evil. Wild creatures posed a spiritual threat.

Domestic animals did not fare much better in the seventeenth-century estimation. Early restrictions against their mistreatment were largely utilitarian in nature. In 1641, for instance, a law in Massachusetts prohibited "tyranny or cruelty towards any brute creatures which are usually kept for the use of man."[5] Certainly the wording here focuses on the interests of humans. In sum, the Puritans' ideas concerning inherent depravity and human insignificance did not dampen their conviction, upheld by Genesis 1:28, that animals exist only to serve and be used by people.

Nor did this attitude change during the Enlightenment of the eighteenth century. During this period, an emphasis on reason and order produced an appreciation of cultivated landscapes. Wild animals, on the other hand, were not valued by most Enlightenment thinkers, who continued to fear the chaos and haphazardness that the wilderness represented. Despite an increasing interest in cataloging the physical details of fauna exemplified by Mark Catesby and William Byrd, there was little concern for the animals themselves, let alone for their protection or preservation. While Enlightenment thinkers no longer viewed nature as being innately evil, they valued it most where humans could impose control.[6]

Beginning in the late eighteenth century, Romanticism encouraged a different posture toward the animal world. This movement, characterized by an attraction to mystery and chaos, pervaded intellectual life in nine-teenth-century America. Romantics looked favorably upon wilderness and its occupants; they emphasized the awe rather than the fear that uncon-trolled environments inspired. Although many Romantics continued to accord humans the central position in nature, a few writers and artists—such as William Cullen Bryant and Thomas Cole—either downplayed people and their works or omitted them altogether.[7] But most Romantics had no desire to experience wilderness or wild animals firsthand. Ralph Waldo Emerson, for instance, was interested in unspoiled nature because he believed it was a conduit through which humans could establish contact with a higher reality. As an exponent of Transcendentalism, an offshoot of the Romantic movement, Emerson was more concerned with the spiritual than the material world. Rarely did he write about the physical aspects of nature.

That task was left to Henry David Thoreau. From 1845 to 1847 this disciple of Emerson put Transcendental ideals into practice by living in the woods at Walden Pond. Here he recorded the wild animals he en-countered. Like Emerson, Thoreau hoped that his painstaking examina-tion of the details in the natural world would yield spiritual knowledge. "The fact," he wrote, "will one day flower out into a truth." Sharing Emerson's notion that nature is emblematic of the spiritual world, Tho-reau did not venerate animals for their own sake; instead, he had found an aesthetic use for them. Still, his writing conveyed a deep sympathy for wild creatures which was unusual in the mid-nineteenth century. It was the "character" of the animal that interested Thoreau, "not its clothes and anatomy." Contact with wildlife, he wrote in *Walden*, "is to make my life more rich and eventful."[8] During his day, however, Thoreau was not widely read; it would take a generation for his enthusiasm for wild na-ture to filter down to the popular level.

By the end of the nineteenth century, rapid industrialization fueled the Romantic love for wilderness. As contact with the natural world became a rare experience, urban Americans began to value it. Because they feared that their society was becoming too developed, an increasing number of city dwellers turned to the outdoors, sparking the nation's first "Back to Nature" movement.[9] John Muir, a mountaineer and a pop-ular nature writer, observed this trend in his book, *Our National Parks*:

"Thousands of tired, nerve-shaken, over-civilized people are beginning to find out that . . . wildness is a necessity," he claimed. "Awakening from the stupefying effects of the vice of over-industry and the deadly apathy of luxury, they are trying as best they can to mix and enrich their little ongoings with those of Nature, and to get rid of rust and disease."[10] Wilderness, then, was especially appealing to those who worried that Americans were becoming too soft in the cities. For many urban dwellers, contact with animals—the embodiment of the wilderness— became a way to regain their lost vitality.

In linking animals and humans, Darwinian science seemed to support the notion that life in cities was unnatural and debilitating. Seizing this theme, such writers as Jack London and Maximilian Foster reveled in the wildness and invigorating savagery of their animals. Meanwhile, Frederic Remington and Ernest Thompson Seton captured the frenetic energy of wildlife in their paintings, which frequently featured such seemingly fierce creatures as wolves.

More often, however, popular portrayals emphasized the lighter side of animal kinship to humans. Reversing the Jekyll and Hyde motif, writers and artists demonstrated that beasts are like people. In fact, late-nineteenth-century cynics noted that animals depicted in popular writing were becoming more amicable and virtuous than many humans; the peaceable kingdom, it seemed, had arrived. While such anthropomorphism was not in itself unique to the late nineteenth century, new characteristics of expression emerged during this period. First, literary and artistic works were presented increasingly from the animal's point of view. While the intention, like that of Aesop, might have been to inspire and instruct humans, the focus was on the animal. If they appeared at all, people occupied the sidelines. Second, writers and artists themselves ventured into the natural world, primarily to observe *living* creatures. Lastly, popular depictions often argued against the mistreatment of animals.

Works about wildlife were changing in volume as well as in form. Never before had the general public been so widely exposed to this genre; animal stories and essays were especially prevalent in popular journals. By 1880 inexpensive postage and the use of the rotary press had increased the number of national magazines, some of which came to boast circulations of a million.[11] These presented natural history to lay readers in terms they could understand.

This increasing regard for wildlife culminated in the desire for protection. Sportsmen were among the first to protest the wanton destruction of animals. So significant were their efforts that one historian has credited them with spearheading the conservation movement.[12] Yet the rationale of sportsmen was almost wholly utilitarian; alarmed by the rapidity with which game animals were disappearing, hunters, for the most part, were more concerned with the continuation of their sport than with the welfare of individual creatures or species.

Nineteenth-century humanitarians, on the other hand, deserve greater attention for their concern for wild animals than they have thus far received from historians. For all the recent debate concerning the "animal liberation" movement, very little has been written about early humanitarian interest in wildlife. Like the hunter-conservationists, this small but vocal group protested the wholesale slaughter of western animals; the humane point of view was in fact represented in such conservation organizations as the Audubon Society. However, humanitarians objected to killing animals not because it was wasteful to humans but because it inflicted pain. Drawing their inspiration from English thinkers, they established sentience as the basis for protection. As science closed the gap between humans and other animals, humanitarians had further ammunition for their cause. Some went so far as to question our right to interfere at all with the lives of other creatures.

But this burgeoning goodwill was not extended to predators. Hunters and humanitarians were united in their rejection of meat-eaters. Although a few farsighted individuals pointed out the value of carnivores, most conservationists favored elimination of animals who were inconvenient or who failed to comply with their standards of morality. Reactions to predators, then, can measure how much attitudes had actually changed; even humanitarians—whose position concerning animals represented a radical intellectual departure from traditional thought—stopped short on this issue. For all their rhetoric concerning enlightened treatment of animals, most nineteenth-century Americans continued to require that animals be useful and well behaved.

Certainly it would be inappropriate for this study to condemn people of the last century for their apparent inconsistencies or their failure to assume modern views. It was not until predators gained acceptance in the 1920s and 1930s, however, that an entirely new ethic regarding animals could emerge. As scientists revealed the necessity of predation, animal lovers began to use ecological precepts to question longstanding assumptions about human centeredness.

To some observers, this shift in perspective signals nothing less than a second Copernican Revolution. Just as sixteenth-century science removed the earth from the center of the universe, discoveries of the last hundred years have displaced humans from the center of the biosphere.[13] Yet old attitudes die hard. Anthropocentrism is crumbling, but it has not collapsed; recent studies have demonstrated that most Americans do not subscribe to a biocentric view of the world.[14] Although nearly all of the sources used for this book—stories and essays, newspaper editorials and letters, humanitarian promotional literature—were widely available to educated readers, the authors were not representative of the general public. Aside from the personal papers of several naturalists and humanitarians, the evidence here focuses on writing intended for a popular audience. But reading John Muir's essays—in the nineteenth or twentieth centuries—was different from embracing his ideas.

Even the most eloquent writers cannot eliminate the tenacious hold of attitudes from centuries past. Our society continues to mistreat animals, perhaps owing to a lingering fear of the impulses they arouse. Numerous creatures—predators in particular—are viewed more in symbolic than realistic terms.[15] The persistent hatred of the wolf, for instance, is reminiscent of the Puritan line of thinking, which held that wild creatures represent a danger to man's spiritual welfare. So complex are modern perceptions of animals that one exasperated zoo director recently characterized them as being "hopelessly and perversely inconsistent."[16] Yet it is important to remember that our ethics regarding other creatures are still developing. As one early twentieth-century observer reminded his readers: "the question of our behaviour towards animals is a comparatively recent one."[17]

Part of the problem is that the moral systems of the variety of animal-protection groups are not understood. A *Seattle Times* reporter recently complained that the "same people who recoil from hunting deer, shooting ducks, or trapping muskrats blithely . . . poison slugs in their vegetable gardens, and spray-bomb aphids on their rose bushes."[18] Skeptics often ask animal-rights advocates how they can eat plants in good conscience. Such puzzlement was expressed at the turn of the century as well, when tongue-in-cheek essays argued for "vegetable rights."[19]

Exasperation at the apparent illogic of humanitarians stems from a failure to recognize their preoccupation with sentience—and the more informed among them are prepared to disprove the notion that plants can feel. Peter Singer, a leading philosopher of Animal Liberation, seems willing to exclude creatures without complex nervous systems.[20] Some conservationists, on the other hand, wish only to preserve species diversity; they do not object to meat-eating or hunting. Compounding the confusion is the fact that the boundary between the two positions is not always distinct. Sometimes concerns for ecosystems and animal pain overlap.

Additional difficulty arises from our definitions of the term 'animal'. We use the same word to denote a variety of creatures, including mammals, reptiles, fish, insects, and amoebae. Yet the labels we use for other creatures "can skew our moral responses to them," as a *Newsweek* article noted. We might mourn the death of a pet mouse, while simultaneously setting traps to kill "pest" mice in the kitchen.[21] For the purpose of simplification, the word 'animal' in this book excludes humans.

That such discussion could occur at all indicates that animals have become a significant topic. A hundred years ago, most Americans would have been astonished at the recent debates regarding wildlife. Since the nineteenth century, however, arguments against sport hunting, fur wearing, the confinement of wild animals, and the destruction of wildlife habitat have increased in number and volume. The intensity of this opposition suggests that values in our society are indeed changing.

1

Science and Sentiment

ANIMALS IN THE "NEW SCHOOL"
OF NATURE WRITING

If we chose to let conjecture run wild, then animals . . . may partake of our origin in one common ancestor—we may be all melted together.
CHARLES DARWIN, NOTEBOOK OF 1837

If we are only a little higher than the dog, we may as well make the dog out to be as fine a fellow as possible.
H. W. BOYNTON, *Atlantic Monthly*, 1902

Until recent years, no period in United States history displayed more enthusiasm for the outdoors than the late nineteenth and early twentieth centuries. During this time nature study became a popular pastime for an increasingly urban population. But it was more than the "Back to Nature" movement which sparked American interest in animals. Darwinian science, affirming the close relation between man and beast, had prompted the desire to learn more about the latter. Popular nature writing, particularly that which focused on animals, obliged this curiosity for Americans who had neither the ability nor inclination to get to the wilds themselves. The new genre, however, provided more than mere description of animals; numerous authors also defended the notion that evolution is a positive force in a benevolent universe—against what seemed to be evidence to the contrary.

The darker implications of Darwinism had produced despondency among intellectuals on both sides of the Atlantic. "We are crushed and trampled on remorselessly by the movement of nature," mourned one Victorian, "and our feelings count for nothing." Another noted gloomily that "Nature means one vast whirlpool of war, death, and agony." Even Emma Darwin, wife of the great naturalist, worried that "the course of all modern thought is 'desolating.'" Throughout the late nineteenth century, articles expressing this dismal tone appeared in popular journals with unnerving frequency. *Outlook*, for instance, characterized the spirit of the age as one of despair and pessimism. An article in the *Nineteenth Century* agreed that people were becoming more cynical and indifferent; even children appeared to "sneer oftener than they smile."[1]

Science, many observers suspected, was responsible for this malaise. "The worthlessness of life," the sociologist E. A. Ross wrote in 1891, "is an idea that agrees with science" and "meets the mood of the age." To him, the implications of biological theories—particularly those of Charles Darwin and August Weismann—were bleak, leaving mankind with nothing "mysterious, nothing unique, nothing divine." Human history, it seemed, has been governed solely by the struggle for existence.[2] Proving the natural world to be amoral, arbitrary, even cruel, science stripped man of his illusions, setting him adrift in a void. The emphasis on strife in Charles Lyell's *Principles of Geology* (1830), for instance, had inspired Alfred, Lord Tennyson's ominous lines:

> *Man, her last work, who seemed so fair,*
> *Such splendid purpose in his eyes,*
> *Who rolled the psalm to wintry skies,*
> *Who built him fanes of fruitless prayer,*

> *Who trusted God was love indeed*
> *And love Creation's final law—*
> *Though Nature, red in tooth and claw*
> *With ravine, shrieked against his creed—*[3]

At the end of the century, literary naturalists on both sides of the Atlantic reinforced this view, depicting man as a helpless, inconsequential creature, subject to the whim of natural forces. Moreover, Darwin's theories, linking humans and animals, led to frightening speculation concerning man's bestial nature; other creatures, after all, could be ferocious and uncontrollable. Such American writers as Stephen Crane, Frank Norris, and Theodore Dreiser portrayed the animality of their characters in an unflattering light. In his *Strange Case of Dr. Jekyll and Mr. Hyde*, Robert Louis Stevenson, too, explored the primal brutality lurking within a seemingly civilized man.

A few authors of animal stories shared these grim interpretations. The favorite theme of Maximilian Foster, for instance, was survival of the fittest; nearly all of his portrayals—presented under such titles as "Terror" and "Tragedy"—ended in death. Even his deer, traditionally a gentle creature, became "a wild, remorseless destroyer," whose eyes had acquired "a red, ugly gleam." And life was no easier for predators: Foster's coyote experienced "continual torment."[4] Jack London's animals, too, were sometimes savage brutes. In his stories, however, life in the wilderness was not tragic for those creatures that survived. Anxieties concerning the enervating quality of urban living account at least in part for the popularity of his writing; it was the vitality of London's characters that made them attractive.

Yet a very different picture of the animal world was offered by a variety of popular writers who asserted that wild creatures—and by extension, humans—were not the victims of indifferent, uncontrollable forces. Releasing their readers from the dismal universe that science had exposed, many nature writers provided, through firsthand observation, evidence of dignity, beneficence, and morality in the wild. Readers responded enthusiastically to this interpretation. Sales of books by John Muir and Ernest Thompson Seton, most of which portrayed nature as a benign force, were unusually high.

Contemporary critics recognized that the appeal of wildlife writing had increased greatly at the turn of the century. Nearly every issue of most popular magazines featured at least one animal story or essay. So prevalent had this genre become that it received "unlimited space in the Sundays and monthlies."[5] Reviewers noted also that animal lore had changed; placing the modern animal storyteller in the "new school" of nature writers, they explained that the "present-day interest" was predicated on accuracy of detail. Much of the writing in the "new school" was neither fiction nor strictly factual. Seton, a Canadian whose animal stories were widely read in the United States, represented this recent trend in nature writing. His animal characters, he explained, were "composites" of actual creatures.[6]

Although not all wildlife authors had formal training in the sciences, many could boast extensive experience observing in the field. Seton ventured to remote places to encounter animals; his wilderness excursions included a six-month trip to the Arctic in 1906. Muir, the most celebrated nature writer in the West, spent numerous seasons in the wilds of Alaska as well as in the Sierra. These two, along with numerous authors who have since sunk into obscurity, enjoyed close contact with the animal world—and their writings drew from their experiences in the wilderness.[7]

Their approach, however, was not strictly empirical. Although the genre is difficult to define, Dallas Lore Sharp, himself a turn-of-the-century nature writer, claimed that he and his fellows differed from mere scientists in their spirituality and emotion. John Burroughs, the nation's best-known nature writer during this period, was especially adept at portraying the facts of animal life in a lyrical manner. What made Burroughs's writing so appealing, offered one reader, was his "sympathetic observation joined with a love of expression." Muir's followers, too, admired his ability to merge "scientific accuracy with poetical expression." This combination, according to a review in the *Independent*, had never been seen before.[8]

Late-nineteenth-century nature writers did share one commonality with the tradition of Aesop: in downplaying the ferocity of animals, they focused on traits that resembled those of admirable humans. But what distinguished these authors from their predecessors was the insistence that their animal portrayals were true to life. "[My] animals," Seton asserted, "were all real characters. They lived the lives I have depicted, and showed the stamp of heroism and personality more strongly by far than it has been in the power of my pen to tell." Moreover, unlike his contemporary, Rudyard Kipling, Seton professed to write "from the animal's viewpoint"; humans were "excluded wholly or reduced to a faint accessory." His aim was to convey how the animal "lives and thinks and feels." Being difficult to substantiate, this claim was bound to get Seton and his fellow animal biographers into trouble.[9] Another quality separating turn-of-the-century authors from the long tradition of nature writers which preceded them was their deep sympathy for individual animals, which often culminated in pleas for protection.

Certainly the creatures portrayed by the "new school," like those of Aesop, served to inspire and instruct. But these later animals also disputed the grim implications of science. Esteem for man, it seemed, could be restored through his association with "virtuous" animals—a possibility which nineteenth-century critics greeted with interest. H. W. Boynton, a reviewer of nature books, perceived that "when, not so very long ago, man waked up to the fact that he was mere mammal, he began to cast about to see what could be said for his nearest relations." Because "we are only a little higher than the dog," he concluded, "we may as well make the dog out to be as fine a fellow as possible."[10] Numerous writers did exactly that.

Animal stories of the period usually featured refined, noble creatures. Seton, for instance, was always careful to point out the honorableness of his characters. A fox in his popular *Wild Animals I Have Known* offered her offspring poisoned meat to save him from the debasement of being chained—and Seton implied that she later committed suicide to escape her "sorrowful life." His famous "pacing mustang" likewise chose death over suffering captivity.[11] The new nature writing, then, allowed readers to project their perceptions and anxieties onto actual animals.

Although the details of Seton's stories were discounted by a variety of critics, he continually swore that all his writing was rooted in fact. A gifted artist as well as a writer, Seton earned a reputation as a competent field naturalist. While working on his four-volume *Lives of Game Animals*, he received the John Burroughs Medal for nature writing—an indication of his wide appeal. Moreover, scientists praised his two-volume study, *Life-Histories of Northern Animals*. Upon its publication, Frank M. Chapman, a curator of the American Museum of Natural History, announced that "Seton has done for mammals what Audubon did for birds but he has done it better." Yet *Life-Histories* also discussed animal suicide.[12] If a scientist of Chapman's reputation could respect Seton's work, then it is not surprising that general readers accepted his fanciful tales as accurate. Many of Seton's followers were urban dwellers who were unfamiliar with life in the wilderness. They found the nobility of Seton's animals to be an appealing characteristic of his writing.

Nor was Seton the only author who exaggerated and exalted the actions of wild creatures. Noble animals appeared frequently throughout the popular books and magazines of the late nineteenth and early twentieth centuries. In addition to animal suicide, topics included "animal chivalry" and "animal marriage." Charles Roberts, another Canadian whose works were read widely in the United States, suggested that even a bee is capable of a "sturdy spirit" which forbids "ignominy." His gander received further elevation, being described as "a gentleman in feathers."[13] Like those of Seton, Roberts's animals were not degraded brutes but highly sensitive beings with aesthetic sensibilities.

Related to this attempt to impart dignity to animals was the insistence upon their individuality. The increasing tendency of scientists to consider animals—and more disconcertingly, humans—merely in terms of species drew criticism from their ranks as well as from lay observers. In *Science* magazine, for instance, an anatomist asserted that "there is as distinct and characteristic an individuality in [animal] natures as in that of human creatures."[14] Olive Thorne Miller, author of voluminous bird books, also pointed out the uniqueness of her subjects. The "undying charm of bird study," she explained, "lies in the individuality of these lovely fellow creatures, and the study of each one is the study of a unique personality, with characteristics, habits, and a song belonging exclusively to itself. Not even in externals are birds counterparts of one another." Thus, she concluded in another article, "it is not safe to judge [a] species 'en masse.'"[15]

Other nature writers supported Miller's notion. An entire chapter in Florence A. Merriam's *A-Birding on a Bronco* was devoted to uniqueness. Perhaps the most vociferous defender of animal individuality was William J. Long, a Congregationalist minister and prolific writer of animal stories up through the 1930s. He announced that "there is no such entity as a species, which is merely a group of individuals."[16] Even such a widely revered nature writer as John Muir argued that each animal is essentially different from his fellows. Mills's observations of individual animals in the Rocky Mountains included "Mrs. Squirrel" and "Dr. Woodpecker, Tree Surgeon." Although frankly sentimental, his writing was based on extensive experience in the high country of Colorado. Mills learned about the individuality of wild creatures while living in a log cabin in the Rockies. His writing, like Seton's, appealed both to adults and to children.

Observations concerning individuality allowed animal biographers to portray wondrous, exceptional creatures who sometimes strained the limits of credibility. Seton's "Redruff," for example, was "the biggest, strongest, and handsomest" of partridges. His ram was still more impressive:

"Krag must have been the idol of his band. For matched with rams he had seemed a wonder, and among ewes, his strength, his size, and the curling horns must have made of him a demigod, and the winged heart and the brimming cup were his."[17] In fact, the title of his book *Animal Heroes* indicates Seton's interest in the uncommon. William J. Long, too, was careful to imbue all his animals with extraordinary traits. In one sense, the emphasis of these authors upon the superior animal corroborates Darwinian theories concerning the survival of the fittest; Seton in particular pointed out that the weak often perish. More likely, however, their portrayals served a counter purpose: the possibility of stupendousness among the animals helped lift them—as well as their human analogues—above the status of mere brutes.

With the same end in mind, writers about animals also focused upon intelligence. Throughout his stories, Seton stressed the wit of his creatures. However, their wisdom was not innate; most of them had been "taught" survival skills, either by their mothers or by leaders like Silverspot, who organized and "drilled" his fellow crows. That Long harkened to a similar theme is evidenced by the title of his book, *School of the Woods*. Numerous essayists supported the notion of animal education. Effie Bignell, for one, claimed to have witnessed a "'little squirrel lady'" training her offspring. Likewise, Ernest Ingersoll—whose veracity in animal reporting would later be commended by President Theodore Roosevelt—described "morning lessons" in nut hunting. A respected bird watcher, Olive Thorne Miller also depicted a variety of teaching endeavors, including a music lesson. Another celebrated writer who discussed animals teaching their young was Gene Stratton Porter. Considering herself to be well versed in natural history, she produced numerous popular novels in which nature was employed as a significant backdrop. In addition, Porter wrote such articles as "The Birds' Kindergarten," indicating her interest in animal intelligence.[18]

Under man's tutelage, creatures could be taught more advanced subjects. At the turn of the century, horses and dogs purported to have learned mathematics and spelling sparked a considerable amount of comment in popular journals. Today's interest in Koko, the gorilla who communicates by sign language, is reminiscent of that generated a century ago by animals trained to count and talk. Although the Elberfeld horses—or their owners—were discredited by such skeptics as John Burroughs, the number of articles concerning Clever Hans and Muhamed indicated a sizable following in England and the United States. Such creatures soon found their way into fiction; Jack London portrayed dogs with "mathematical" minds who were taught "shorthand speech" by humans.[19]

John Muir, a naturalist of great credibility, also portrayed some domestic animals as being "notably sagacious." In *The Story of My Boyhood and Youth*, Buck, for instance, "seemed to reason sometimes almost like ourselves." While at feeding time the other cattle had to have their pumpkins split open for them, this resourceful ox crushed them himself with his head. Another ox who lived by his wits was given to "opening all the fences that stood in his way to the corn-fields."[20] Not only do animals think, concluded an article in the *Literary Digest*, "but they plan and scheme."[21]

Such fascination with animal intelligence can be explained in terms of the popular reaction to scientific materialism. Americans of the late nineteenth and early twentieth centuries did not want to believe that behavior is dictated solely by what Muir called "blind instinct"; nature writers assured them that reasoning accounts for the survival of most animals. Furthermore, during the 1890s, a bitter debate erupted between followers of August Weismann, the German biologist who asserted the importance of heredity, and neo-Lamarckians, who emphasized external condition. Because Weismannism appeared more deterministic, many Americans embraced the latter view.[22]

William J. Long noted that these two issues were linked. "Most people think that the life of a wild animal is governed wholly by instinct," his preface to *School of the Woods* reads. "They are of the same class who hold that the character of a child is largely predetermined by heredity."[23] Much of Long's work was in fact devoted to refuting their contention. Although the abstruse ideas of scientists did not radiate down to the popular level in pure form, writers like Long represented a counterforce to intellectual currents generated by nineteenth-century science. In sum, Americans found the premise that the development of an animal or plant could be affected by externalities comforting; it provided the feeling that they were in control and could improve their lot through changing their environment. It is significant, then, that Long presented intelligence not as an inborn but as an acquired quality.

Long's emphasis upon animal reason went far beyond that of his contemporaries. His article titled "Animal Surgery," published in 1903, recounted observations of animal behavior that were unusual to say the least. Here he told of a muskrat who, after amputating his trapped leg, smeared the wound with gum. Bears, Long explained, also use clay to heal themselves. Even more striking was his account of a woodcock he discovered plastering a mixture of mud and grass upon its broken leg. After allowing the clay bandage to harden, the bird flew away, good as new.[24] Needless to say, this assertion—presented in all seriousness—outraged scientists and provoked a storm of protests from wildlife authors, who feared that Long would undermine the credibility of all amateur observers.

William Morton Wheeler, a Harvard biologist, was among the leaders of the attack. Particularly disturbed by Long's woodcock story, he denied, in *Science* magazine, that a bird could understand the properties of clay, let alone bone-setting techniques. "Could the creature have been captured," he sneered, "we venture to affirm that he would have been eligible to a chair in surgery in one of our leading medical schools, and a phenomenally rapid progress of the science would have been insured." Long's article, in Wheeler's estimation, was not only devoid of scientific merit, but was "bad even as fiction."[25] Not one to take criticism lightly, Long immediately shot back, citing numerous witnesses to animal doctoring similar to those reported in his article. One of these claimed to have presented another woodcock with a self-bandaged leg to a physician, who "upon examining it expressed himself in a most emphatic way by saying that it was a better job than nine tenths of the surgeons could do."[26] The debate raged on until the exasperated editors refused to print anything further on the subject.

Meanwhile, Burroughs entered the controversy. Distinguishing between "real" and "sham" natural history, he denounced Seton and Long for misleading their readers.[27] Animals, he argued, are creatures of instinct. During the dispute, Burroughs noted, in an attempt to disallow the notion of animal reason, that intelligence is indicated by language. Later, Long produced a book entitled *How Animals Talk*. So vehemently did Burroughs contest the idea of intelligence that he disturbed his friend John Muir, who had noticed evidence of reason among animals.[28] Moreover, Burroughs recognized that the accentuation of animal individuality permitted embellishment and exaggeration; after all, if no two animals are alike, it is difficult to discount the word of any observer, however preposterous it may seem.

Other nature writers took the opportunity to vindicate their genre. Dallas Lore Sharp, for instance, was quick to dissociate himself from Long's brand of nature writing. Poking fun at Long, he lamented that the author had seen "quite so much with his own eyes, for many of us live the year round in the woods, and—well—most of our animals must have gone over into Mr. Long's woods."[29] Flagrantly outstepping the bounds of fact, Long thus incurred the scorn not only of scientists but also of his fellow nature writers.

The most prominent figure to become involved in the debate was Theodore Roosevelt. A naturalist in his own right, the president, echoing Burroughs, derided Long as being "the yellow journalist of the woods" who wrote only about "story book beasts." As a hunter, he was especially incensed by Long's account of a wolf that bit through the chest of a caribou, reaching the animal's heart and killing him instantly. Long's woodcock article was another source of irritation to the president. It "seems a pity," he observed, "not to have added that [the bird] also made itself a crutch to use while the splint was on." Referring to those who romanticized wildlife as "nature fakers," Roosevelt asserted the importance of accuracy in natural history.[30] Always ready to defend himself, Long retorted in the *New York Times* that the president was merely a game butcher, whose "literary style" was in any case "fit for the wastebasket."[31]

Nor were Seton and Long the only sentimental nature writers. Reviewers frequently, albeit gently, chided Olive Thorne Miller for stretching the facts.[32] Similarly, Gene Stratton Porter's portrayals of wildlife, based on her observations of the outdoors, were frankly moralistic. Certainly she received heavy reproof from critics of literature, who dismissed her work as "molasses fiction." Porter, however, differed from Seton and Long in that she did not insist too loudly that her animals were true to life.

The president's participation in the nature faker controversy attests to its magnitude. Frank M. Chapman of the American Museum of Natural History suggested that the argument revealed a growing interest in animals among general readers. "From an insignificant smudge," he wrote, this issue "has become a roaring blaze and its sparks are kindling throughout the land." Sympathetic readers were quick to defend the animal biographers: "Children and mere lovers of nature," offered one woman, "owe no small debt to men like William J. Long." In the writer's defense, she poignantly noted that his anecdotes were no more incredible than those of Darwin. Certainly Long's impact on his readers was enduring. To this day, the writer has retained a following; when he was in office, former president Ronald Reagan stated that Long's *Northern Trails* had been his favorite childhood reading.[33]

Similarly, reviewers defended Seton's work throughout his career. According to a *Dial* critic, it was the human qualities which Seton imparted to his animals that were responsible for his "well-deserved popularity." William T. Hornaday, director of the New York Zoological Park, also praised him: in a review of *Wild Animals I Have Known*—a book which Burroughs claimed should have been entitled *Wild Animals I ALONE Have Known*—he pronounced Seton's work "altogether fine." Hornaday in fact was becoming weary of "the same old annual parade of toothless and decrepit stories of fierce wild cats, aggressive pumas, dueling bears and alligators, and child-stealing eagles."[34] In other words, like many Americans, he wanted to read stories that muted the struggle for existence.

Popular nature writers thus stressed what Burroughs called "universal beneficence." Animals, they argued, are not engaged in grim competition; cooperation is the first rule of the natural world. Turn-of-the-century nature essays were filled with examples of altruistic birds rescuing fellows with broken wings and rodents bringing food to aged or blind relatives. This kindness was not limited to members of the same species. In the *Atlantic Monthly*, E. P. Evans, a linguist who had taught at the University of Michigan, described a rat who brought daily offerings of corn kernels to a lame dove. Long, too, cited numerous instances of animals aiding each other. In a statement that exemplifies his penchant for hyperbole, he likened wild beasts to "the cherubim."[35] Although

Seton conceded a degree of death and terror in the wild, many of his stories featured a maternal tenderness that was frequently extended to the young of different species. In fact, "wild adoption" was a prevalent theme in the works of both Seton and Long.

Although the extent to which these writers were influenced by the ideas of Prince Peter Kropotkin is difficult to determine, their benign animals are similar to those presented in the Russian thinker's *Mutual Aid* (1902). Emphasizing cooperation, Kropotkin's book was intended to counter the bleak assertions of Thomas Henry Huxley—"Darwin's bulldog"— concerning competition and conflict in the natural world. Like Kropotkin, John Muir was dismayed by the notion that wild creatures are embroiled in a struggle for existence. "We gaze morbidly . . . upon our beautiful world," he lamented, "and see ferocious beasts and wastes and deserts." Liberty Hyde Bailey, author of *The Holy Earth*, also assured readers of the cooperation among wild creatures. A retired professor from Cornell University, Bailey enjoyed considerable notoriety for his horticultural studies. He reached a wide audience when he refuted "the almost universal opinion that nature exhibits [a] merciless and relentless struggle."[36]

To prove their point, a few popular naturalists looked to the creatures who had reputations for bloodthirstiness. Their special fondness for wolves led Seton and Long to produce story after story depicting the compassion of these animals. In his essays, Muir, too, vindicated rattlesnakes as well as bears, noting their timidity and gentleness. Even seemingly aggressive bugs received consideration: among spiders, according to Olive Thorne Miller, "there are instances of gregarious living, as well as of small spiders being not unwelcome guests in the web of larger ones."[37] If, on the other hand, it appeared impossible to mitigate the ferocity of carnivores, some nature writers simply omitted them from their studies.

When they were discussed, predators were dismissed as aberrant villains, as in the case of Mabel Osgood Wright's *Birdcraft*. This book suggested that one species of hawk "is a worthy target for rifle practice." In *Citizen Bird*, Wright, president of the Connecticut Audubon Society, explained that she was interested only in "well-behaved birds." Meat-eaters would not become widely acceptable to nature writers for another half a century. That Wright believed in the benignity of most creatures, however, is evidenced in her book, *The Friendship of Nature*.[38]

In their negation of strife, a few nature writers went so far as to deny that animals suffer pain. "I never saw one drop of blood, one red stain," Muir declared, "on all this wilderness." In his writing, wild creatures rarely suffered. Muir's ouzel, the subject of one of his best-known essays, died without "gloom," vanishing "like a flower, or a foam-bell at the foot of a waterfall." Another of his favorites, the Douglas squirrel, was depicted as being "as free from disease as a sunbeam."[39]

William J. Long provided the most poignant example of this tendency. "The animals which perish under the teeth and claws of other beasts meet a merciful end," he assured his readers. Victims "perish instantly for the most part." Viewed in this light, Long's account of the wolf that so quickly killed the caribou assumes a significance unnoticed by the critical Roosevelt. Burroughs himself stressed the absence of pain in the natural world, claiming that "tooth and claw usually overwhelm by a sudden blow, and sudden blows benumb and paralyze." For all his criticism, Burroughs was in sympathy with the motives of the nature fakers, if not with their tactics. Especially toward the end of his life, much of Burroughs's writing refuted the notion that nature is cruel. "As a whole, the universe is all good," he observed in his last book.[40]

These writers, then, attempted to assuage the pessimism of their age by demonstrating that it had no basis in the natural world. To Muir, the wilderness was full of "happy" birds and beasts. Even his grasshopper was a "jolly fellow," full of "glad, hilarious energy." In the life of this insect, "every day is a holiday; and when at length his sun sets . . . he will cuddle down on the forest floor and die like the leaves and the flowers, leaving no unsightly remains for burial." Other writers shared Muir's sunny view. Long, for instance, proposed to write "animal comedies" to discount the charge that life in the woods is tragic. The linguist E. P. Evans supported this position, claiming that wild creatures possess a sense of humor and can even "appreciate a practical joke."[41]

They sought also to dispel the fear that nature is chaotic, haphazard, and amoral. In his Romanes lecture (1893), Thomas Henry Huxley unveiled a godless universe where ethics counted for nothing: "the wicked," he observed, "flourishes like a green bay tree, while the righteous begs his bread." Concluding his address, the hard-bitten Darwinist claimed that "the ethical progress of society depends, not on imitating the cosmic process, still less in running away from it, but in combating it." This idea, according to Holmes Rolston III, a modern-day ethicist, influenced several generations "who frequently concluded that ethics had nothing to do with the laws of nature unless it was to alter and overcome our natural instincts and drives, lest we too behave 'like beasts.'"[42]

Turn-of-the-century nature writers, on the other hand, set about to find morality in the wild. Seton especially was concerned with this task. "Conventionality and social rules," he claimed in 1901, are not "silly man-made tyrannies. They are really important laws that, like gravitation, were here before human society began, and shaped it when it came." Although in Seton's writing vice was "not by any means limited to the human race," his stories illustrated that "bad" animals are punished in the wild.[43]

Other nature writers supported the notion that animals have moral perception. "Bird courts," wherein guilty creatures are arraigned and executed by their fellows, were a popular subject. E. P. Evans reported an experiment in which a goose's egg was placed in the nest of a stork. When the "questionable progeny" hatched, the stork husband, who had been "thrown into the greatest excitement," returned to the nest with nearly five hundred storks. These birds, Evans claimed, held a "mass meeting," where they were "addressed by several speakers, each orator posting himself on the same spot before beginning his harangue." Concluding their deliberations, the storks pounced on the unfaithful female and her hapless gosling, killing them both. In addition to valuing "conjugal fidelity," animals, Evans pointed out, possess a "lively sense of what is lawful."[44] That such an absurd interpretation of goose behavior could be featured in the *Atlantic Monthly*, a major journal, is revealing. As a linguist affiliated with the University of Michigan, Evans appeared to be a reputable source of information. His reassurances of order appealed to readers who were nervous about violence in the wild.

Pursuing this theme in "The Natural History of the Ten Commandments," Seton demonstrated that traditional virtues have a place in the process of natural selection. Using the rhetoric of Darwinism, he explained that the most "successful" animals are obedient, honest, and monogamous. Furthermore, the higher animals, according to Seton, possess a sense of a "superior power." This idea was explored more extensively in a fable published in *Century* magazine, which described a pair of phoebes whose trust in an "invisible power" saved them from a variety of "devils." In the late nineteenth and early twentieth centuries, the possibility that animals had souls in fact became a lively topic of discussion among observers of the animal world.[45]

Evidence of animal spirituality allowed nature writers to argue that the natural world, far from being pointless and amoral, contains purpose. It is no accident that many popular naturalists, including Dallas Lore Sharp and William J. Long, were clergymen. As such, they opposed the erosion of spirituality provoked by late-nineteenth-century science. Still, neither Sharp nor Long rejected the notion of evolution; they were concerned instead with establishing the fact that order existed. Even Burroughs, less moralistic than his contemporaries, maintained that nature is not arbitrary: "I am persuaded that there is [a Cosmic Mind or Intelligence] in the universe, pervading every atom and molecule in it," he wrote in the *Atlantic Monthly*. Muir, who embraced the "truths of evolution," also detected an "Intelligence that laid out the plan."[46]

The acknowledgment of order in the wild, coupled with the previously discussed assertions of animal individuality and intelligence, led to speculation concerning the responsibilities of humans. In other words, if we are not simply the victims of chaotic external forces or uncontrollable inner impulses, we are then capable of restraint and are accountable for our actions. Nature writers applied this point to human abuse of the natural world; nearly all of their works contained pleas for the protection of wildlife.

Popular natural history writing thus became a means to enlist reader sympathy. In one sense, the anthropomorphism that riled critics, earning authors like Long the epithet "nature faker," served to drive home the point that man and animal are related. However, nature writers reversed the macabre Jekyll and Hyde theme: rather than portraying man as beast, they tried to demonstrate that beasts are like men. Many of the drawings accompanying Seton's stories emphasized the humanlike qualities of animals, a propensity which often annoyed reviewers. "Man has nothing that the animals have not at least a vestige of," Seton explained.[47] Likewise, the titles of Olive Thorne Miller's books, *The Bird Our Brother* and *Little Brothers of the Air*, indicate her attempt to link animals and men. In *Citizen Bird*, Mabel Osgood Wright also suggested that wild creatures are no different from human residents of the country; similarly, her *Four-Footed Americans and their Kin* featured "horse and cow people."

Muir, too, demonstrated the relationship between man and his "horizontal brothers." He believed that "any glimpse into the life of an animal quickens our own and makes it so much the larger and better every way." One of his most popular tales involved the dog Stickeen, who accompanied him on a harrowing excursion across an Alaskan glacier. As night was falling, the two encountered an enormous crevasse, passable only by means of a precarious ice-sliver bridge. At first reluctant to follow Muir across, the terrified dog finally reached the opposite side of the chasm. Safe at last, he "ran and cried and barked and rolled about fairly hysterical in the sudden revulsion from the depths of despair to triumphant joy." This shared ordeal, continually recounted for admirers, taught Muir that animals are "friends and fellow-mortals indeed"; like Wright, he argued that they are "fellow citizens."[48]

Animals, these authors agreed, should be treated accordingly. Seton in particular was concerned with the abuse of wild creatures. "Since . . . animals are creatures with wants and feelings differing in degree only from our own, they surely have rights," his preface to *Wild Animals I Have Known* reads. "My chief motive," he explained in another book, "has been to stop the extermination of harmless wild animals." As its title suggests, *Lives of the Hunted* undertook to familiarize readers with the creatures that humans destroyed for sport or profit.

In 1917, James Oliver Curwood would be just as direct. His article "Why I Write Nature Stories" explained his desire to discourage readers from hunting.[49] A former hunter himself, Curwood hoped that his writing would convince Americans to view animals as worth saving. His anti-hunting pleas, which appeared in such publications as *Good Housekeeping*, reached a large audience. Today, Curwood's portrayals of mistreated wild creatures remain compelling; in 1989 Columbia Pictures released the film, *The Bear*, based on Curwood's book, *The Grizzly King*. Both tell the story of an enormous bear who is relentlessly pursued by a hunter. Although the man wounds the grizzly, he is unable to kill the elusive animal. At the climax of the story, the bear catches his assailant unawares and unarmed. As the two confront each other face to face, the hunter recognizes that he is doomed. To his astonishment, however, the bear simply walks away from the confrontation. While the grizzly had every reason to attack the hunter, he was a peaceful creature who preferred not to fight. The point here was that the bear was an inherently "good" animal who deserved to live. The hunter, on the other hand, had acted badly. He leaves the scene a reformed man.

Like Curwood, Muir attempted to instill respect for wildlife through his writings. The *Story of My Boyhood and Youth* offered numerous sympathetic portraits that urged people to "put their animal fellow mortals in their hearts instead of on their backs or in their dinners." Gene Stratton Porter, too, hoped to make readers aware of the need for wildlife protection. In *The Song of the Cardinal*, her story of bird courtship, the animals are indistinguishable from the human characters—a tactic that met with readers' approval. "If the Audubon Society should circulate thousands of copies of this work," one review ventured, "it would do far more to revolutionize public sentiment than the exposure of the same amount of money in dry arguments or heated protests."[50] In other words, readers were receptive to endearing portrayals of animals; emotional stories made them care about the plight of wild creatures.

For this reason, popular naturalists avoided purely factual accounts. Lay readers did not want to be bothered with—or further threatened by—the bleak implications of science. As Long pointed out, the public was not concerned with "the fur and feathers that clothed the Wood Folk," but with "the spirit that animated them." One of Porter's characters espoused a similar view, advising readers not "'to bother none 'bout the discoveries of science.'" Disconcerted by this tendency in nature writing, Burroughs attempted an explanation. "Science is impersonal and cold," he wrote, "and is not for the heart but for the head. The heart symbolizes so much for us, it stands for the very color . . . of life, for the whole world of sentiment and emotion—a world that lies outside the sphere of science."[51]

While Darwinism seemed to lower the status of humans, nature writers—and nature fakers—thus raised the status of animals. In doing so they indirectly shifted the position of humans in the natural world. For centuries, people had believed that animals existed solely for their benefit. By the turn of the century, however, wild creatures had become, in the words of one author, "almost human."[52] From this point on, it would be increasingly difficult to justify mistreating them.

2

Wilderness Hunters and Bird Lovers

EARLY MOTIVATIONS FOR WILDLIFE PROTECTION

Wild beasts and birds are by right not the property merely of the people today, but the property of the unborn generations, whose belongings we have no right to squander.

THEODORE ROOSEVELT, QUOTED IN GEORGE BIRD
GRINNELL'S "AMERICAN GAME PROTECTION"

Theodore Roosevelt was the best-known proponent of wildlife conservation in his day. He was also the nation's most famous hunter. Today, many animal lovers would find that a strange and unappealing combination. Indeed, among environmentalists, it is becoming increasingly fashionable to be against hunting. Although sportsmen are included in such organizations as the Audubon Society, Sierra Club, and Earth First!, they are continually criticized by other members. One of the most aggressive groups to oppose hunting is The Fund for Animals. Its members actually meet sportsmen in the wild, in the hopes of convincing them to refrain from killing animals. This tension is not new; in the United States, organized protests against blood sports emerged in the late nineteenth and early twentieth centuries. Hunting, however, is not antithetical to conservation. A hundred years ago, much of the groundwork for the protection of wildlife was laid by sportsmen. Their call for conservation was conveyed through a variety of hunting journals, including *American Sportsman, Forest and Stream, Field and Stream,* and *American Angler*— all of which were founded in the 1870s and 1880s. Some hunter-conservationists were particularly concerned about birds; the Audubon Society was founded by a sportsman.

What pushed hunters and bird lovers toward conservation in the late nineteenth century was an alarming decline in wildlife populations. Especially poignant was the destruction of the passenger pigeon and the buffalo—two species which had been usually profuse when the nation was founded. Most Americans had come to view their supply of game as being endless. Indeed, one of the most striking features of the New World was its abundance of animals. Rarely did the written accounts of the first European settlers fail to marvel at the number and variety of wild creatures. This perception of cornucopia was remarkably resilient; attempts throughout three centuries to impose limitations on hunting had been sporadic and ineffectual. As late as the 1850s, the supply of passenger pigeons was considered to be inexhaustible.[1]

Not until the late nineteenth century could anyone have predicted that this species would one day be extinct. So lavish were the numbers of passenger pigeons that a single flock, recorded by John Josselyn in 1673, appeared to have "neither beginning nor ending"; so dense were the birds that he "could see no sun." As settlement spread west for the next two centuries, descriptions remained exuberant. The ornithologist Alexander Wilson observed a flight in 1806 which spanned forty miles and contained two billion birds. Similarly, during a roost witnessed by John James Audubon in 1813, the passenger pigeons arrived "by thousands, alighted everywhere, one above another, until solid masses as large as hogsheads were formed on the branches all around. . . . It was a scene of uproar and confusion." A century later, John Muir would portray these birds in a more poetic light. "The beautiful wanderers," he remembered, "flew like the winds in flocks . . . so large that they were flowing over from horizon to horizon in an almost continuous stream all day long, at the rate of forty or fifty miles an hour, like a mighty river in the sky, widening, contracting, descending like falls and cataracts, and rising suddenly here and there in huge ragged masses like high-plashing spray."[2]

Buffalo, too, were numerous. Before white settlement there were an estimated sixty million roaming the continent. Nor were these animals limited to the plains; they were found in the trans-Appalachian frontier as well. Such abundance had aided the expansion of the country. Not only did the availability of wild meat advance western settlement, but animals with valuable fur, hides, and plumes provided an important source of income as well.[3] Yet overuse of wild creatures began at the outset of white occupation. As early as 1650 nearly all the beaver of New England had been trapped out; by the late 1830s these animals had become scarce even west of the Rocky Mountains. Similarly, the turkey and deer populations along the eastern seaboard were seriously impaired by human encroachment. Most of the damage to wildlife had been, and still is, caused by loss of habitat through such activities as farming, logging, and mining. The introduction of exotics like the German carp and the English sparrow also crowded native species.

Direct killing, however, was responsible for much of the destruction of wildlife. Passenger pigeons in particular were harvested in exorbitant numbers during a very short period. Their density, similar to that of the bison, made them easy targets. While passenger pigeons were occasionally shot, more often they were first captured in nets; one dramatic catch, lasting several weeks, yielded over a billion birds. By 1878, when the final nesting colony was wiped out, the population of the species had dropped below the critical mark.[4] Martha, the last surviving passenger pigeon, died in the Cincinnati zoo in 1914. Several years earlier, Muir noted with considerable bitterness that these "bonnie creatures" brought a mere "cent apiece" in New York markets.[5]

Just as poignant was the large-scale slaughter of the buffalo. Access to these animals was provided by transcontinental rail lines which not only brought hunters to the West but also carried the meat, and more importantly, the hides back to eastern markets. Railroad construction had separated the buffalo into northern and southern herds. By the mid-1870s, few animals remained south of the Platte; the less accessible herd of Dakota, Montana, and Wyoming was destroyed after completion of the Great Northern Railway.[6] Within a ten-year period, then, the immense population of bison had been wiped out. Although the overgrazing of cattle contributed to the decimation of the buffalo herds, alarmed Americans in the late nineteenth century believed that intense hunting was responsible. And while other animals, including elk and antelope, were also hunted for their marketable hides, their decline was not so abrupt as that of the buffalo.

The problem was not killing for sport, but killing for profit. Late-nineteenth-century America had provided the optimum conditions for professional hunting: a large eastern market and a relatively open West where game thrived.[7] Unimpeded by strong restrictions, market hunters supplied urban Americans with a variety of birds and mammals that seems inconceivable today. In the last century wild meat figured prominently in the diet of even those living in the cities. Fowl available for purchase in the public markets of the East included coot, loon, quail, woodcock, twenty-six species of duck, and numerous shore birds; among the mammals sold were bison, elk, caribou, antelope, big horn sheep, mountain goat, black bear, wild cat, woodchuck, porcupine, beaver, skunk, otter, muskrat, hare, and squirrel.[8]

A holiday menu from the Grand Pacific Hotel in Chicago further revealed the extent of game available for consumption: the dishes offered included "white-tailed deer (soup, boiled tongue, roast saddle, broiled steak, cutlet) . . . mountain sheep (boiled leg, roast), black bear (boiled ham, roast, ragout 'Hunter Style'), cinnamon bear (roast), buffalo (boiled tongue, roast loin, broiled steak), antelope (steak), elk (roast leg), opossum (roast), raccoon (roast), rabbit (broiled, 'Braise, Cream sauce'), jack rabbit (roast), English hare (roast)," and a variety of wildfowl. Equally spectacular were the kills that provided such meals: during a single year in California, one hunter brought nearly thirteen thousand wild animals to market.[9]

Although the precise effect of this extravagance on most wildlife populations is difficult to determine, it seemed clear to nineteenth-century critics that market hunting was immediately responsible for the decimation of the passenger pigeon and the buffalo. Because wholesale devastation is more unsettling than gradual damage, such writers as George Bird Grinnell used the "wanton butchery" of wildlife to bring the need for protection into national prominence. Grinnell, who became the editor of the hunting and fishing journal, *Forest and Stream,* had shot buffalo himself. Although he conceded that these animals (and, he might have added, the passenger pigeon) would have given way to human settlement eventually, Grinnell was harsh in his condemnation of professional hunting. The commercialization of game, he asserted, assures its extinction.[10]

William T. Hornaday, Director of the New York Zoological Park, agreed. His book, *Our Vanishing Wildlife,* published in 1913, brought the need for conservation before the public. No wild species of bird or mammal, he pointed out, "can withstand exploitation for commercial purposes." Hornaday in fact had nothing but contempt for market hunters. "The men who pursue wild creatures for the money . . . never give up," he warned. "They work at slaughter when other men are enjoying life, or are asleep." Nor did pot hunters, or those who killed for food, fare better in his estimation. Those "men who sordidly shoot for the frying pan," he claimed, do so "at the expense of the public." A crotchety and outspoken fellow, Hornaday was especially annoyed at New York City's Italian population. He characterized immigrants from Southern Europe as "guerrillas of destruction" who shot "our most useful and sweetest songsters" for the dinner pail. He worried that the "dignified chase" of legitimate game might "degenerate, as it has in Italy, to the popping of robins, sparrows and bobolinks." Like Grinnell, Hornaday believed that hunting was a gentleman's activity which should be carried out in a spirit of sportsmanship.[11]

Numerous hunters shared their concern. The subject of good etiquette in the field received an increasing amount of attention during the last half of the nineteenth century. Its chief spokesman was a well-born Englishman who had emigrated to the United States in 1813. Henry William Herbert—or "Frank Forester" as he came to be known—outlined the proper methods of gunning and angling in his two-volume *Field Sports,* published in 1848. Among the activities condemned were shooting game out of season and killing geese in the water and grouse on the ground. Also to be avoided was the use of artificial lights to lure prey as well as the practice of driving deer into the water, where they became easy targets. Moreover, Herbert indicated that the genuine sportsman was always attentive to his horses and dogs. Those who wished to dissociate themselves from the "common," destructive habits of poachers and market hunters readily adopted Herbert's "code of the sportsman." Drawing from the tradition of Izaak Walton, his message thus appealed to gentleman hunters who lamented the crass materialism of the Gilded Age.[12]

But Herbert offered more than English hunting values to American sportsmen. He urged also that they band together to protest the mercenary destruction of game. The men who did so possessed money and position. The Boone and Crockett Club, for instance, was founded in 1888 by Roosevelt and Grinnell. This wildlife conservation group wielded considerable political power; members included Senator Henry

Cabot Lodge and former Secretary of the Interior, Carl Schurz. Market hunters, on the other hand, could boast no such luminaries among their ranks; as a group, they exerted little political influence.[13] Moreover, sportsmen benefitted from the numerous journals devoted to their interests, for their writings helped rally supporters to the cause of conservation.

So effective were sportsmen in their efforts to protect wildlife that the historian John F. Reiger credits them with the establishment of the conservation movement. Nearly all nineteenth-century conservationists, he argues, were anglers or hunters whose concern for wildlife habitat resulted in the formation of the initial national forests and parks.[14] The Boone and Crockett Club, for instance, aided the passage of the Forest Reserve Act of 1891, allowing the president to set aside timber lands.

The most pressing concern of the Boone and Crockett Club was the management of Yellowstone Park. Established in 1872, this reserve harbored the nation's largest elk herds as well as most of the remaining wild buffalo. For years, these animals had attracted poachers, who had nothing worse to fear for their offense than confiscation of equipment and expulsion from the park. Desiring to protect large game animals, the Boone and Crockett Club lobbied for stricter penalties for poaching. Grinnell produced numerous editorials calling national attention to the problem. This concern led in 1894 to the passage of the Lacey Act, which permitted jail sentences and fines for the wanton destruction of animals in the park. John F. Lacey, an Iowa congressman and a member of the Boone and Crockett Club, constructed the legislation. Owing to the efforts of these sportsmen, Yellowstone became the nation's first inviolate wildlife refuge.[15] Appalled by the unprecedented destruction of animals in the late nineteenth century, sportsmen also sought to prohibit the sale of game. They lobbied for the Lacey Act of 1900, which involved the federal government in wildlife conservation. This law prohibited the smuggling of protected game into states without restrictions.

Historians disagree over the extent to which gentlemen hunters influenced conservation measures. Because a great number of Americans of the late nineteenth and early twentieth centuries enjoyed recreational hunting and fishing, it is difficult to substantiate the claim that these activities fostered an organized desire for wildlife protection.[16] What is clear, however, is that sportsmen during this period demonstrated remarkable farsightedness. While most Americans viewed animals as expendable commodities, organizations such as the Boone and Crockett Club at least viewed animals as worth saving.

As a co-founder of the Boone and Crockett Club, Theodore Roosevelt provides a good example of the values of the sportsman. During his presidency (1901–09) he strongly supported the conservation of forests and parks as habitats for wildlife. Roosevelt's interest in animals dated back to his childhood. As a youth, his dreams of becoming a naturalist had prompted him to establish the "Roosevelt Museum of Natural History" in his home. The young Roosevelt was especially intrigued by birds— and while attending Harvard he became a member of the Nutall Ornithological Club of Cambridge. Also while in college, he produced a list of summer birds in the Adirondacks, recording ninety-seven species.[17]

Although his career ambitions shifted to politics in the 1880s, Roosevelt persisted in his enthusiasm for natural history. His hunting stories, published on the side, provided painstaking details concerning the appearance, habits, and behaviors of animals. This interest was not limited to game, for he also included observations of songbirds in his writing. Moreover, Roosevelt's love for the outdoors was unmistakable. His books, *Hunting Trips of a Ranchman* and *Ranch Life on the Hunting Trail*, extolled not only the pleasures of the chase but also the beauty of the landscape. So developed was his appreciation of scenery that some reviewers likened him to Thoreau. According to his friend John Burroughs, Roosevelt's writing conveyed a "sympathetic insight" into the natural world.[18] This praise suggests that Roosevelt was out for more than bagging trophies.

Even so, Roosevelt's writing remained focused on hunting. Grinnell recalled that although he enjoyed discussing birds and small mammals, Roosevelt's chief concern was big game. Almost invariably, his most sensitive nature prose was followed by his desire to kill an animal—a tendency which riled critics during his day. William J. Long was not the only nature writer who objected to Roosevelt's hunting exploits. The dent's trip to Yosemite in 1903 prompted a scolding from John Muir, who asked, "Mr. Roosevelt, when are you going to get beyond the boyishness of killing things?" Similarly, political cartoons lampooned the President for his excessive shooting. But Roosevelt complained that those who protested hunting were ignorant of the essential differences between genuine sportsmen and gunners who lacked good field etiquette. The true enemies of wildlife, he maintained, were those who resorted to unfair practices to obtain their quarry.[19]

Probably there was no way that Muir could ever have convinced Roosevelt to give up hunting. The problem was that the two men, for all their mutual admiration, did not share the same worldview. Even on the surface, their portrayals of animals revealed very different qualities. While Muir conveyed a pensive, reflective attitude, Roosevelt was primarily a man of action who sought direct participation in nature. Although he devoted much space to describing the kill, rarely did Roosevelt's narrative stop to ponder the death of the animal or what it meant. Instead, his writing emphasized movement and excitement. His book, *The Wilderness Hunter,* published in 1893, closed with the regret that he had not yet had the opportunity to kill a bear with a knife, or to spear a wild pig, or to shoot an alligator by torchlight.

For all its bluster and boisterousness, however, *The Wilderness Hunter* made clear that gunning was a serious activity. Shooting game, in Roosevelt's estimation, was part of the "strenuous life" which his soft, over-civilized society needed. As industrialization increasingly drew people to the cities, it became necessary to "cultivate that vigorous manliness" that close contact with nature had once provided. Fearing that the nation might lose its vitality, Roosevelt suggested that Americans could regain the "hardihood, self-reliance, and resolution" of the pioneers through hunting in the wilderness. His own spiritual and physical health had been strengthened by contact with the outdoors—and Roosevelt had a romantic belief in the rejuvenating power of nature.[20]

To Roosevelt's mind, American men could also recapture the frontier spirit by reading narratives about the pursuit of animals. While providing vicarious hunting experiences, his writings urged readers to venture into the wilds themselves. Nor was Roosevelt the only sportsman who noticed the importance of hunting stories. In his introduction to *Hunting Sports of the West,* Cecil B. Hartley pointed out that gunning and angling books offer "a certain share of positive utility," for they encourage such characteristics as perseverance, presence of mind, endurance, "and that hardy spirit of enterprise, which has led to some of the noblest undertakings recorded in the history of our country." No western adventure story was complete without its hunting exploits. *Wild Life in the Far West,* for instance, detailed the pursuit of a "lordly bull" who was "a very giant among his fellows." Similarly, *Wild Life in the Rocky Mountains* featured a chapter entitled "An Exciting Hunt," which promised "exciting adventures with animals."[21]

The emphasis on the wilderness here was significant. Roosevelt believed that shooting animals in a game preserve was not as worthwhile as learning to survive on one's own in unfamiliar territory. It was important, too, that the sportsman find and stalk his own game. In order to deserve the title of "hunter," Roosevelt wrote, one must be able to fend for himself and to confront the difficulties of the wilderness without assistance. To complete this image of self-sufficiency, Roosevelt continually pointed out that he hunted mostly to keep his camp in meat. Hence, shooting animals was a secondary concern for Roosevelt, for he was more interested in developing the hunter's character. Accordingly, he also suggested mountaineering as one of the "manliest of sports." Roosevelt hoped that Americans with a "taste for hard work and adventure" would "attempt conquest of [the] great untrodden mountains of their own continent," for "there would be far more discomfort and danger" here than "on well-known and historic ground like the Alps." Fishing, on the other hand, had less appeal for Roosevelt than did the "rougher and hardier" sports.[22]

It was the physical challenge, then, that attracted Roosevelt to hunting. He was careful to describe the length of his excursions, as well as the bitter weather which he endured "with no tent and generally no fire." So hardy did Roosevelt become that he eventually "ceased to mind the freezing misery." His buckskin suit, worn on shooting trips, completed the image of the wilderness hunter. This was the clothing, Roosevelt explained, of Daniel Boone and Davy Crockett.[23]

Of course, much of the challenge on the hunting trail was derived from encounters with fierce animals. Roosevelt portrayed large predators as being especially hazardous—and for this reason they were among his favorite quarry. Stalking one of these beasts, he warned, required extraordinary skill and swift judgment. The rewards, however, were unequalled. In Roosevelt's writing, encounters with predators heightened the hunter's senses and his awareness of his wild surroundings. His hearing was especially acute: "Every slight noise made my pulses throb," he recalled. To Roosevelt, physical risk was an important component in reaching this state of awareness. Although he advised his readers to be cautious, Roosevelt suggested that "the keenest zest in sport comes from [the presence of danger,] and from the consequent exercise of the qualities necessary to overcome it. The most thrilling moments of an American hunter's life are those in which, with every sense on the alert, and with nerves strung to the highest point, he is following alone . . . the fresh and bloody footprints of an angered grisly; and no other triumph of American hunting can compare with the victory to be thus gained."[24]

In keeping with this theme, Roosevelt delighted in the willingness of some animals to "show fight." The bears he hunted brandished their formidable claws; they attacked with their lips drawn back and their teeth gnashing in savage snarls. Nor was shooting wild pigs an activity for lightweights. One feisty javelina, whose "teeth kept going like castanets, with a rapid clamping sound," inflicted a severe cut on Roosevelt's dog. Similarly, his wolves featured "jaws like those of a steel trap and teeth that cut like knives." Always sensitive to sounds, Roosevelt found their howling to be "sinister and dismal." The best way to hunt wolves, he advised, was to use greyhounds. According to Roosevelt, "Nothing more exciting than this sport could possibly be imagined."[25]

Roosevelt's preoccupation with the ferocity of predators was not unusual in the late nineteenth century. Many westerners exaggerated the rapacious character of these animals, in part to justify killing them. However, in Roosevelt's day there were writers—including Jack London, Ernest Thompson Seton, and William J. Long—who reveled in the wildness of the wolf. Their portrayals celebrated this animal as the embodiment of the wilderness. Although Seton hunted wolves, he regarded his quarry with respect—and after the kill, he exalted the animal in his writing. In his story, "Lobo, the King of the Currumpaw," for instance, Seton employed the theme of savagery to celebrate the strength of the wolf.[26]

Roosevelt, on the other hand, exhibited little affinity for predators. Far from exalting the wolf as worthy prey, Roosevelt denounced this animal as "archetype of ravin, the beast of waste and desolation." Because they raided livestock, wolves, in his estimation, were "criminals." Similarly, cougars were "slinking" and "cowardly" creatures. Although his assessment of bears was not nearly so harsh, Roosevelt's portrayals of these animals also could convey a striking lack of sympathy. After shooting one bear cub, he recorded that its skin was not "big enough to use for anything but a doily." Throughout the remainder of the hunt Roosevelt referred to yearlings as "doily bears."[27] Not always, then, did he demonstrate a love for his quarry.

Roosevelt's writing also revealed a streak of bloodthirstiness. His journal for the summer of 1884 included these sample entries: "Knocked the heads off two sage grouse. 12 sage hens and prairie chickens, 1 yearling whitetail 'through the heart.' 'Broke the backs' of two blacktail bucks with a single bullet. 1 blacktail black buck, 1 female grizzly, 1 bear cub, 'the ball going clean through him from end to end.'" Nor did Roosevelt seem too worried that his quarry was not always killed instantly. One disturbing passage in his book *Hunting Trips of a Ranchman* described a wounded blacktail buck running with his exposed entrails protruding.[28] These examples suggest that to Roosevelt, wild animals were merely creatures to be conquered.

But there was another side to Roosevelt's character. One of his most famous hunting exploits involved his refusal to shoot a bear cub that his friends had tied to a tree. The publicity sparked by that incident resulted in the creation of the teddy bear—a symbol of Roosevelt's benevolent and tender side. Of course, Roosevelt's conception of the wilderness hunter as rugged and self-reliant would have prevented him from shooting confined prey. Still, his concern for sportsmanship and for the protection of wildlife was unquestionably sincere. Although his writing might appear insensitive to modern readers, Roosevelt's hunting stories brought the need for conservation before thousands of readers. His highly visible, flamboyant character attracted further attention to his cause.

Like Roosevelt, many sportsmen were concerned with more than big game. In the late nineteenth and early twentieth centuries they were also interested in the conservation of birds. To this end, they joined numerous bird lovers—many of whom were women—who hoped to protect these animals from destruction. Birding had become a fashionable pastime—

especially for those living in cities. Frank M. Chapman, a curator of the American Museum of Natural History, recalled that birds were regarded as "Nature's most vital and potent expressions." For urban dwellers, they were also among the most accessible. The appeal of birds, Chapman believed, was something new. Neltje Blanchan, another bird enthusiast, agreed. "The popular enthusiasm for out-of-door life generally and for the birds particularly," she wrote in 1917, was "one of the signs of our times."[29] Increasing desire for contact with nature prompted urban Americans to look to their own backyards as well as more remote places; one advantage of bird study was that it could be conducted even in the city.

Most nature essays in fact were devoted to these animals. John Burroughs, dubbed John O'Birds, was best known for this genre; his book *Wake-Robin* was a favorite among bird lovers. Similarly, John Muir's lyrical essay on the ouzel—or the "hummingbird of the California waterfalls"—was well received by readers. Other writers, including Florence A. Merriam, Olive Thorne Miller, and Mabel Osgood Wright also encouraged their largely female readership to appreciate birdlife. Not surprisingly, interest in these animals led to an outcry against market hunting.

In the late nineteenth century birds were killed in staggering numbers to satisfy demands for food and fashion. During this period Americans could buy a wide range of fowl for their tables. Market hunting was not limited to game birds; many songbirds also were viewed as appropriate food for humans. Robins, for example, were served in soups, while cedar waxwings and goldfinches made "hearty" pies. Also available for purchase were batches of bobolinks, bundled and tied together like carrots.[30]

The millinery trade created much of the demand for nongame birds. Decorative plumes had become especially profitable at the end of the century. So extensive was the use of feathers as well as whole birds on women's hats that, according to one historian, "church gatherings and other social events often resembled aviaries."[31] This custom dated back to eighteenth-century France. There, fashionable women topped their piled hairdos with elaborate feathers and entire stuffed birds—a trend which required them to ride in carriages either seated on the floor or with their heads out the windows. By the 1890s newly created magazines like *The Ladies' Home Journal* and *Vogue* had encouraged in the United States a widespread demand for birds with attractive plumage. Among the most desirable were herons and birds of paradise. To sustain this fashion, the harvesting of these animals, according to an editorial in *Forest and Stream,* reached "tremendous proportions."[32]

In response, several organizations emerged to prevent the slaughter of nongame birds. The American Ornithological Union proposed a "model law" for their protection in 1886. This group, which was comprised mostly of scientists, developed from the Nutall Ornithological Club of Cambridge. Although several states, including New York, Pennsylvania, and Texas, adopted versions of the "model law," enforcement was difficult. Not until the Lacey act forbade illegal interstate shipment of wildlife products in 1900 did state game laws become effective.

Especially active in the campaign against plume hunting was the Audubon Society. Formed in 1886 by Grinnell, this organization boasted a larger, more general membership than the American Ornithological Union. The club grew very quickly; within two years it had attracted 50,000 people. Those who joined pledged to refrain from three activities: the killing of nongame birds, the destruction of nests and eggs, and the wearing of decorative feathers. Because he wanted to devote more time to his duties as editor of *Forest and Stream,* Grinnell abandoned the Audubon Society in 1889. By this point, however, the movement against plume hunting had gained momentum; during the 1890s individual states, led by Massachusetts, established permanent clubs. In 1905 these state organizations merged to form the National Association of Audubon Societies. To advertise its cause, the club adopted the American Museum of Natural History's journal, *Bird-Lore.* This forum for bird protectionists featured articles condemning "Woman's Heartlessness."[33]

The efforts of these organizations led to stronger federal involvement in the preservation of wildlife. Using the Forest Reserve Act, President Roosevelt in 1903 set aside Pelican Island in Florida as a refuge for egrets, pelicans, and terns. Although appreciative, the Audubon Society quickly recommended that additional federal lands important to bird populations be protected; by 1904 President Roosevelt had created fifty-one additional wildlife sanctuaries. Wardens—some of whom were hired by the Audubon Society—patrolled these lands to ensure the enforcement of game laws. In 1913 Congress passed the Weeks-McLean Act, which accorded federal protection to migratory game birds. This law granted the Bureau of Biological Survey—a precursor of the Fish and Wildlife Service—unprecedented powers of enforcement. Government-sponsored field studies also increased in number and scope. In the 1870s the ornithologist Elliot Coues had produced *Birds of the Northwest* and *Birds of the Colorado Valley* through the support of federal geological surveys.[34] By the early twentieth century more extensive field studies of birds were conducted by the Biological Survey.

To T. Gilbert Pearson, the first secretary of the National Audubon Society, these events signaled nothing less than a "reformation" in perceptions. The thoughts of Americans, he explained, "were turning from the pioneer's attitude of destroying wildlife to the present widespread desire for its preservation." Naturally, Pearson credited the Audubon Society with helping to bring about this change. He also recognized that sportsmen had offered essential support to bird lovers. As Grinnell and Roosevelt demonstrated, the two interests could overlap. What is significant about the movement to protect nongame birds is that for the first time in the nation's history, animals—even nongame species—were preserved for aesthetic reasons. Grinnell recognized this motivation in the bird enthusiasts. An "increasing number of people," he wrote, "were interested in wild life protection because these objects are beautiful to look at and ought to be preserved so that we and our successors may have the pleasure of seeing them."[35] Like Roosevelt, Grinnell thus demonstrated a rare ability to take the long view.

For all this talk of a new development in attitudes, however, Americans had retained their anthropocentric outlook. Grinnell's reference to animals as "objects" is revealing. Although wild creatures could be protected for their beauty, it was still their usefulness to humans that made them valuable. Aesthetics, Grinnell pointed out, enhance "our national well-being." Even this motivation was not enough; in selling their ideas to the public, bird protectionists often found it necessary to use economic arguments. According to Pearson, the lengthy reports of the Biological Survey concerning the relationship of birds to successful agriculture were "essential" to the Audubon Society's "educational and legislative campaign." Similarly, the monetary value of insectivorous birds was extolled by such writers as William T. Hornaday. In any case, appreciation for the beauty of animals was no less utilitarian a motivation for protection than was concern for economics. As Hornaday pointed out, wild creatures exist "partly for our benefit and partly for those who come after us."[36]

Organizations devoted to sportsmen were similarly motivated by utilitarian concerns. As conservationists, hunters, too, generally viewed animals in a manner that some environmentalists today would find offensive. To sportsmen of the late nineteenth and early twentieth centuries, animals were essentially, as Roosevelt put it, "property." Americans should protect wildlife because, in his words, "we have no right to squander" the "belongings" of future generations. Concerned only with human needs, Roosevelt argued that conservation should be limited to the "useful and beautiful" animals. Thus, as conservationists, sportsmen were not motivated by a recognition of the rights of individual creatures. Nor did they demonstrate an incipient understanding of ecosystems. As John F. Reiger has pointed out, hunters merely regarded wildlife habitat "as the necessary context of their sport." Grinnell, too, had noticed that the initial rationale for protecting wildlife was "selfish," for hunters wished to "lessen the killing of game" only "to furnish abundant sport for themselves."[37] Grinnell's words suggest that hunters were concerned chiefly with the availability of future targets. Although their actions benefitted wildlife populations, sportsmen did little to challenge traditional values regarding animals.

Of course, early conservationists must be considered in the context of the late nineteenth and early twentieth centuries. However, during this period there were Americans who valued animals apart from humans. While hunters and some bird lovers believed that animals existed for human convenience, a small but vocal group of humanitarians asserted that wild animals should be protected for reasons other than their utility. Unlike other conservationists, humanitarians viewed animals as more than objects to hunt or to admire. In doing so, they were the first Americans to expand the realm of ethics to include the natural world.

3

The New Humanitarianism

Erase sentiency from the universe and you erase the possibility of ethics.
J. HOWARD MOORE, *Better-World Philosophy* (1899)

Theodore Roosevelt identified three sources of wildlife conservation in 1913: "the true sportsman, the nature-lover," and "the humanitarian."[1] Although environmental historians have long recognized the importance of the first two groups, they have devoted little attention to the humane point of view. Because humanitarians focused mostly on domestic animals, this group is not readily associated with conservation.[2] Yet their arguments for protecting wildlife represent a significant development in attitudes toward nature, for humanitarians, unlike other conservationists, argued that animals are worthy of moral consideration. Humanitarians of the late nineteenth and early twentieth centuries challenged the assumptions regarding human superiority and dominance that pervaded Western thought. In this respect they anticipated the modern environmental movement by eighty years.

Humane concern for wild animals has been overlooked in part because it differed from the concerns of other conservationists. To be sure, at the time Roosevelt identified the three groups, the boundaries between them were not altogether distinct; when it came to the plume trade, for instance, sport hunters and bird lovers united with humanitarians in their protests. Still, shooting game and bird watching were activities consistent with what Roderick Nash has called the "utilitarian" and "aesthetic" rationales for conservation—neither of which apply to humanitarians.[3] The organizations for sportsmen emphasized the need to maintain wildlife populations to ensure that humans could continue hunting. The National Audubon Society focused on protecting attractive creatures that humans could observe. Although admirably farsighted, their conservation efforts seem today to be little more than self-serving common sense.

Humanitarians, on the other hand, were more concerned with the suffering of individual animals than with the protection of species. William J. Shultz, an early observer, suggested that what distinguished them from sportsmen was their reluctance to consider animals to be mere property.[4] Humanitarians thus broke with the Judeo-Christian tradition, established by Genesis 1:28, concerning the dominance of humans over animals. During the thirteenth century Thomas Aquinas had defended the rule of men over beasts by pointing out that animals are less godlike than humans; five hundred years later Immanuel Kant similarly had downplayed human obligations to other creatures, owing to their supposed lack of rationality.[5]

By the late eighteenth century, however, the English philosopher Jeremy Bentham had rejected traditional justifications of human dominance over other creatures. According to him, the "question is not, Can they *reason*? nor Can they *talk*? but Can they *suffer*?" Bentham's philosophy was drawn from his observation that sentient creatures seek pleasure and avoid pain. In England, then, capacity for feeling became a basis for protection of animals—wild as well as domestic. In that country the general label "humanitarian" applied to those who worried about suffering. According to the historian James Turner, such preoccupation with pain was a recent development, stemming in part from a decline in religious belief in compensation for the hardships of this world. In previous centuries pain was endured stoically in the hopes that one day those who suffered would be rewarded in heaven. During Bentham's era, tolerance for pain began to decrease markedly. The Industrial Revolution, with its emphasis on earthly gain, helped focus attention on the rewards of this life. Scientific advancements, including the introduction of ether as an anesthetic, also increased sensitivity to pain.[6] In England, this new sensibility had implications for the treatment of animals.

During the nineteenth and early twentieth centuries, American humanitarians took their cue from the English. The literature of English thinkers circulated widely among them, and English leaders helped establish animal welfare societies in the United States. Like their English counterparts, American humanitarians looked upon the infliction of suffering as morally wrong. One of the most vocal advocates of this point of view was J. Howard Moore, a high school teacher of zoology and ethics. He was convinced that our treatment of other creatures should be based on their capacity for feeling. "Erase sentiency from the universe," he asserted, "and you erase the possibility of ethics." Henry Childs Merwin, another prolific writer, agreed. He informed the large readership of the *Atlantic Monthly* that the "instinct of pity" is the "only safe judge of right and wrong."[7]

This "New Humanitarianism," as it came to be known on both sides of the Atlantic, differed from the compassion of previous eras. Although it drew the ideals of kindness and mercy from Christianity, the new movement was distinguished by a concern for animal pain. The humane creed was unique to the nineteenth and twentieth centuries; humanitarians believed that even Bentham was a man "ahead of his time."[8] Stephen Coleridge, an early observer of humanitarianism, noticed that it was a recent development. Kindness to animals "as advocated, practiced, and enforced at the present time," he noted in 1914, "is a comparatively modern social manifestation. It is, as we know it, the growth of the last century only." Nineteenth-century science prompted this change in worldview. Affirming the link between humans and animals, Charles Darwin had demonstrated that people were neither unique nor specially created. Throughout the late nineteenth century that message was brought to the general public through such journals as the *Popular Science Monthly*, which informed its readers that humans share "numerous similarities of nature" with other creatures. In his writing J. Howard Moore, too, commented on the uniqueness of his time. "Tradition is losing its power over man's conduct and conceptions as never before," he wrote, "and Science is growing more and more influential." Accordingly, humanitarians drafted a "new charter," based on the "new ethics."[9]

Although it was especially aggressive, the movement was slow to take hold. Only a small portion of the population subscribed to the new humanitarianism; most late nineteenth- and early twentieth-century Americans appeared unsympathetic. So radical were the precepts of humanitarianism that to follow them, in the words of one observer, "would be so exceedingly inconvenient."[10] Yet the literature of the movement reached a large audience. Among the publications of the American Humane Education Society, for instance, was *Black Beauty*, which sold more than two and a half million copies before 1910. Described as the "Uncle Tom's Cabin of the Horse," this book portrayed cruel treatment of animals and the need for reform. In fact, one judge found *Black Beauty* so impressive that he sentenced a man charged with overloading a horse-drawn wagon to read it.[11]

Humane organizations also published their own journals, including *The Animal Kingdom* and *Our Dumb Animals*, which featured "those who cannot speak for themselves." While these organs served to inform members, they were designed for recruitment as well. Exposure was provided by such humane leaders as George T. Angell—known around Boston as the "Angell of Mercy"—who distributed hundreds of thousands of free copies of *Our Dumb Animals* to residents of his city. He in fact hoped to place a copy of this journal "into every home."[12] Humanitarians, then, were intent on promoting their ideas.

The best-known individual to defend sentient creatures was the Englishman Henry S. Salt. His *Animals' Rights*, first published in 1892, became a manifesto of the movement. This book went through numerous editions and was translated into Dutch, German, French, and Spanish. Salt influenced many American humanitarians; Moore was especially inspired by his ideas. In fact, Salt's writings, which sparked considerable debate in journals and newspapers on both sides of the Atlantic, were widely noticed. He helped organize the Humanitarian League in 1891, and for the next three decades edited *The Humanitarian* and *The Humane Review*. While his ideas were not generally accepted by the public, they were deemed significant enough to attack in the popular press.[13]

Controversy was in any case good publicity for the growing number of animal protection organizations, the most prominent of which was the Society for the Prevention of Cruelty to Animals (SPCA). Encouraged by the president of its English counterpart, the New York lawyer Henry Bergh established the SPCA in this country in 1866. That same year the state legislature made abuse and neglect of animals a misdemeanor. Although as early as 1829 New York had passed a law forbidding cruelty to animals, it had not been effectual. To provide enforcement, Bergh obtained a charter of incorporation, allowing the New York police force to aid SPCA members in the inspection and curtailment of cruelty cases.

As president of the SPCA, Bergh was interested especially in horses. He campaigned to ease the loads of those attached to street cars, for example, and to provide them with drinking water. Bergh became a familiar figure to drivers, for he patrolled the city streets and prosecuted offenders himself. He also established an ambulance for injured animals. Further concerns of his organization included humane shipment and housing of cattle, as well as the abolition of such activities as cock fighting. Bergh's success in New York quickly led to the formation of SPCA branches in other states. Their solicitude was not limited to animals; when the SPCA was confronted in 1874 with a case of cruelty to a young girl, Bergh established the complementary Society for the Prevention of Cruelty to Children. So strong was the response to Bergh's efforts that by 1881 *Animal World*, a humanitarian journal, reported that "our cause has made more progress in the United States during fifteen years, than in England during fifty years."[14]

In time a variety of smaller, more specific organizations also emerged. Their concerns, ranging from antivivisection to animal rescue, indicate the wide scope of the humanitarian movement. The American Bands of Mercy, for example, promoted humane education for children, while the need for animal shelter was addressed by the Bide-a-Wee Home in New York, which fed its residents donated scraps from the Waldorf-Astoria. By the early 1920s there were an estimated 539 active humane societies with a combined membership of over two hundred thousand; participants included the moderate and mainstream as well as what critics called the lunatic fringe.[15]

There also appeared at this time the First Church for Animal Rights, which featured "animal ritual" and an "animal Bible." Its founder, Royal Dixon, had produced two books with revealing titles: *The Human Side of Birds* and *The Human Side of Animals*. According to him, the Scriptures "imply that man and beasts have, equally, a share in a future life beyond the grave." He saw a need, then, to provide for the "spiritual welfare" of animals. Dixon's animal church, which attracted three hundred people, was rooted in the compassion and mercy of Christianity.[16] Yet he rejected mainstream theology which excluded animals from salvation and moral consideration. To Dixon's mind, those who denied the spiritual life of animals were blinded by arrogance. He hoped to convince people that animals had souls and were therefore worth saving—for this life as well as the hereafter. These ideas did not gain a large following, for they went far beyond mere kindness to abused animals. Dixon's animal church in fact questioned the human-centered foundation of traditional religious thought in the United States.

Uniting the diverse groups of humanitarians was their concern for sentient creatures. They were also unified in their interest in individuals rather than species. Most humanitarians agreed that animals should be accorded legal protection from suffering; even the moderates desired stricter enforcement of existing laws. In their arguments against abuse of animals, however, humanitarians differed. Some focused on the duty of humans to be merciful to inferior animals. Others took the more radical position that sentient creatures have rights. But the term "animal rights," albeit frequently used, was fraught with ambiguity. Although pain remained the central issue, not all humanitarians who employed this phrase were antivivisectionists or vegetarians. Not all those who spoke of "animal rights" were convinced that other creatures could suffer from mental stress as well as physical pain. Nor did all humanitarians agree with Salt's notion that animals should be granted "restricted freedom" for "individual development," particularly when it came to domestic creatures.[17] Only extremists refrained from using animals for food, clothing, or as beasts of burden. The humanitarian movement, then, was far from single-minded.

Yet the mere idea that animals have rights, however ill-defined, was to have important implications for wildlife. Although most humanitarians emphasized urban, domestic animals, their organizations also had a keen interest in the "tormented wild things of the forest and plain." The SPCA in fact urged Congress to create a department to preserve the buffalo. As the leader of this organization, Bergh viewed "the useless and inhuman torture and destruction of . . . unoffending animals, roaming on the public lands" as an "outrage . . . on man and beast." To him, the protection of wildlife was a cause "of serious magnitude."[18] Indeed, nearly every issue of SPCA journals and newsletters, from Boston to San Francisco, contained articles about the plight of wild creatures. Humane organizations were concerned also with the protection of wild birds. Exemplifying the link between humanitarianism and conservation, Bergh, in addition to heading the SPCA, became an honorary vice-president of the Audubon Society.

With their protests against the suffering of individual animals, humanitarians approached conservation from a new angle. For the most part, bird conservationists relied upon economic and aesthetic—that is, utilitarian—arguments. Humanitarians, however, added their characteristic concern for animal pain. Band of Mercy leaders, for instance, exhorted their members to "feed wild birds in the wintertime," for the "poor things cannot find food for themselves on the hard ground or on the snow"; similarly, the SPCA worried that herons and egrets plucked live for decorative feathers were left to their "lingering deaths in the swamps."[19]

Their objections to pain put humanitarians at odds with some conservationists. At best, practical-minded sportsmen had objected to wasteful killing of wildlife owing to their concern for posterity. But as a group, sportsmen were not motivated by solicitude for individual animals. To humanitarians, on the other hand, protection of wildlife was part of a newly emerging moral system which, as one disgruntled sportsman put it, denied man's "right of sovereignty over the lower animals." Although their numbers were small, humanitarians wielded enough influence to worry hunters. When Bergh attacked the popular sporting activity known as the pigeon shoot, for example, a writer in the *American Sportsman* groaned that the SPCA leader would stir up "old fogy humanitarians everywhere."[20]

Such scornfulness was not confined to sportsmen. To nonbelievers, humanitarians, like many reformers, appeared to be a self-righteous, often humorless lot. Bergh seemed to his detractors to be a particularly somber man; cartoonists satirized his long, drawn face and sober countenance. This perception was significant, for Bergh was so closely associated with his organization that the two could not be separated. The *New York Herald*, for example, claimed that the SPCA "was distinctly a one man power."[21] Certainly it was the leaders of the humane movement who defined and articulated its ideas. Accordingly, criticism of this humane organization frequently was leveled at Bergh himself.

His striking appearance and eccentricity made him an especially visible target. The son of a wealthy ship builder, Bergh had served as Secretary of Legation and Acting Consul in Russia during the 1860s.

Throughout his long presidency of the SPCA, he maintained the reserve of the well-born. Observers were taken by Bergh's "commanding stature of six feet," and a silk top hat added to "the severity of his presence." Anecdote suggested that Bergh could use physical force when verbal persuasion failed. Upon discovering an improperly loaded cattle cart, Bergh was said to have dragged down the driver and his assistant, banging "their heads together with a thud" to demonstrate "how the heads of those poor sheep and calves feel." On another occasion, he personally removed some of the passengers on an overloaded street car, throwing one cantankerous fellow into a snowbank.[22]

Bergh's unorthodox, sometimes arrogant methods were bound to attract attention to the SPCA. Even other humanitarians were puzzled by him. In an article in *McClure's*, Clara Morris, a sympathizer, described the SPCA leader as a "riddle." According to her, Bergh was not motivated by affection for animals. Despite his efforts on their behalf, Bergh "did not love horses," she explained; nor did he have much fondness for dogs. His "sort of justice," then, was "calm" and "impersonal." Certainly Bergh was not a vegetarian, although he had a fastidious aversion to meat that was not well done.[23]

Because their rationale was similarly unclear, humanitarians often were accused of misanthropy. Frances Power Cobbe, for example, was charged with "exclusive sympathy for animals and total indifference to human interests." Critics feared that this English humanitarian "would sacrifice any number of men, women, and children, sooner than a few rabbits should be inconvenienced." Similarly, a reviewer in the *Atlantic Monthly* complained in 1906 that "we have changed from lovers of men to lovers of beasts."[24]

Some humanitarians did convey a peculiar disgust for people. Among Americans, J. Howard Moore was especially disparaging of humankind. According to him, man "is not a fallen god, but a promoted reptile." Although "he is cunning and vainglorious, and towers about on his hinders," man, Moore concluded, "is a cold, hard-hearted *brute*." Nor was his morose tone a mere affectation; Moore's despondency eventually led him to take his own life. English humanitarians were equally unflattering in their assessment of humankind. Marie Louise de la Ramée, who published widely in Britain and the United States under the pseudonym "Ouida," described the average person thus: "His ears are wadded by prejudice, his eyes are blinded by formula, his character is steeped in egotism." Few humanitarians, however, went as far as Anna Kingsford, an English antivivisectionist who announced that she preferred animals to people and offered herself as a subject for medical experimentation.[25]

Certainly these sentiments did not endear humanitarians to the public. Humane leaders frequently were dismissed as crackpots; Salt himself was thought to be a "compendium of the cranks."[26] But criticism served to bring humanitarian issues to light. Although Bergh was unusually sensitive to personal attacks, he welcomed good-natured barbs that provided exposure for his society. One New York dining salon, for example, put on display a large live turtle destined for slaughter. Not wishing to offend the SPCA or its president, the restaurant furnished a bed of corn silk and a pillow for the "comfort of the poor [animal]," along with a placard explaining that he was to "be served in soups and steaks on Thursday," at which time Bergh, his organization, and other interested parties were "invited to come to do justice to his memory."[27]

Although such satire reflected the extent to which Americans had become aware of humane ideas, it also indicated that the New Humanitarianism would not readily replace deeply ingrained attitudes toward animals. Still, their failure to rouse widespread enthusiasm did not discourage most humanitarians. "No great reform," claimed an article in the *Arena*, "has ever been carried through which at the beginning was not greeted with derision."[28] Nor did opposition to their cause prevent humanitarians from taking themselves seriously. They believed that their work addressed larger issues than the need to preserve sentient creatures. To them, protection from pain had a spiritual significance.

Given this point, it is interesting to note that a large number of humanitarians were women. Sydney H. Coleman, an early observer of the movement, pointed out that over half the memberships of several major humane organizations were female. If their support were "suddenly withdrawn," he wrote, "the large majority of societies for the prevention of cruelty to children and animals would cease to exist." Women, *Our Dumb Animals* explained, are "endowed with a much greater sensibility" than men. According to that humanitarian journal, the sex was "born to pity, to relieve, to console."[29]

This idea emerged early in the nineteenth century. From the beginning of the industrial era, Americans had come to view women as moral caretakers. While men immersed themselves in the cutthroat atmosphere of business or factory, their wives would strengthen the ethical fibers of the nation. It was no accident, then, that many reformers were female. The humanitarian Frances Power Cobbe noted this point and concluded that women's "moral superiority" made them especially suited for humane work. Cobbe was an English reformer whose feisty brand of humanitarianism quickly gained an audience among American advocates. She was convinced that the female perspective would have a civilizing effect on what had become a rapacious industrial society. Cruelty and pain, she announced, is "naturally" revolting to the feminine mind.[30]

Most humanitarians believed that no truly refined or cultivated person would condone abuse of other creatures. To them, concern for animals became a measure of the advancement of civilization. Good character, suggested an article in the *Independent*, is derived from "courtesy to the whole creation." Mistreatment of animals, on the other hand, developed cruel natures. In her article on Henry Bergh, Clara Morris explained that before the SPCA, mere exposure to brutality was "coarsening the fiber and hardening the hearts of the people," thereby "lowering their spiritual standard."[31] Humanitarians, then, worried about the demoralization of people as well as the abuse of animals.

This anxiety, which was strongly evident in the initial years of the humanitarian movement, continued into the early twentieth century. Humane advocates feared that cruelty to beasts could lead to a disregard for people. They warned, for instance, that compassion for humans "is never to be found in a mind totally callous with regard to the sufferings of the lower animals." They also believed that, given our treatment of wild creatures, "in the future the human race will have no tenderness for those of its own kind who are feeble or aged, and will destroy all those who weary it, obstruct it, or importune it."[32] Frances Power Cobbe in fact considered the well-being of people to be the foremost goal of humanitarianism. The "hearts of men," she pointed out, "will grow more tender to their own kind by cultivating pity and tenderness to the beasts and birds." Given this view, it is ironic that Cobbe was accused of misanthropy. "Human claims for happiness," she maintained, take precedence over "the claims of brutes."[33]

Critics on both sides of the Atlantic, however, wondered why more humanitarians did not directly devote more attention to human misery.

The historian James Turner has offered an interesting explanation: because the doctrine of political economy strongly resisted interference with exploited laborers, he suggests, mistreated animals were easier, safer targets for humane zeal. Humanitarians thus "subconsciously transferred their charitable impulses from the forbidden ground of the working class slums to a more acceptable object of benevolence." For evidence, Turner cites their references to the "labouring classes" of animals. Yet George T. Angell, president of the Massachusetts SPCA and founder of the American Bands of Mercy, wrote and lectured on "The Labor Question." To his mind, solicitude for other creatures was related to concern for humans. "When the rights of dumb animals shall be protected," he argued, "the rights of human beings will be safe." Salt, too, believed that the emancipation of humans and animals was "inseparably connected," for no single reform could "be fully realized apart from the rest."[34]

To humanitarians, all forms of cruelty, whether visited upon people or animals, had become a degenerative force. Living in cities far removed from the processes of nature, they had acquired an acute sensitivity to strife along with an aversion to the corporeal. The new-found kinship with other creatures had its unpleasant side. A recurrent theme in humanitarian writing was fear of savagery, for clearly not all animals behaved in a manner which met the standards of civilization. Although nature writers who presented wild creatures to the public denied that the natural world is brutal, the existence of predation could not be refuted completely. Nor could the close relationship between humans and animals, established by nineteenth-century science, be ignored.

Yet humanitarians could at least protest that people did not have to be bestial or ferocious. Barbarous tendencies in humans could be offset by magnanimity toward fellow creatures. "That the work of the humane societies has aided in our progress away from the savage to the civilized and humanized condition cannot be doubted," wrote a commentator in the *Independent*.[35] Humanitarians, then, sought to suppress specific activities that, in their estimation, indicated a vestigial savagery in man. Hence, the various factions of the humane movement became increasingly specialized, as they organized to oppose hunting, vivisection, meateating, and the confinement of wild creatures.

4

The Barbarisms
of Civilization

AN ANALYSIS OF

HUMANITARIAN PROTESTS

Much good will be done by the . . . protest against the numerous
barbarisms of civilization—the cruelties inflicted by men on men, . . . and
the still more atrocious ill-treatment of the so-called lower animals, for
the purpose of "sport," "science," "fashion," and the gratification of an
appetite for unnatural food. Manifesto of the Humanitarian League, 1891

The humanitarians who in 1890 dubbed *Black Beauty* "The Uncle Tom's
Cabin of the Horse" had made a significant comparison.[1] Like Harriet
Beecher Stowe's antislavery novel, *Black Beauty* conveyed the pain and
anguish that resulted from cruelty. Relying on pathos and sentimentality,
both books also demonstrated the depravity and degeneration of those
responsible for the suffering. Just as *Uncle Tom's Cabin* had revealed the
plight of slaves, *Black Beauty*, an English book widely distributed by the
American Humane Education Society, evoked sympathy for abused animals. Both books were employed in a crusade for reform. In fact, abolitionism and the humane movement were closely related; after the Civil
War, Stowe herself began writing on behalf of animals. Despite their
small numbers, humanitarians became an especially vocal, visible group
by the late nineteenth century. They hoped to convince people that the
world would be much improved—if only we could eradicate specific
evils. These included hunting, vivisection, meat-eating, and the confinement of animals.

Humanitarians approached their cause with an evangelical zeal often
typical of reformers. Those outside the humane movement were sometimes put off by their intensity and abrasiveness. Yet these qualities got

humanitarians—and their views—noticed. Before the Civil War abolitionists possessed personalities similar to those of humanitarians. No cru-
sader in the fight against slavery, for example, had been more vociferous
than William Lloyd Garrison. As the editor of the fiery newspaper *The
Liberator*, he acknowledged that people objected to his uncompromising,
intemperate language. The first issue, released in 1831, made his position
clear: "I am in earnest—I will not equivocate—I will not excuse—I will
not retreat a single inch—AND I WILL BE HEARD." In Garrison's
estimation, these strong words were needed to jolt white Americans out
of their apathy. Most people, however, dismissed Garrison as a crackpot.
So offensive were his views that a mob in Boston dragged him through
the city on a rope. Still, Garrison retained the strength of his convictions.
Posterity, he claimed, "will bear testimony that I was right."[2]

Later in the nineteenth century, humanitarians would demonstrate
the same earnestness. They, too, would employ strong words in the crusade for animals. Stowe, the writer whom President Lincoln had credited
for starting the Civil War, became so concerned about mistreatment of
wild animals that she claimed she would "do *any* thing that can benefit
the cause."[3] Like the abolitionists, humanitarians attempted to expand
the boundaries of ethics to include an oppressed group. Like the abolitionists, they also believed that their cause would be vindicated in the
future, when Americans would look back on the barbaric behavior of the
past with horror.

To humanitarians, no activity was more depraved than hunting. It was
not so much the killing of animals for food that they found objectionable;
meat-eating humanitarians viewed slaughtering as an unfortunate necessity. But shooting for pleasure was another matter. Humanitarians
viewed blood sports as more than a frivolous pastime; in their estimation,
killing wild animals needlessly was an act of inexcusable wantonness. Of
course, protests against hunting go back centuries. Before the New Humanitarianism, however, the activity was condemned not because it was
cruel to animals but because it was considered to be a worldly sin. Some
Puritans, for instance, had frowned on hunting as an indulgence.[4]

By the nineteenth century complaints against hunting focused on the
brutishness of the man who would deliberately inflict suffering on an
animal. Henry David Thoreau, for example, wrote that no "humane

being, past the thoughtless age of boyhood, will wantonly murder any creature, which holds its life by the same tenure that he does." His words, published in *Walden* in 1854, suggest that hunting was a stage in human development. Once a person reached physical and spiritual maturity, he would naturally "outgrow" it. According to Thoreau this progression affected societies as well as individuals. During his own day, however, Thoreau was not widely read; few Americans were aware of his ideas. He was too unusual to be appreciated by a wide audience. "I warn you, mothers," he wrote, "that my sympathies do not always make the usual phil-*anthropic* distinctions." Thoreau could not even "fish without falling a little in self-respect."[5]

By the end of the century Henry S. Salt, a leading humanitarian in England, had discovered Thoreau. His biography of Thoreau was among the first to call attention to this previously little-known author. The two men shared an interest in animals as well as a concern for the liberty of the individual. Like Thoreau, Salt condemned hunting. Blood sports, he claimed in *Animals' Rights*, published in 1892, reveal the "tiger that lives in our natures," which "nothing but a higher civilisation will eradicate." His American friend J. Howard Moore agreed that hunting derives from a "vestigial instinct" devoid of "either sense or decency." In the early years of the twentieth century, humanitarians increasingly echoed this sentiment. While Theodore Roosevelt presented shooting in the wilderness as a means of strengthening and revitalizing soft urban Americans, they warned that those who indulged in blood sports would slip into a state of savagery. An author in the *Nineteenth Century*, for example, feared that during the hunt the "higher feelings" of the participants "are doused by the smell of corruption. . . . The lower animal within us is developed, but at the loss of the higher instinct of the soul."[6]

Although humanitarians did not enjoy strong credibility with the American public, their themes were also taken up by such revered writers as John Muir. He did not align himself with humanitarian organizations or comment on their writings. Yet he shared not only their concern for the suffering of individual animals but also their fear of barbarity. Although Muir had shot wild creatures as a youth in Wisconsin and later accompanied hunting expeditions in the Sierra, he had no liking for the "murder business" and rarely carried firearms. Blood sports, he maintained, are a debasing pastime, capable of transforming even "the decent gentleman or devout saint" into "a howling, bloodthirsty, demented savage." At times his aversion to shooting animals took the form of ridicule. Lacking regard for the character and intelligence of their prey, hunters, he sneered, remain unaware that they "are themselves hunted by animals," who "in perfect safety follow them out of curiosity."[7] Hence, some animals, according to Muir, are more clever than the hunters who pursue them.

Nor was Muir the only naturalist who spoke out against hunting. Even John Burroughs, who at one point defended Roosevelt's sporting activities, claimed that "a man in the woods, with a gun in his hand, is no longer a man—he is a brute." Ernest Thompson Seton, well-known for his animal stories, similarly regretted the practice of turning "a beautiful, glorious, living creature . . . into a loathsome mass of carrion."[8] Seton's sympathy for animals pursued for sport or profit was indicated throughout his book, *Lives of the Hunted*.

Angling was not attacked as vehemently as other blood sports. Perhaps because fishing had been viewed traditionally as a contemplative activity, it was difficult to portray participants as bloodthirsty savages. Fishing also failed to inspire strong protests because it involved animals that were not attractive in the traditional sense. The humane movement's emphasis on the kinship between people and animals encouraged the perception that only humanlike creatures deserved moral consideration. Nevertheless, humanitarians were suspicious of anyone who would kill for pleasure, and protested this sport as well. Stowe had considered the subject important enough to work into her book, *Oldtown Folks*. Here one of the characters announced that fish have "their rights" just as people do. Muir, too, maintained that angling was inappropriate in Yosemite, for it violated the "rights of animals." Both writers emphasized the sentience of the victims. "I can't bear to see no kind o' critter in torment," explained Stowe's character. Similarly, Muir wondered at people seeking "pleasure in the pain of fishes struggling for their lives."[9]

The portrayals of suffering wildlife at times became maudlin. The words "pitiful" and "hopeless" were evoked in numerous journal articles and letters to newspapers. Condemning hunting as a "barbarous" activity, one woman sent the following description of prey to the *New York Times*:

"Small, innocent, helpless, friendless animals maimed and dying in the ice and snow and biting winds! Tiny, inoffensive creatures, wounded to the death, crawling into icy graves to beat out their gentle breaths as the 'sport' of man's wantonness!" Similarly, the *Animal's Friend*, a humane journal, condemned hunters who remained unmoved by the "piteous cry" and "dying agonies of a creature so miserably torn."[10]

These sentiments were sure to elicit contempt from sportsmen. Humanitarians remained convinced, however, that time was on their side. One article in the *Fortnightly Review* noted in 1914 that "this movement of charity towards our dumb fellow-creatures has been gaining a deeper hold upon the human heart with each succeeding generation." Today, according to the historian and sportsman John F. Reiger, "it is becoming increasingly fashionable to be against all hunting."[11]

Yet humanitarians joined forces with sportsmen in their attacks against hunting for profit. Like gentleman hunters, they were offended by the plume trade—or "murderous millinery," as Salt put it. J. Howard Moore called market hunters "marauders" who roamed "the forests of the earth to ravage and depopulate them." Through its publications the Society for Prevention of Cruelty to Animals (SPCA) attempted to enlist sympathy for "feathered martyrs."[12] Again, it was the suffering of wild birds that bothered humanitarians. What angered them most was the fact that these animals died in misery simply to satisfy the dictates of women's fashion.

While the animals killed or injured for ornamental purposes were mostly wild, humanitarians were also alert to domestic creatures abused for the sake of vanity. In 1922, for example, the Humane Society was able to prosecute a young woman for dyeing a cat blue to match "the general color scheme" of her wardrobe. "Otto," the victim, watched the proceedings from beneath the overcoat of a Humane Society policeman.[13] The humane movement, then, wanted to stop the mistreatment of animals for frivolous purposes.

For humanitarians, the worst offense in this category was the killing of wild creatures for furs. As early as 1915 humane journals attempted to inform readers about the gruesome manner in which pelts were taken. *Our Dumb Animals*, a publication of the SPCA, called the steel trap humankind's "most cruel" invention.[14] One of the most vocal groups against animals suffering for fashion was the Anti-Steel Trap League. Formed in 1925, this group was a predecessor of Defenders of Wildlife. By the end of the decade, the Anti-Steel Trap League was waging an especially well-organized, focused campaign. Although its members maintained that furs were entirely unnecessary, their official goal was to see that pelts were taken in a humane manner. As it was, the legs of such animals as muskrats, skunks, and beaver were captured in traps that, in some cases in the Far West, were visited only infrequently. The animal then either starved or gnawed off his limb. What the Anti-Steel Trap League wanted was a trap that killed the animal instantly, or fur farms where pelts could be obtained through less painful methods.

Lucy Furman, who later became vice-president of the group, linked its activities to the general "awakening of the human conscience in regard to the treatment of animals." A former school teacher and a writer, she hoped to convince Americans of the sentience of fur-bearing creatures. They "have highly organized nervous systems," she pointed out in the *Atlantic Monthly*, as well as "senses . . . more acute and keen than those of civilized man." It was therefore barbaric to subject them to the prolonged misery of the steel trap for such a needless purpose. Furman's seriousness was indicated by her claim that "this evil" was "the most outstanding atrocity of modern times." Her essay concluded with an appeal to "the thinking women who read the *Atlantic*." By the 1940s the campaign for more humane trapping had resulted in new laws in thirty-seven states. Some of these required trappers to check their lines more frequently; a few actually prohibited trapping or the leg-hold trap altogether.[15]

Another activity that seemed especially pernicious to humanitarians was experimentation on sentient creatures. Although vivisectors used domestic animals, humane arguments against these scientists related to treatment of wildlife as well. "Nearly all animal lovers who set pen to paper," James Turner has pointed out, "felt obliged to denounce vivisection, at least in passing." Most American humanitarians were sympathetic, if not active, regarding this issue. Its importance was noted by an article in the *American Magazine*, which claimed in 1909 that the public has "heard a great deal about anti-vivisection of late, both in New York and London. The propaganda has won the support of widely circulated newspapers and men and women of high standing in their communities." Similarly, the *Nation* reported on their "constant clamor."[16]

When it came to antivivisection, humanitarians in the United States were even more vehement than those in England. Henry Bergh sent SPCA spies—disguised as reporters—to observe experiments; it was his intention not merely to restrict the activity but to obtain a complete ban. The American Anti-Vivisection Society, formed in 1883, also changed its platform within four years from mere limitations on experiments to abolition.[17] Because they generally viewed the natural world as a benevolent place, humanitarians considered pain—particularly when deliberately inflicted—to be an aberrant evil. To them, the special horror of vivisection was that it could not be attributed, as could most atrocities, to ignorance, habit, or ill-breeding. Instead, it was a calculated, cold-blooded, and relatively recent form of abuse, practiced by well-educated scientists. Vivisection was, moreover, a foreign activity, derived from France and Germany.

Although American researchers protested this humane "hysteria," antivivisectionists remained unconvinced of the benefits of experimentation on animals. Their pain, asserted Henry Childs Merwin, known for his work on behalf of horses, was "too high a price" for knowledge and freedom from disease. Vivisection was not only cruel to animals but also detrimental to the moral character of humans. Mere exposure to suffering, humanitarians believed, led to insensitivity. Their sensibilities hardened, vivisectors thus became capable of barbarous acts against humans as well as animals. According to *Our Dumb Animals*, "it often happens that medical students, corrupted by hospital teaching, imbibe such a love of [cruelty] that when they visit their homes they practice it for its own sake." Vivisection, in sum, "reverses the order of the refining forces of civilization."[18] So effective was the campaign against experimentation on animals that several states, including Massachusetts and Washington, banned the practice in some schools and colleges.

Despite the fervor of these protests against hunting, trapping, and vivisection, meat-eating was the one issue on which most early humanitarians stopped short. In this respect they differed from present-day advocates. While the horrors of the slaughterhouse repulsed such activists as

Bergh, the practice of eating animals has not been widely questioned until recently. Turn-of-the-century vegetarians occupied the fringe of the humanitarian movement. Even other reformers looked upon them as crackpots. H. M. Hyndman, and later George Orwell, regretted that the socialist cause had been tainted by the presence of these "odd cranks."[19]

Modern-day humanitarians, however, are puzzled by their predecessors' refusal to take this last step on behalf of animals. Peter Singer, a leading philosopher of Animal Liberation, has labeled the nineteenth century the "era of excuses" for its failure to embrace vegetarianism despite its increased sensibility. As early as 1785 humane thinkers felt it necessary to write justifications of meat-eating, indicating their uneasiness. Even those who took the plunge exhibited an inconsistency that could not have aided their cause. In 1909, for instance, the *New York Times* described a socially prominent vegetarian as a "strong believer" who nevertheless served "a roast once in a while to vary the vegetable diet." Part of the problem was that abstention from meat-eating represented the most radical break from traditional treatment of animals. Of all the "novel manifestations of sympathy" to appear in the late nineteenth century, vegetarianism, according to James Turner, was "the most profoundly subversive of conventional values."[20]

Yet to a few humanitarians reform seemed impossible without a resolution of the food question. Early vegetarians were convinced that their movement "lies at the base of all reform." Vegetarianism, they believed, was linked to "a grand set of social and moral reformations," including temperance, women's rights, and concern for human suffering. Indeed, Salt was adamant that the humane cause would not advance without vegetarianism as a major tenet. In verse, he chided sympathizers who would not give up their meat:

> *Oh, yes! You love them well, I know!*
> *But whisper me, when most?*
> *In fields at summer-time? Not so.*
> *At supper-time—in roast.*

This concern was not limited to such "cranks" as Salt. Muir, too, looked forward to "a better time" when people would become "truly humane, and learn to put their animal fellow mortals in their hearts instead of . . . in their dinners."[21]

While aversion to meat-eating goes back to the ancients, it was not until the last century that vegetarianism gained enough followers to become noticeable as a movement. We cannot, observed a Victorian historian of food reform, "trace anything like an organized Vegetarian propaganda prior to the present century." Similarly, a letter to the editor of *Outlook* noted the "wakening interest" in vegetarianism. Although he conceded that the "fatal influence of Butchery is no new theory," the physician Howard Williams announced in 1896 that the late nineteenth century differed from previous eras in its recognition, prompted by science, of the "oneness of the higher non-human races, essentially, with the human in mental no less than physical organization." Meat-eating, he concluded, was no longer morally justifiable.[22] Growing numbers of vegetarian converts in Britain and the United States agreed. Their writings, like those of antihunters and antivivisectionists, revealed the fear that infliction of pain leads to barbarity.

In the United States, William Metcalfe inspired the movement. He was an English clergyman and physician, who in 1817 established a vegetarian church in Philadelphia. Becoming a vocal advocate of the cause, he helped found the American Vegetarian Society in 1850 and edited its journal, the *American Vegetarian*. It was in fact at this time that the term "vegetarian" came into existence. The British Vegetarian Society maintained close contact with its American counterpart, and even in these early days membership on both sides of the Atlantic numbered in the hundreds.

Although Metcalfe's organization disbanded a decade later, by the 1880s Henry Clubb, another English immigrant, revived the Philadelphia society and established a new journal, *Food, Home, and Garden*. Soon, however, the center of the movement shifted to Chicago, where a new national organization was founded; in 1893 an international vegetarian congress took place at the World's Fair. Members included such prominent figures as Bronson Alcott, Upton Sinclair, and George Bernard Shaw. For the most part, they abstained only from what was called the "three F's": fish, flesh, and fowl; dairy products were acceptable to them. So numerous had vegetarian dinner guests become by the end of the century that popular journals were advising hostesses what to serve them. The success of meatless restaurants in both New York City and London, coupled with the wide availability of vegetarian cookbooks, demonstrated the extent to which the movement had taken hold.[23]

It was more than mere numbers that distinguished nineteenth-century vegetarians from their predecessors. Many Greeks and Romans who avoided meat were motivated by a belief in the transmigration of souls: Pythagoras, for example, was convinced that animals contained human spirits. Early European vegetarians, however, had been preoccupied with health. Even in nineteenth-century America, the Graham bread craze, which drew from physiological arguments, was concerned in part with hygiene. Horace Greeley, the prominent editor and a follower of Sylvester Graham, claimed that "a strict vegetarian will live ten years longer than a habitual flesh-eater, while suffering, in the average, less than half so much from sickness as the carnivorous must."[24]

Yet by this time the writings of vegetarians indicated that they were concerned primarily with the morality of killing animals for food. Metcalfe, for one, objected to the practice on ethical grounds. Similarly, Salt, who wrote extensively on the movement, claimed that although "questions of hygiene and of economy both play their part," it is "beyond doubt that the chief motive of Vegetarianism is the humane one." The British Vegetarian Society, too, listed among its resolutions "the many advantages of a . . . moral character resulting from Vegetarian habits of diet." In the *New York Times* observers agreed that "the main line of argument offered by the vegetarians is of an ethical" nature.[25] To them, slaughtering seemed a brutal and unnatural activity.

What made vegetarians so sensitive to this issue was their newfound awareness of the sentiency of animals. They were concerned about the suffering of creatures killed for food. "Millions of the most sensitive and lovely organisms," Moore pointed out, though "palpitating and full of nerves, are hourly assassinated, flayed, and haggled, and their twitching fragments hauled away." According to vegetarians, that horrific process demoralized both the butcher and his customer, igniting their "baser propensities."[26]

Certainly meat-eating offended the aesthetic sensibilities of vegetarians. This "barbarous habit," they complained, assailed the "finer feelings" and "sense of beauty." Butcher shops, moreover, represented an "incongruity" in a "civilized age." Claiming that the "whole process of ingesting food is disgusting," one writer pointed out that we need not make matters worse by feeding upon "carrion and offal." Salt also wondered that artistic gatherings and social functions were "tainted" with animal food. "You take a beautiful girl down to supper," he complained, "and you offer her—a ham sandwich! What are we to say of the politeness which casts swine before pearls?" Meat-eating, he concluded, is not in "good taste."[27]

Objection to animal food was not limited to active vegetarians. Earlier in the century Thoreau had argued that as humans advance spiritually, they lose their taste for meat. According to this Transcendentalist, "it is a part of the destiny of the human race, in its gradual improvement, to leave off eating animals." Yet he warned his readers "of an animal in us, which awakens in proportion as our higher nature slumbers." We must be vigilant, he pointed out in *Walden*, and avoid "gross" feeding. Like many vegetarians, Thoreau was uneasy with the corporeal. "Nature is hard to overcome," he conceded, "but she must be overcome."[28]

Repulsed by the "depraved appetite" which craved meat, Muir, too, preferred "bread without flesh." Man, he lamented at several points in his journal, "seems to be the only animal whose food soils him." Muir's disgust regarding meat-eating was particularly evident in a passage from *My First Summer in the Sierra*. Here Muir described a slovenly shepherd who allowed the fat and gravy from his meal to drip down his trouser leg "in clustering stalactites." As a result, his pants became so adhesive that they wore thick instead of thin, and "in their stratification" had "no small geological significance." It is no accident that this man also functioned as a butcher in Muir's anecdote. Muir believed that, ideally, "one ought to be trained and tempered to enjoy life . . . in full independence of any particular kind of nourishment." Such fastidiousness, coming from a person who reveled in wildness, stemmed from more than a simple offense to a delicate sensibility. Muir's distaste was in keeping with his denial that the natural world is brutal; most of his animals were portrayed as being "dainty feeders." He and the members of the vegetarian societies had one thing in common: a belief in the "spiritualizing" effect of a vegetarian diet.[29]

The converse was also true. Vegetarians issued frequent warnings concerning the hazards of meat-eating: if people were not careful, even seemingly civilized humans could slip into a state of savagery, assuming "pugnacious and animal-like" characters. The problem, according to Hereward Carrington, author of *The Natural Food of Man*, was that meat excites "the individual to acts which he would not think of performing, were his body less stimulated and more under control." Sexual promiscuity and incontinence were considered to result from animal food. Although vegetarians derived "potential energy" from their diet, they did not experience the "desire to expend it so frequently." Similarly, alcoholism was traced to meat-eating. It was no accident that Metcalfe produced tracts concerning abstinence from intoxicating drinks side by side with those concerning abstinence from flesh food. An article in the *Popular Science Monthly* also noted a relationship between the consumption of meat and a "violent desire for spirits and the excitement which they create." The "appetite of the drunkard," as one observer put it, "is directed almost exclusively to animal food." Even Victorian "Pessimism, Indifferentism, and Unbelief" was traced to the diet of "blood and slaughter." Sin, concluded one of Metcalfe's followers, "came into this world through the appetite, and must be driven out the same door."[30]

Desiring to escape this alarming animality, vegetarians pointed out that only the most ferocious and degraded creatures prey on flesh. What was needed, they decided, was "restraint against the ills of the body." Not surprisingly, a great deal of print was devoted to assuring readers that their physiology did not require animal food. In any case, charges that a meatless population would soon become listless were countered by observations that "a vegetarian diet makes for quieter and more law-abiding citizens." Because "the majority of people have to lead a subordinate and routine life," an article in *Harper's* suggested, it is wise to minimize the "inconvenient desires and restless imaginings" which meat produces. In short, those who wished to avoid the "danger zone" adopted a vegetarian diet.[31]

To be sure, these notions did not go uncontested. As early as the 1850s the "food question" had been addressed by Herman Melville, who scoffed at the "Pythagorean" diet in such works as *Pierre* and *Moby Dick*. "Ah, foolish!" he wrote, "to think that by starving thy body, thou shalt fatten thy soul!" Lesser-known writers agreed. Dismissing the "spiritualizing quality of parsnips" as "nonsense," one detractor suggested that "any lingering ferocity in our beef and mutton dissolves in the process of cooking." Another critic argued that eating is more than "a humiliating necessity, to be done behind the door and with a sense of degradation." While vegetarians are often "good men," he asserted, "no one will contend that they are jolly." For this reason, "the redoubtable feeders are to be preferred,—men whom neither roast nor pudding can intimidate."[32]

Vegetarians, however, remained convinced of the ill-effects of meat consumption. And if animal food could make a person ravenous, slaughtering had worse consequences. In the *Popular Science Monthly* one writer claimed that this "brutalizing occupation . . . morally degrades the man who earns his bread by it." Butchers, she informed her readers, "often become murderers," at times killing "individuals whom they [do] not even know." Transporting livestock to the slaughterhouses was fraught with similar hazards; daily exposure to animals who suffered overcrowding and lack of food and water could render a man callous and unfeeling. This threat also applied to the commercial fisherman, who, according to one observer, "unwittingly grows cruel" upon contact with dying animals. William Alcott, a particularly vocal vegetarian, worried that although we "are not all trained to be butchers," we come to a table "day after day, which is loaded with the flesh of animals. If this is not Cannibalism, it is certainly pretty near it."[33]

Salt, a socialist as well as a vegetarian, took this point one step further. Claiming that it was not the butcher but his customer who was guilty of pernicious action, he condemned as "cannibals" those who live "by the sweat and toil of the classes who do the hard work of the world." Salt himself, although a graduate of Cambridge and a former Eton master, lived in a simple cottage in Surrey. In his mind socialism and vegetarianism were related, for both were predicated on a sense of justice. "If those who live selfishly on the labour of others are rightly denounced as bloodsuckers," Salt asked, "do not those who pamper a depraved appetite at the expense of much animal suffering deserve a similar appellation?"[34] In any case, he pointed out, vegetarianism, like temperance, could benefit the health as well as the pocket of the working class.

Certainly Salt was unusual—even for a vegetarian. The fervor with which he championed the cause of animals was unmatched both in Britain and in the United States. Descriptions of beasts awaiting slaughter often assumed a purely sentimental tone. One writer emphasized the "large, pathetic black eyes" of the "beautiful milk-white oxen" doomed to die; besides, she found the end product—"a huge *grosse piece* on an enormous dish"—to be revolting. Others assured readers that solicitude for animals should never exceed that extended to humans.[35]

Still, a handful of zealots, among whom Salt figured prominently, valued animals for their own sakes, arguing that they had rights quite apart from those of men. Several writers viewed this concept as an inevitable extension of the same spirit which granted rights to slaves and women. Salt, for instance, predicted that the "emancipation of men will bring with it another and still wider emancipation—of animals." His "Creed of Kinship" held that "in years to come there will be a recognition of the brotherhood between man and man, nation and nation, human and sub-human, which will transform a state of semi-savagery . . . into one of civilization, when there will be no such barbarity as . . . the ill-usage of the lower animals by man." His friend Moore agreed, claiming that humanity is at present "only in its larval stage."[36]

The food question, in Salt's estimation, was an essential step in this progression. Noting the incongruity of asserting the rights of a creature "on whom you propose to make a meal," he urged those who were concerned with the claims of animals to adopt vegetarianism. Taking a different approach, Muir, who himself was not altogether strict in his abstinence from flesh food, also detected an inconsistency in "preaching, praying men and women" who killed and ate animals "while eloquently discoursing on the coming of the blessed, peaceful, bloodless millennium."[37]

Salt found the protest that if all the world were vegetarian there would be fewer animals to be particularly insipid. "Blessed is the Pig," he sneered, "for the Philosopher is fond of bacon." In an essay entitled "The

Logic of the Larder," he mocked the person who announced, upon passing a butcher shop, that "I have been a benefactor to this pig, inasmuch as I ate a portion of his predecessor; and now I will be a benefactor to some yet unborn pig, by eating a portion of this one." Salt assured his readers that to the creature's "porcine intellect," the matter appears differently. After all, he concluded, we cannot assume that "the real lover of animals is he whose larder is fullest of them." Scorning those who would stoop to such rationalizing to defend their vile habit, Salt imagined them revising Coleridge's lines to read:

> *He prayeth best, who* eateth *best*
> *All things both great and small.*[38]

There was no doubt in his mind that animals were better off not existing than to be fated for slaughter.

Salt's definition of "ill-usage," then, went far beyond that of his contemporaries. While many late-nineteenth- and early-twentieth-century humanitarians were concerned only with easing the obvious physical pain of tormented animals, he concluded that all sentient creatures should be allowed "individual development." To Salt, mere imprisonment of wild animals was an act of cruelty. Few people, he claimed, could delight in a captive creature "if they . . . fully considered how blighted and sterilized a life it must be." If "we desire to cultivate a closer intimacy with the wild animals," he suggested, it cannot be based on "the superior power . . . by which we can drag them from their native haunts, warp the whole purpose of their lives, and degrade them to the level of . . . curiosities."[39] Wild animals, he maintained, should not be forced to do the bidding of humans.

Nor was Salt alone in his concern. The number of humanitarians who agreed with him on this point was sufficient to create a controversy regarding the value of zoos and circuses. As far back as colonial days, traveling menageries had delighted audiences. In the late nineteenth century large zoos became increasingly popular, as a means not only for preserving species but also for recreation. In crowded cities such as Philadelphia and New York, the opportunity to view wild animals prevented residents from becoming "disconsolate." In addition to providing contact with nature, zoos, according to an article in *Outing*, had an added value in keeping citizens out of "the back room of the saloon."[40] Yet humanitarians worried about the confinement of wild creatures.

Much of their protest against zoos emphasized either neglect of the animals' physical needs or training methods. However, some writers also lamented the sheer indignity that confinement brought to wild animals. An article in the *Westminster Review* regretted that "the noble lion, king of the forest," should be caged in a few yards of space, "instead of roaming through jungle and thicket." Because wild beasts have "sympathies and keen senses," their imprisonment made "demoralizing spectacles." According to Ernest Bell, a friend of Salt, performing animals suffered similar debasement at the hands of trainers whose "triumph it is . . . to control them to do silly things." In the early twentieth century the SPCA tried repeatedly to secure legislation prohibiting trained animal acts. This sense of outrage was long lasting. Recently, the SPCA derided the Barnum and Bailey Circus as "an animal freak show," indicating that the scrutiny of performances has continued to the present day. Since the early twentieth century, humanitarian groups have also objected to rodeos.[41]

Such concern was reflected in the founding of the Jack London Club in 1918. This unusual organization required neither payment of dues nor election of officers; participants simply pledged to avoid trained animal performances. During the 1920s nearly every issue of *Our Dumb Animals* featured a lead article on the Jack London Club, which in less than a decade attracted three hundred thousand "members." To advertise its cause, the organization distributed copies of Jack London's *Michael—Brother of Jerry*.

Like Salt, London was a socialist who was sensitive to the suffering of animals as well as humans. His book detailed the miseries of a variety of creatures—most of them wild—undergoing training for public shows. In his introduction London pointed out that he was hardly "a namby-pamby." While many humanitarians were viewed by the public as excessively softhearted and ignorant of the processes of nature, London had spent his life "in a very rough school," observing "more than the average man's share of inhumanity and cruelty." Yet what really angered him was the "cruelty and torment" of "animals being broken for the delight of men." Like the antivivisectionists, he regretted that those humans responsible possessed a "controlled intelligence." Besides, watching animals in pain was degenerating to the audience. In "The Madness of John Harned"—the story of a bull fight—London wrote, "It is degrading to those that look on. It teaches them to delight in animal suffering."[42]

London's interest in trained animals was related to his interest in the wilderness. Just as he relished landscapes that were free from human control, he preferred animals that acted naturally. London objected to animals performing because it reduced them to the level of mere spectacles and perverted their characters. Taming—or breaking—the spirit of a wild creature was like conquering the wilderness, and he viewed this process with regret. Owing to his literary stature, London's protests against trained animal acts attracted public attention.

Eventually, such attacks affected the trained animal industry. Ringling Brothers, Barnum and Bailey Circus, for example, dropped their wild animal acts from 1925 to 1929. Charles Ringling explained that "criticism by the public" was his motivation, for an increasing number of Americans feared that wild creatures "are taught by very rough methods, and that it is cruel to force them through their stunts."[43]

So persistent was the outcry against wild animal acts that William T. Hornaday, Director of the New York Zoological Park, felt compelled to respond. He scoffed at the "sentimental Jacklondon idea" that a confined animal is a miserable captive. This attitude was supported by such journals as *Scientific American*, which pointed out that zoo animals are compensated for the loss of their liberty with safety from the perils of the wilderness. Yet Hornaday admitted that creatures taken from the wild often objected to life in the zoo. One perverse polar bear refused to swim in his "fine, big pool," becoming a "sore trial to those responsible for his personal appearance before visitors." Elephants, too, sometimes proved to be troublesome to Hornaday. When these animals became "unruly," he did not object to their receiving "a sound whack."[44]

Nor did forcing animals to perform on stage bother Hornaday. All creatures who work, he asserted, are better off "than those who do nothing but loaf and grouch." To Hornaday, there was "no higher use to which a wild bird or mammal can be devoted than to place it in perfectly comfortable captivity to be seen by millions of persons who desire to make its acquaintance." In response to this sentiment, one critic sneered that some humans might be more useful "under Dr. Hornaday's paternal wing."[45] Although his work for the cause of conservation was unquestionably admirable, Hornaday had surprisingly little respect for individual wild creatures. Certainly he disagreed with the notion that animals had their own interests and desires and should be allowed to pursue them.

Many late-nineteenth- and early-twentieth-century Americans would have found nothing unusual about Hornaday's attitude. But some humanitarians were offended by the assumption that other creatures should provide amusement for humans—and their numbers were large enough to annoy Hornaday. All animals, they believed, should enjoy at least "limited freedom." Henry Childs Merwin, who was interested particularly in horses, urged his readers to recognize that each animal has "a character, a mind, a career of his own." Similarly, Moore lamented that animals were regarded as being mere "slaves" rather than "associates." Sentient creatures, he claimed, have "feelings and vanities" as well as an existence independent of man.[46]

So bent was Salt on according liberty to animals that he opposed keeping them as pets—a practice which implied subservience and smacked of condescension. His play *A Lover of Animals* poked fun at sickly and effete lap dogs, suggesting that pethood perverted the natural character of animals. Other creatures, he claimed, should be "our friends not our pets." Because "animals have their own lives to live as men have," they should be neither confined nor pampered. In his view humans should admire other creatures only from a distance. Although some of Salt's readers might have dismissed this notion as eccentric or even preposterous, today it is steadily gaining exposure, if not acceptance. Still, the distinction between "companion" and "pet" was unclear. Salt himself encouraged numerous animals—including a cat named "Hodge"—to live at his home in what seemed to be a "petlike capacity."[47]

To further establish the independence of other creatures, Salt suggested changes in our references to them. When applied to animals, the pronoun "it," he pointed out, encouraged humans to view them as "things." He also maintained that the terms "vermin" and "varmint," indications of inconvenience to men, should be discarded. But it was not pity and mercy—indications of human superiority—that Salt sought for animals; instead, he argued that other creatures be accorded moral status. Our relations with animals, he maintained, should be based "on a broad sense of justice." For the same reason, Salt objected even to the phrase "dumb animals," for "nothing more surely tends to their depreciation than thus to attribute to them an unreal deficiency or imperfection." Used by humanitarians, this term "may be meant to increase our pity," Salt acknowledged, "but in the long run it lessens what is more important, our respect."[48]

This position had taken several decades to develop. In its early stages the humanitarian movement had emphasized the need for kindness to animals. Henry Bergh, for example, objected to the wretched conditions of slaughterhouses; he also argued that they made degrading spectacles which should be removed from sight. Salt, on the other hand, wanted slaughterhouses eradicated altogether. He was concerned not only with the physical suffering of animals but also with their mental anguish. To his mind, humans did not simply have a duty to treat other creatures kindly; animals should be allowed to pursue their own interests.

Although such animal rights advocacy was limited to a small number of enthusiasts, their publications were extensive enough to provoke attacks. Rupert Hughes, a renowned editor and prolific contributor to popular journals, satirized the notion that beasts are entitled to claims similar to those of humans. While their "manners are far from polished," most animals, he mused, need only "a little education" and "a few newspapers printed in their own language . . . to prepare them for an exercise of the right to vote—a right they could surely exercise as well as many of the electors." Here Hughes was addressing the claim—presented by several writers in all seriousness—that animals should be considered citizens. As for vegetarianism, no one should "permit himself to be guilty of the odiously bad taste of eating his relations, especially his poor relations." Ignoring the issue of sentience, Hughes concluded that plants, too, might have a case, and therefore called "upon all conscientious persons to abstain from animal and vegetable food."[49] That a person of Hughes's repute could address this issue in *Harper's,* a major journal, attests to its significance. Certainly the argument for animal rights had hit a nerve.

In the long run, humanitarians have weathered such criticism. A recent forum on humanitarianism in *Harper's* took seriously those views which Americans of a century ago considered to be outlandish. Even Salt, once thought to be the "compendium of the cranks," has been vindicated. So compelling were his ideas that Gandhi sought him out on a trip to England. Historians have become sympathetic. Recently Keith Thomas praised *Animals' Rights* as "a masterpiece of its kind," not only "cool and reasonable in tone" but also "lucid and persuasive." Far from dismissing humanitarianism, Brian Harrison places the movement in the larger context of the zeal for moral reform which was pervasive on both sides of the Atlantic during the late nineteenth and early twentieth centuries. Among reformers, he claims, the common goal was "to uphold the dignity of the individual in an industrial and urban" setting.[50]

When it came to animals, this tendency was predominantly English and American. Early humanitarians viewed themselves as being unique. "Other countries do not usually show much solicitude about the welfare of animals," noted Ernest Bell in 1918.[51] Rapid industrialization had decreased direct contact with nature, while heightening awareness of suffering.

It was their newfound empathy that enabled nineteenth-century humanitarians to look beyond themselves to other creatures. Increased sensitivity to pain alone could not have changed traditional attitudes; the ability to feel *another's* anguish was also necessary. Cruelty itself required an appreciation of the suffering of victims. In other words, people could not be labeled "cruel" unless they could imagine how the pain that they inflicted felt. When the physical links between humans and animals became obvious, ideas concerning their spiritual kinship were not far behind. "Where men see no difference between themselves and animals," one Victorian pointed out, "what is more natural than they should wish to spare them?"[52]

Some humanitarians consciously attempted to understand the perspective of other creatures. One animal lover wrote that the "only way to judge fairly of any practice involving the feelings of another living being, is to look at it from his point of view." From "the animals' standpoint, man's behaviour towards them has been tyrannical and selfish in the highest degree." Another writer urged humans to consider "how odious to the horse must be the mere forcing of the bit into his mouth and of the headstall over his ears."[53] This empathy was most readily employed with creatures that closely resembled humans.

The acknowledgment that animals have consciousness weakened the notion that they were created for human use. Nineteenth-century science provided the evidence. Just as theories of evolution produced apprehension regarding man's animality as well as a recognition of his responsibilities toward fellow creatures, so did they demonstrate that the world was not created exclusively for man's convenience. Although man may attempt to "convince himself that all other animals were made for him," Moore noted in *The Universal Kinship*, "Darwin has lived." Similarly, E. P. Evans, who published voluminously on the topic of animal psychology, marveled that humans should wonder why anything harmful to them should exist. In the *Popular Science Monthly* he reported that "science has finally . . . taken this conceit out of man."[54] Animals, concluded these humanitarians, exist not for humans but for themselves.

Although the humane movement was not often taken seriously, Americans were also exposed to this view through the popular writings of John Muir. Inquiries as to the "purpose" of other creatures annoyed him; the egocentric assurance that other creatures live for man "is not supported by the facts," he argued in his journal. (However, in the published version, this disquieting passage was amended to read "by all the facts.") Muir rejected the "teachings of churches and schools" which held that animals "have neither mind nor soul, have no rights that we are bound to respect, and were made only for man, to be petted, spoiled, slaughtered or enslaved."[55] To the modern reader, Muir's insistence that animals are individuals in their own right is perhaps the most striking feature of his writing.

Of all the ideas associated with the New Humanitarianism, this was the most far-reaching. The notion that animals exist independently of humans and therefore have a right to liberty can be viewed as an extension of liberal values.[56] For the last two centuries, the Western world has granted rights to an increasing number of people, from white men to blacks to women. Humanitarians such as Salt recognized this progression and predicted that animals would be the next group to be accorded moral status. They consciously linked the cause of animal rights to the democratic ideals of the American Revolution. The First Church for Animal Rights, founded in 1920, proposed to allow other creatures "life, liberty, and the pursuit of happiness."[57] Such a development, however, required that people relinquish their human-centered outlook.

The recognition that animals have rights apart from those of humans laid the foundation for the further extension of ethics to the natural world which took place in the 1930s. Before ecological consciousness could take hold, however, another change in traditional perceptions was necessary. The final step would be the acceptance and appreciation of predators, the most inconvenient and offensive of animals.

Nature Writers

Nature writing of the late nineteenth and early twentieth centuries was a new form of expression. Unlike earlier portrayals of wild creatures, the stories and essays of this period began to focus on the animal. If they appeared at all, humans occupied the sidelines. Many of the new writers ventured into the wilds themselves, to observe living creatures. And for all their differences in tactics and style, all the authors pictured here argued for the protection of wild creatures.

Their writings reached a wider audience than was available to nature observers of previous generations. Owing to technological innovations, the publishing industry produced more books and popular magazines than had ever been possible. Added to

Ernest "Wolf Thompson" Seton (1906). On the right is his signature and trademark—a wolf paw print. Courtesy, Seton Memorial Library, Philmont Scout Ranch, Cimarron, New Mexico.

this advantage was a growing interest in the natural world among urban Americans. Here the new nature writers found a ready market; they presented wild creatures to these readers in terms that were not only poetic and scientific but also understandable.

John Muir and "California" Stickeen, named after the celebrated dog hero who shared Muir's adventure on a glacier (1905). Courtesy, the Bancroft Library.

Mabel Osgood Wright, as she appeared in *Bird-Lore* (1913). Her book, *The Friendship of Nature*, pictured here, assured readers that the natural world is benign. She served as president of the Connecticut Audubon Society.

John o'Birds (Burroughs) and John o'Mountains (Muir) in Yosemite (1908).
The "Two Johns" were the most prominent nature writers of their era.
Courtesy, the Bancroft Library.

Enos Mills and friend. This
writer, based in the Colorado
Rockies, emphasized the
individuality of his animal
subjects. Courtesy, Rocky
Mountain National Park.

Hunters

Hunting is becoming increasingly unfashionable in the United States. Joseph Wood Krutch, a celebrated drama critic and nature writer, spoke for a large group of readers when he wrote in the 1950s that "it is inconceivable how anyone should think an animal more interesting dead than alive." To him, killing for sport was "the perfect type of that pure evil for which metaphysicians have sometimes sought." In nineteenth-century America, however, recreational hunting was a widely accepted activity, endorsed by conservationists and influential statesmen. At that time, most protests focused on those hunters who, lacking the field etiquette of the sportsman, shot animals for the market or the dinner pail.

Theodore Roosevelt, "On the Trail," from the frontispiece to his book, *Hunting the Grisly*, published in 1893. In his estimation, shooting game was part of the "strenuous life" which "cultivates that vigorous manliness" necessary to a soft, overcivilized nation. Roosevelt hoped that wilderness hunting would restore to urban Americans the "hardihood, self-reliance, and resolution" of the pioneers.

Hunting stories often exaggerated the ferocity of wild animals. This arresting illustration appeared in an article in the *Pacific Rural Press*, published in 1873. Emphasizing adventure and daring, the author explained that the hapless fellow pictured here had found himself "unexpectedly taking an inside view of a Grizzly's face, under circumstances of startling interest." Courtesy, the Bancroft Library.

This staged bear fight highlighted the strength and bravery of the hunters. Courtesy, California Historical Society, San Francisco.

Lithograph entitled "S. E. Hollister, The Great American Hunter and Trapper" (1863). Unable to use his firearm, this plucky hunter tackled the bear with only a knife. Courtesy, the Bancroft Library.

Since the late nineteenth century, *Field and Stream* has been a popular journal among sportsmen. This cover from 1936 promised readers "The Greatest Lion Story Ever Written." Here the predators were portrayed as "Man-Eaters."

This advertisement, appearing in *Field and Stream* in 1935, notes that "You can Hunt most anywhere, but if you really want to SHOOT—and SHOOT big game, then come with us into the Interior of Alaska or to the Kenai Peninsula." The ruler (pictured right) suggests a preoccupation with the size of the trophy.

ALASKA

BIG GAME HUNTING

You can Hunt most any-where, but if you really want to SHOOT—and SHOOT big game, then come with us into the Interior of Alaska or to the Kenai Peninsula . . . the world's finest big game regions. Here are found Kodiak, Brown, Grizzly and Black Bear, Sheep, Goat, Caribou and Moose.

Alaska fall hunting season extends from August 20th to November 1st. Ten successful years operating in the remotest areas of Central, Western, and Southwestern Alaska, THE ALASKA GUIDES are now booking fall season hunts . . . both pack and airplane expeditions. Write or wire for details.

THE MINIMUM COST OF AN ALASKA BIG GAME HUNTING TRIP IS ABOUT $1000.

Please give details of the type of hunt that you wish.

Market and Pot Hunting

This photograph demonstrates the variety—as well as the numbers—of wild creatures killed by market hunters in the early twentieth century. From the William T. Hornaday Collection, courtesy, the Library of Congress.

Appearing in *Western Wild Life Call* (February 7, 1913), this disturbing illustration revealed the carnage of market hunting. Courtesy, the Bancroft Library.

Here a man poses with his morning's hunt. Courtesy, Idaho State Historical Society, Boise.

Owing to women's fashion, plume hunting was lucrative in the late nineteenth and early twentieth centuries. As this photograph demonstrates, entire birds were sometimes used to adorn hats. Herons and birds of paradise were especially valuable targets. Courtesy, the Forest History Society.

On their first morning in the Sierra Nevada, these hunters shot a she-bear and both cubs (1882). Courtesy, the Bancroft Library.

Later, the hunters skinned the bears (1882). John Muir heard from a hunter in Yosemite that "b'ar meat is the best meat in the mountains; their skins make the best beds, and their grease the best butter." Courtesy, the Bancroft Library.

Hunters in Yosemite, a decade before the region was accorded national park status in 1891. John Muir, for one, applauded the restrictions on "the barbarous slaughter of bears, and especially of deer, by shepherds, hunters, and hunting tourists, who, it would seem, can find no pleasure without blood." Courtesy, Yosemite Research Library.

Humanitarians and the Treatment of Animals

Humanitarianism first became noticeable as a movement during the last century. Although much of their work focused on domestic animals, humanitarians also devoted considerable effort to protecting wildlife. They differed from other conservationists, however, in that they were more concerned with the suffering of individual animals than with the maintenance of species. A small but vocal group, humanitarians protested the wholesale slaughter of animals in the West not because it was wasteful to humans but because it inflicted pain.

Engraving of Henry Bergh, first president of the American Society for the Prevention of Cruelty to Animals (first branch formed in New York, 1866). Pinned to his coat is the ASPCA seal. Bergh also became an honorary vice-president of the Audubon Society, exemplifying the link between humanitarians and wildlife conservationists. Courtesy, the New York Historical Society, New York City.

Bergh's success in New York led to the formation of SPCA branches in other regions, including the West Coast. This SPCA ambulance operated in San Francisco. In 1881 one humanitarian journal reported that "our cause has made more progress in the United States during fifteen years, than in England during fifty years." Courtesy, the California Historical Society, San Francisco.

A Bear Dance in Georgetown, Colorado. Many humanitarians objected to the use of wild animals as spectacles for amusement. Courtesy, the Library of Congress.

Jack London and "Brown Wolf." As pictured here, this writer had no qualms about killing chickens. However, his book *Michael—Brother of Jerry* railed against trained animal performances. London explained that although he was hardly "a namby-pamby," he was angered by the "torment" of "animals being broken for the delight of men." His book inspired the formation of the Jack London Club, dedicated to persuading Americans to boycott trained animal acts. Courtesy, Oakland Public Library, Oakland History Room.

RODEO CRUELTY STIRS HUMANITARIANS

JACK LONDON CLUB DENOUNCES INHUMANE AND LOW-GRADE FORMS OF PUBLIC AMUSEMENT

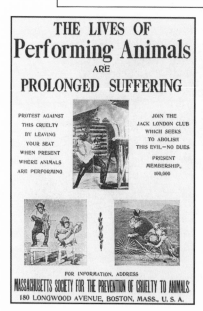

THE LIVES OF
Performing Animals
ARE
PROLONGED SUFFERING

PROTEST AGAINST THIS CRUELTY BY LEAVING YOUR SEAT WHEN PRESENT WHERE ANIMALS ARE PERFORMING

JOIN THE JACK LONDON CLUB WHICH SEEKS TO ABOLISH THIS EVIL—NO DUES. PRESENT MEMBERSHIP, 100,000

FOR INFORMATION, ADDRESS

MASSACHUSETTS SOCIETY FOR THE PREVENTION OF CRUELTY TO ANIMALS
180 LONGWOOD AVENUE, BOSTON, MASS., U. S. A.

Throughout the early 1920s, the Jack London Club attempted to dissuade audiences from patronizing trained animal acts, which humanitarians believed to be cruel and unnatural.

King Leo, St. Louis Zoo. From the late nineteenth century to the present, humanitarian groups have objected to zoos and circuses. Although some have worried about neglect of the animals' physical needs, many have protested the sheer indignity that confinement brings to wild animals. One early-twentieth-century humanitarian explained that "the noble lion, king of the forest" should be "roaming through jungle and thicket" instead of being forced to do "silly" tricks. Courtesy, the Library of Congress.

William T. Hornaday, Director of the New York Zoological Park (pictured left). He scoffed at the "sentimental Jacklondon idea" that a confined animal is a miserable captive. To his mind, there was "no higher use" for a wild creature than "to be seen by millions of persons who desire to make its acquaintance." From the William T. Hornaday Collection, courtesy, the Library of Congress.

When his zoo animals became "unruly," Hornaday (pictured left) did not object to their receiving "a sound whack." Unlike humanitarians, he applauded
the use of wild animals on stage. All creatures who work, he asserted, are
better off "than those who do nothing but loaf and grouch." From the
William T. Hornaday Collection, courtesy, the Library of Congress.

This circus poster indicates the appeal of humanized animals. In a sense, forcing animals to perform for people was like conquering wild nature. Courtesy, Circus Galleries of the John and Mable Ringling Museum of Art.

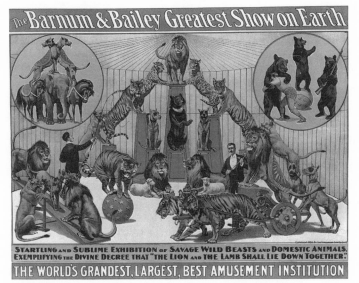

Here the Barnum & Bailey Circus promised a "Startling and Sublime Exhibition of Savage Wild Beasts and Domestic Animals, Exemplifying the Divine Decree that 'the Lion and the Lamb Shall Lie Down Together'" (1894). Courtesy, Circus Galleries of the John and Mable Ringling Museum of Art, Sarasota, Florida.

Wildlife in the National Parks

From the inception of the National Park Service in 1916, supporters recognized the importance of protecting wildlife in the reserves. That year, Joseph Grinnel, director of the Museum of Vertebrate Zoology, University of California, Berkeley, suggested that animals were essential to the national parks. "To the natural charm of the landscape," he wrote in Science, *"they add the witchery of movement." Yet reconciling the management of animals and the interests of visitors has been a difficult task. As Americans learned that national parks offered not only monumental scenery but also an opportunity to view a variety of animals, they began to expect contact with wildlife as part of their experience in the reserves.*

Although hunting was outlawed in Yellowstone in 1894, the ruling did not apply to predators. Here army personnel, then in charge of the park, gloat over a wolf carcass in 1905. Courtesy, Yellowstone National Park Photo Archives.

From the earliest days, bears were an attraction in the national parks. In this photograph, Captain George S. Anderson displays his pet bear. Courtesy, Yellowstone National Park Photo Archives.

During the early years of the national parks, however, the setting in which most visitors encountered wildlife was hardly natural. Americans in fact came to view the reserves as large, outdoor zoos. Eager for support, the National Park Service encouraged such spectacles as bear feeding grounds, which created an atmosphere more appropriate to a carnival or circus. Worse, this close and artificial contact led to conflicts between humans and wild creatures. Aggressive—or "troublesome"—bears were sometimes "disposed of," indicating that in the national parks the interests of the visitors came first.

Today, the National Park Service attempts to preserve wild creatures in their natural state. Dating back to the 1930s, the idea of the park as a biological sanctuary was reaffirmed by

A. Starker Leopold in his report, "Wildlife Management in the National Parks," published in 1963. Some environmentalists object to this phrasing, claiming that it is humans, not animals, that need to be managed. Yet the old conflicts, particularly between visitors and bears, remain. Animals dangerous to humans are still killed—a practice which presents questions as to the purpose of the national parks. Do they exist primarily for the enjoyment of the visitor? Or should they be devoted to preserving unimpaired ecosystems and their wild inhabitants?

Founded in 1918, the Yosemite Zoo featured not only deer (pictured here), but also tule elk, which were exotic to the region. The enclosure encouraged visitors to view animals as spectacles. In 1932 this unnatural exhibition was abolished. Courtesy, Yosemite Research Library.

Bear dump, Glacier Point, Yosemite National Park (1936). The bear feeding grounds in Yosemite attracted tourists, who were assured a glimpse of park wildlife. According to John Muir, sighting one of these animals in the days before they were lured by garbage was a rare occurrence. Courtesy, Yosemite Research Library.

Yellowstone, too, offered visitors a "bear show" (1936). Courtesy, Yellowstone National Park Photo Archives.

The "lunch counter" at Old Faithful encouraged bears to approach humans, which led to conflict (1929). The bear dumps were abolished in 1943. Courtesy, Yellowstone National Park Photo Archives.

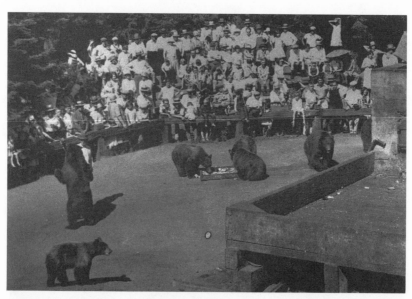

Here visitors to Sequoia National Park enjoy the spectacle at the bear grounds. One man (pictured left) entered the arena to feed a bear by hand. Courtesy, Sequoia and Kings Canyon National Parks.

The wording of this sign is revealing (ca. 1930). In the early twentieth century, the Park Service discouraged feeding animals by hand not because it was unnatural, but because it might be dangerous. Courtesy, Yosemite Research Library.

In Yellowstone, even the cubs became aggressive. Until recent decades, begging bears were a common sight in this park. Courtesy, Yellowstone National Park Photo Archives.

Although they could be dangerous to humans, bears were among the most appealing spectacles in the national parks. Here a woman feeds a bear a bottle in Yosemite. Courtesy, Yosemite Research Library.

So attractive was the image of the drinking bear that Coca-Cola used one in an advertisement (1931). Appearing in the *Ladies' Home Journal*, the bear in this illustration (pictured left) mimics a Yellowstone visitor. From the Collection of Alfred Runte, courtesy, the Coca-Cola Company.

In Yosemite a "troublesome" bear is removed to a remote area and marked with paint (1931). Repeat offenders were sometimes killed—a practice which continues today. Courtesy, Yosemite Research Library.

At times, even National Park Service officials encouraged a "carnival" atmosphere which would be considered inappropriate today. Here a ranger gives a deer a pipe in Yosemite (ca. 1929). Courtesy, Yosemite Research Library.

A National Park Service publication anthropomorphized animals, making even the predators seem cute (1939). Courtesy, Yosemite Research Library.

Today, the National Park Service is careful to warn visitors not to approach the wildlife. This poster indicates that for all the recent attention focused on the grizzlies of Yellowstone, buffalo, too, can be dangerous. Courtesy, Yellowstone National Park.

Predator Control

In the early decades of the twentieth century, "inconvenient" animals—or "varmints"—were killed in record numbers. Encouraged by ranching interests, the Bureau of Biological Survey (precursor to the Fish and Wildlife Service) waged a war against coyotes, killing as many as 35,000 per year. Wolves and mountain lions were also favored targets.

So great was the hatred of predators during this period that

In the early twentieth century, the Bureau of Biological Survey conducted a war against "varmints." Throughout the West, this agency killed as many as 35,000 coyotes per year. Although poisoned bait became the favored method, these animals were caught in traps (1924). Courtesy, National Archives.

even conservationists applauded government control. John Burroughs, a celebrated nature writer, complained in 1906 that the varmints in Yellowstone "certainly needed killing." The "fewer of these there are," he explained, "the better for the useful and beautiful game." William T. Hornaday, director of the New York Zoological Park and noted conservationist, offered similar advice regarding "wild-animal pests." He considered "firearms, dogs, traps and strychnine thoroughly legitimate weapons of destruction. For such animals, no half-way measures [would] suffice." His wording and tone indeed suggest that a war was on.

Not until the 1930s did the public begin to understand the consequences of predator control. Slowly, Americans came to appreciate carnivores for their role in controlling destructive populations of rodents and deer. Today, some environmentalists argue that predators have intrinsic value, apart from any usefulness to their ecosystems.

This photograph demonstrates the level of animosity against predators in the early-twentieth-century West. Courtesy, Glacier Natural History Association.

Jay C. Bruce, lion hunter, killed predators in Yosemite National
Park (1927). Courtesy, Yosemite Research Library.

In some parts of the West, the lack of predators led to an explosion of rodent
populations. These men pose with 1,200 jackrabbits, representing one night's
catch (1912). Courtesy, Idaho State Historical Society, Boise.

Joseph Grinnell (pictured right), Director of the Museum of Vertebrate Zoology, University of California, Berkeley (1938). Grinnell and his assistants were among the first to protest predator control. Courtesy, Museum of Vertebrate Zoology, University of California, Berkeley.

Defenders of Wildlife is among the organizations urging the reintroduction of wolves into the national parks. This advertisement appeared in *Time* in 1987. Courtesy, Defenders of Wildlife.

Illustrations of Predators

Americans of the last century would have been astonished by our recent goodwill toward the wolf—the quintessential predator. Most of them agreed with Theodore Roosevelt's condemnation of this animal as "the archetype of ravin, the beast of waste and desolation." Although largely undocumented, accounts of the wolf's treachery and cruelty were widespread.

Yet recent studies suggest that wolves are shy creatures who pose no threat to humans. The idea of the wolf, then, has been more terrifying than the behavior of the actual animal warrants. Of all creatures, wolves best embody the essence of the wilderness: alien, disordered, and beyond the control of man. For centuries, abhorrence of these qualities has been projected on real beasts. Today, as the number of Americans who value wilderness continues to rise, wolves, too, have come to be appreciated.

John Woodhouse Audubon's "White Wolf" was a terrifying, savage creature (1843). Courtesy, Department of Library Services, American Museum of Natural History.

No nineteenth-century adventure story was complete without a confrontation with wild animals. Pictured here is an illustration from Mayne Reid's *Adventures Among the Indians*. These wolves are depicted as hellish spirits, rising from the underworld. Courtesy, University Research Library, University of California, Los Angeles.

Painted by Edward Hicks, *Peaceable Kingdom* expressed the hope—based on religious prophecy—that one day the predator would lose the taste for blood (ca. 1834). Here bear and livestock (pictured right) share an ear of corn. Until very recently, Americans have required animals to act like well-behaved humans. But by the 1930s predators began to gain acceptance for their ecological usefulness. If the bloody tooth and claw could not be denied, at least they could be put to good use. Courtesy, National Gallery of Art, Washington, D.C. Gift of Edgar William and Bernice Chrysler Garbisch.

Ernest Thompson Seton's *La Poursuite* (The Pursuit) reveled in the wildness of wolves (1895). His paintings celebrated the savagery and frenetic energy of the predator. In Seton's day, the wolf was rapidly disappearing in the West. To him, man was a contaminant in the natural world. Courtesy, Seton Memorial Library, Philmont Scout Ranch, Cimarron, New Mexico.

Ernest Thompson Seton's *The Triumph of the Wolves* depicted a grisly scene (1892). Although the wolf here gnaws on a human skull, Seton believed this predator to be an ideal animal: courageous, loyal, monogamous, and cooperative with his fellows. Courtesy, Seton Memorial Library, Philmont Scout Ranch, Cimarron, New Mexico.

Ernest Thompson Seton's *The Black Wolf of Currumpaw* (1893). A portrait of his fictional wolf Lobo, a "grand old outlaw, hero of a thousand lawless raids," displaying his "huge ivory tusks." Courtesy, Seton Memorial Library, Philmont Scout Ranch, Cimarron, New Mexico.

In the late nineteenth and early twentieth centuries, popular literature often reproached predators for their "bloodthirsty" habits. In this illustration, from *Picturesque California* (1887), a grizzly devours a deer. Courtesy, the Bancroft Library.

Here a grizzly, claws extended, attacks two Indians who killed her cub. From *Picturesque California* (1887). Courtesy, the Bancroft Library.

5

Working Out the Beast

AMERICAN PERCEPTIONS

OF PREDATORS

Of all the wild creatures of North America, none are more despicable than wolves. WILLIAM T. HORNADAY, *The American Natural History*, 1904

. . . the woods were full of big, gray wolves, all howling and gnashing their teeth in the hope of picking my bones.
O.S. WHITMORE, "TREED BY WOLVES," 1909

I have seen wolves that were dainty as deer in matters of diet. . . . And I have knowledge of one wolf at least whose chiefest binding urge in life was loving devotion to his blind and helpless old mother.
ERNEST THOMPSON SETON, *Great Historic Animals, Mainly About Wolves*, 1937

Predators, as every hunter, conservationist, and animal lover knows, have become fashionable. Even the wolf—once believed to be a bloodthirsty, demonic creature deserving of extermination—has found numerous champions of late. During the last thirty years environmentalists have come to look favorably on the wolf and the grizzly as symbols of the wilderness. But not all Americans share their newfound enthusiasm for carnivores. Throughout the twentieth century coyotes in this country have suffered numerous atrocities, including being ignited alive and left to starve with their mouths wired shut; some have even been scalped. During the last decade residents of Minnesota choked wolves to death in snares, in defiance of their "endangered" status. Bounties on these animals were not repealed in Minnesota until 1977—four years after the passage of the Endangered Species Act.[1] Although wolves are gaining in popularity, such actions reveal the tenacity of deep-seated attitudes. For all the increased appreciation and sympathy that emerged during the late nineteenth and early twentieth centuries, some wild creatures remained beyond the pale. Even early conservationists did not accept predators.

Most Americans during this period believed that animals were either "good" or "bad." In fact, an article in *McClure's* pointed out that among animals there were "good" and "bad" individuals as well as "good" and "bad" species. Because they failed to adhere to human standards of morality, predators often were placed in the latter category. Barry Lopez, a modern nature writer, has suggested that lingering animosity toward these animals stems from our identification with their "defenseless" and "innocent" victims. As the most "savage" of beasts, predators seemed almost unnatural, somehow "'wrong' in the scheme of things." Similarly, a national park naturalist in the 1930s explained that "the hardest thing" regarding attitudes toward predation "is to change our natural psychological reaction to the killing of an ungulate by a carnivore."[2] This anthropocentric position sidesteps the point that humans themselves killed a great many ungulates. To some Americans, predators were "bad" because they got in the way of humans who did not want to compete for game. But the words of the park naturalist indicate that the issue went far deeper than that. Because we feel empathetic with prey, we have difficulty accepting that the natural world involves killing. The death of "innocent" animals was especially unnerving to humanitarians, who emphasized the importance of the individual life. Indeed, early arguments against predators indicate that it was more than their inconvenience to humans that made them so objectionable.

To be sure, not everyone at the turn of the century shared this aversion to meat-eaters. A few writers and artists reveled in their primordial savagery. Walter S. Kerr, for instance, recounted with considerable enthusiasm a battle he had witnessed between an enormous mountain lion, "ferocious beyond any description," and a buck of "unexampled bravery." Because the two animals were "equally matched in their agility, strength and cunning," they put on a spectacular fight. The "plunging, rearing, clawing, dodging," Kerr wrote, "the flying skin, the lashing tail, the crackling bushes, the leaves and pine-needles flying everywhere—all made a harrowing picture of deadly struggle too fast to see and too horribly cruel and desperate ever to be forgotten." When Kerr shot the cat, the violence continued, for the buck then charged him and killed his dog. Similarly, Maximilian Foster produced violent, sensational stories with such titles as "Terror," many of which featured predators.[3]

Even Ernest Thompson Seton relished the fierceness of carnivores. His "animal heroes" included bears and coyotes as well as his favorite— the wolf. To him, this animal embodied the wilderness. Wolves therefore appeared in Seton's stories as monumental creatures capable of wondrous feats. Billy, for example, was a wolf of unusual size and strength. When pursued up a steep mountain by a pack of fifteen dogs, he faced his assailants with "dusky mane a-bristling, his glittering tusks laid bare." One by one, Billy hurled the hapless dogs over the cliff: "Slash, chop and heave," Seton wrote, "from the swiftest to the biggest, to the last, down— down—[the great Wolf] sent them whirling from the ledge to the gaping gulch below, where rocks and snags of trunks were sharp to do their work."[4]

Similarly, Lobo, a wolf from Seton's popular book, *Wild Animals I Have Known* (1898), led a savage and romantic life. A "grand old outlaw, hero of a thousand lawless raids" on cattle, he eluded his human captors until his mate, Blanca, was killed. When caught, Lobo fought nobly, his eyes glaring "green with hate and fury." Significantly, Seton's most famous illustration of Lobo emphasized the wolf's "huge ivory tusks." This theme also was reflected in his paintings *La Poursuite*, which portrayed a pack of wolves chasing a sled, and *The Triumph of the Wolves*, which featured a wolf gnawing on a human skull. So gruesome was the latter scene that when Seton submitted the painting to the Canadian exhibition at the World's Fair in 1893, it was at first rejected for suggesting "a false idea of life in Canada."[5]

The best-known writer to glory in the antagonism between animals was Jack London. *The Call of the Wild* (1903), his most popular work, noted that a "moral nature" was a "vain thing and a handicap in the ruthless struggle for existence." Buck, the canine hero of his novel, was "a killer, a thing that preyed, . . . surviving triumphantly in a hostile environment where only the strong survived." He was indeed a formidable character, "ranging at the head of the pack, running the wild thing down, the living meat, to kill with his own teeth and wash his muzzle to the eyes in warm blood." A strictly carnivorous animal, Buck was "overspilling with vigor and virility." Contact with the wilderness had made him strong, in contrast to the house dogs who, in London's world, "did not count."[6]

As a literary naturalist, London was interested in conveying the power of primal forces. His animal characters were meant to be larger than life; according to one critic, *The Call of the Wild* "is not so much the story of a dog that becomes a wolf as a myth about life and death and nature." Still, after the publication of his novel in 1903, London began to identify himself with the predator. He signed his letters "Wolf," acquired a dog named "Brown Wolf," and hoped to move into "Wolf House"—a structure which burned down shortly after its construction.[7] Unlike Seton, London never acquired extensive field experience; he could not, therefore, insist too loudly on the accuracy of his stories. Yet these different writers both portrayed predators as being ideal animals—intelligent, adaptable, dignified, and courageous.

In fiction, this theme was appealing to urban readers who could easily romanticize life in the wilds. When it came to real animals, however, they were far from tolerant. Although "desirable" creatures could be appreciated, much of the population took a dim view of predators. Part of the problem was that animals were increasingly viewed as being responsible for their actions. This attitude was not completely new. For centuries humans had expected other creatures to distinguish right from wrong; during the Middle Ages a variety of animals had been formally brought to trial and executed for their crimes against men. Often, however, the guilty creatures were thought to be functioning as the familiars of evil spirits.[8]

By the nineteenth century the evolutionary link between humans and animals had been demonstrated by science. Well-respected individuals also began to argue on the basis of new research that animals possess "moral endowment." James H. Leuba, a psychology professor at Bryn Mawr College, pointed out that their similarities to people went beyond "anatomical structure and physiological functions." William T. Hornaday, a widely known writer and conservationist, agreed. "The ethics and morals of men and animals," he wrote, "are thoroughly comparative." Given this point, the protection of animals was inevitable. Yet it would also follow, as Hornaday indicated, that a few species were "degenerate and unmoral" and therefore undeserving of solicitude.[9] "Guilty" animals, he believed, must be "brought to justice." Because ethics were defined in terms of man, those animals who did not live by human principles were condemned.

Wolves evoked the greatest outrage. Americans had inherited from Europe a long tradition of horror tales regarding these animals. Generations of children learned from "Little Red Riding Hood" that wolves are deceitful and rapacious. This idea found its way into highbrow literature as well. Willa Cather's novel *My Ántonia* (1918) recounted a harrowing attack on a Russian wedding party. As the wolf pack closed in on the sled, the doomed guests screamed "piteously" as the "little bride hid her face on the groom's shoulder and sobbed."[10]

Western adventure and hunting stories also portrayed wolves as voracious and dangerous animals. So intense was the fear of them that accounts of their ferocity were much exaggerated. One Texas ranger, for example, was said to have been attacked by a pack who "[ate] his horse out from under him" in a "bloody frenzy." Another hapless individual wrote of his experience in northern Michigan, where "the woods were full of big, gray wolves, all howling and gnashing their teeth in the hope of picking my bones."[11]

In the early twentieth century conservationists supported this image of wolf behavior. "There is no depth of meanness, treachery or cruelty," Hornaday asserted, to which wolves "do not cheerfully descend." He maintained that the wolf not only "murders his wounded pack-mates" but also "will attack his wife and chew her unmercifully." More important, this predator could become "deadly dangerous to man." Yet for all their violent natures, wolves were also "contemptible cowards." No wild creatures, Hornaday concluded, "are more despicable than wolves." Because this animal was "a black-hearted murderer and criminal," he would have liked to "exterminate all . . . but one pair." As Director of the New York Zoological Park, Hornaday was a prominent figure whose ideas were taken seriously. Even Theodore Roosevelt, another ardent conservationist, denounced the wolf as being "the archetype of ravin, the beast of waste and desolation." So savage were these "vicious, bloodthirsty" creatures that he sometimes feared to leave his camp fire.[12] Although Seton and London appreciated the wolf as a symbol of the wild, most Americans had no sympathy for the actual animal.

Nor did coyotes fare much better in their estimation. Here, according to one western observer, was a true varmint, "a pariah whose name is an insult when applied to a man, be he ever so low." Whereas this animal could not equal the brutality of the wolf, he nevertheless possessed contemptible traits. The coyote was an especially perverse animal; his voice, which had an "eerie" and "blood-stilling" quality, was sometimes raised in direct defiance of humans. Descriptions held that coyotes were "slinking," "sneaking," "skulking" animals, "crafty," and "cowardly to the last degree." Worse, they were "piratical," given to stealing "helpless lambs" and other poor beasts, "who had no chance against cruelty and cunning." Even *Scientific American* denounced this animal in 1920 as the "original bolshevik." Condemnations of coyote habits could become sentimental and self-righteous in tone. The "destructive work" of this "marauder," mourned one writer, was indicated by the "tell-tale fragments of Bunny's fur coat." The coyote's taste for poultry further stirred the wrath of ranchers. While traditional Indian views of the coyote as a trickster had been good-natured, these accounts attacked the animal's character. The coyote, concluded one western observer, has "no higher morals" than a wildcat.[13]

His comparison was significant. Despite their fewer numbers, wildcats also were denounced for their apparently bloodthirsty habits. An article in *Scientific American* in 1915, for instance, derided the lion as a "brutal murderer" who victimizes "harmless, beautiful animals." Similarly, Roosevelt pointed out that the cougar "is a beast of stealth and rapine," a "destroyer of deer" with a "heart both craven and cruel." Hornaday regarded the cougar as an "intolerable pest." Because they were "fearfully destructive to deer and young elk," these predators, he advised, "must be hunted down and destroyed regardless of cost." In Hornaday's estimation, even the domestic cat was a morally depraved animal for eating birds and rodents.[14]

Attitudes toward bears were more ambiguous. So striking was the image of these animals that in the mid-nineteenth century the State of California pictured one on its flag. Yet bears could be contentious, troublesome creatures. Grizzlies were known to be dangerous. Some descriptions, however, revealed a thoroughgoing aversion to these creatures rather than a healthy respect for them. While recording her travels through the headwaters of the Yellowstone, Frances Fuller Victor complained that bears were "uncomfortably numerous." To her, the grizzly was not simply an animal to be avoided but a "wrathful monster."[15]

As was the case with wolves, reports of these animals at times resorted to hyperbole. "Club-Foot," for instance, was a nineteenth-century grizzly who assumed legendary proportions. If the numerous accounts of him can be believed, this phenomenal animal killed scores of people and had required most of California for his range. Similarly, Captain J. Hobbs's *Wild Life in the Far West* (1873) included a perilous encounter with a grizzly. Attracted by the venison in camp, this bear chased Hobbs and his companions up a tree, where they remained for an entire evening. "From our elevated position we could look down on him," Hobbs wrote, "but it was with no kindly feelings." When the grizzly finally wandered out of camp in the morning, and Hobbs was able to retrieve his rifle, he followed the animal and shot him in "retaliation." His party, he explained, "had been compelled to pass the night in a way that did not . . . increase our regard for our visitor." In addition to the hazards they presented, bears frequently were derided as being "pests," even by such conservationists as Hornaday.[16]

Although less menacing than wolves, wildcats, and bears, small predators did not escape disdain. The intensity of this attitude was demonstrated by a bizarre attempt by John Burroughs, the most gentle of naturalists, to kill a weasel by flinging "him violently upon the ground." Weasels, he pointed out, are "extremely remorseless and cruel." In any case, the fewer the varmints, according to Burroughs, the more the useful and attractive animals. Hornaday agreed with Burroughs's assessment of small predators. To him, weasels were "wicked" animals; he believed that wolverines, too, were among the most "devilish" of animal criminals. Reptiles also seemed particularly repulsive. To Hornaday's mind, such creatures as the pilot blacksnake, "long, thick and truculent," were "deserving of death." Certain snakes, he explained, have a "bad heart."[17]

Meat-eating birds, too, were viewed with derision. Burroughs denounced the shrike as a "butcher because he devours but a trifle of what he slays." Not surprisingly, vultures prompted considerable disgust, even among the most ardent of nature lovers. "There is no end to them," complained Mary Austin in *The Land of Little Rain* (1903), "and they smell to heaven. Their heads droop, and all their communication is a rare, horrid croak." So great was his scorn for predatory birds that Hornaday suggested in 1913 that several species, all hawks, be "at once put under sentence of death for their destructiveness of useful birds." Yet Hornaday's utilitarian bent was sometimes stronger than his loathing of predators, for owls, albeit under "grave suspicion," were saved from "instant condemnation" by "the delightful amount of rats, mice, moles, gophers and noxious insects they annually consume." As late as the 1930s the Yosemite Natural History Association could describe a hawk as "winged death" and a golden eagle as an "enemy."[18]

The tenor of these passages reveals the high level of emotion that predators inspired. In one sense, Americans might emphasize the ferocity of wild animals to justify killing them for food, sport, or convenience. But it was also fear of carnivores that prompted their condemnation. "Bearonoia," as it is called today, involved more than the actual hazard that these animals presented; over the last century numerous studies have confirmed that bears and wolves are shy of humans and will attack only rarely. One recent study of Yellowstone Park has pointed out that while visitors have been gored by buffalo and moose, it is the bear attacks that receive most of the press. The *idea* of the predator, then, has been more terrifying than the habits of the actual animals warrant.[19] And it suggests the rapaciousness that meat-eating people fear in their own characters. In other words, bears and wolves represent the worst side of human nature. More than other creatures, predators embody the essence of the wilderness: alien, disordered, and beyond the control of humans. For centuries, abhorrence of these qualities has been projected on real beasts.

Nothing demonstrates this point better than the reaction of early humanitarians to predators. While they were the first to extend rights to sentient creatures other than man, humanitarians continued to judge animal behavior by human standards. And because they were preoccupied with animal pain, their characteristic broad-mindedness stopped short when it came to carnivorousness. Seemingly bloodthirsty creatures who did not live by humanitarian principles were deemed unworthy of protection. In Victorian England the noted antivivisectionist Frances Power Cobbe had limited her solicitude to harmless creatures. She was interested in protecting "good" animals—a revealing qualifier. "We may," she assured her readers, "clear every inhabited country of wild beasts and noxious reptiles and insects whose existence would imperil our security . . . or who would devour our own proper food." Even Henry S. Salt, the most radical and vocal of animal rights advocates, did not extend his good will to "wolves, and other dangerous species." Like many vegetarians, he linked base savagery, in men as well as animals, to a meat diet. Another vegetarian, echoing Tennyson, exhorted his fellows in 1904 to "move upward, working out the beast, and let the wolf and tiger die." Humanitarians on both sides of the Atlantic attempted to reform meat-eating pets. Salt believed that "cats should not be allowed to torture birds." To this day animal-rights groups continue to publish leaflets outlining vegetarian diets for dogs and cats.[20]

Humane organizations in the United States were as intolerant of predators as their English counterparts. George T. Angell, president of the Massachusetts SPCA, was interested only in "harmless" animals. Even more disdainful of predators was Henry Bergh, who founded the SPCA in New York. He in fact threatened P. T. Barnum with prosecution for feeding "terrified" rabbits to snakes. When the circus caretakers pointed out that these animals eat only live prey, Bergh suggested that the "hateful reptiles" be allowed to starve. So serious was this humanitarian that Barnum's people were forced to convey their snakes in suitcases across the border to New Jersey—away from SPCA jurisdiction—for feeding.[21]

Newspapers unsympathetic to the humanitarian cause did not hesitate to point out Bergh's apparent inconsistencies. The *Sunday Mercury* sneered at Bergh's belief that "Nature," which "permits the hawk to pluck alive the gentle sparrow, and inspires pussy with a harmless taste for mice, will be rectified as soon as the new millennium is realized."[22] Although satiric, this statement indicates Bergh's perception that predation was "incorrect" in the natural world. Humanitarians could not accept predators because they valued the individual life above all else. They did not think of prey—the "innocent" rabbit or deer—merely in terms of species or populations. If humanitarians were to accept predators, they would have to accept also that the natural world did not conform to their values. Hence, they rejected these animals as "mistakes."

Humanitarians had retained the religious conviction that strife in nature was the result of human sin and would one day be amended. Eventually, the lion and the lamb could live side-by-side in peace, as prophesied in Isaiah 11:6–10. They were not the only animal lovers who held this view. In 1901 Hornaday, too, wrote that "Fighting Among Wild Animals" would one day cease; the struggle for existence, he assured his readers, will not last forever.[23] Whether condemning predators or attempting to reform them, animal lovers of the late nineteenth and early twentieth centuries were constructing their version of the peaceable kingdom. The intellectual revolution that had allowed humanitarians to broaden the realm of ethics to include animals was thus incomplete.

There were also practical reasons for not extending protection to all wild animals. Man "no longer tolerates wanton cruelty," noted one humane observer. "But he has not yet reached a point where he actually thinks anything cruel that is useful." Another humanitarian pointed out that "to admit that we are morally bound to consider the animals' feelings at all times would be so exceedingly inconvenient." In addition to the fear they provoked, predators were the animals most likely to get in the way of humans. "None of our fellow mortals is safe who eats what we eat," explained John Muir, or "who in any way interferes with our pleasures."[24] Indeed, at the turn of the century hatred of predators erupted into a full-scale war against these animals.

Ironically, the campaign against them was directed for the most part by individuals and agencies associated with the conservation movement. As the historian Donald Worster puts it, "instead of relying on the varmint-blasting frontiersman, the government itself undertook to eliminate the predator once and for all." This policy was very much in keeping with the progressive ideals of Theodore Roosevelt and Gifford Pinchot, two principle architects of resource conservation. Both men favored the efficient use of nature; as head of the Forest Service, Pinchot was interested not in the aesthetic value of trees but in how to maximize productivity.[25] Similarly, the purpose of government-supervised "game management" was to control wildlife populations for the benefit of man. Ridding the West of immoral and inconvenient animals thus became a means of imposing order and rectifying what was "wrong" in nature.

Much of the impetus for predator control came from ranchers whose lands had become too extensive to permit continual protection of sheep and cattle. In response, the Bureau of Biological Survey, established under C. Hart Merriam in 1905, stepped in to eliminate offending varmints. Originally a fact-finding agency, the Survey provided information regarding the use of poisons against predators; within two years its efforts resulted in the destruction of 1,800 wolves and 23,000 coyotes on national forest lands. Such activity was not unusual for government agencies. Established in 1916, the National Park Service also eliminated bears, wolves, coyotes, and wildcats on its lands; officials assumed that protection of desirable wildlife involved control of carnivores. Not until the 1930s was this policy seriously questioned. Encouraged by conservation agencies, even the Audubon Society destroyed predators, including meat-eating birds, in its sanctuaries.[26]

Still, it was the Survey that became a "professional army," sending forth trained hunters, trappers, and poisoners on private as well as public lands. Its goal in the early years was extermination. One hunter, whose work was reported by the *New York Times* to be "typical of many," distributed 4,000 poisoned baits and established fifty poison stations—which lured wary predators to . . . carcasses—in a single year. In its campaign against these animals the Survey was no less moralistic than the rest of the population. One report noted that coyotes, the agency's primary target, were engaged in a "wholesale slaughter" of game. During the 1920s the Survey poisoned 35,000 coyotes per year; by the next decade, three-fourths of its budget was devoted to predator elimination.[27]

Initially, public reaction to this program ranged from indifference to whole-hearted support. Newspapers and popular journals argued its economic benefits for all Americans. Quoted in the *New York Times*, Dr. Barton Warren Evermann, director of the California Museum of Sciences, defended the Survey's "war on wildlife" by claiming the savings in livestock amounted to three million dollars per year. The "notorious Custer Wolf," he pointed out, had killed 25,000 dollars worth of cattle in seven years before he was trapped by a government hunter. The accuracy of such figures, however, was difficult to demonstrate. Similarly, an essay in *Outlook* announced that predator elimination would bring "greater prosperity, more stock on the range, more beef, wool, and mutton for the markets." Furthermore, the author predicted, national forests "will again become the game paradise of the world." Although he did concede that "for a time perhaps a natural balance will be upset," he had faith that "man will be able to take care of the problem . . . and bring all the resources of the country to his highest use." Another article addressed the "disgruntled trapper or sentimentalist" who complained of government involvement in predator control, indicating that game had "greatly bene-fitted from elimination of enemies."[28]

Private citizens were encouraged by the Survey to participate. The media, too, promoted public action. Texans who enjoyed hunting, urged the *Literary Digest*, should pursue the coyote "and help rid the country of one of its chief pests at the same time." Killing predators also could be lucrative. The *Overland Monthly* reported that "Jim the Wolfer" earned a "fortune" in Montana by shooting, trapping, and poisoning "the huge, gaunt animals that devastate flocks of sheep and herds of cattle." A California hunter similarly received twenty-one dollars for killing a sin-gle coyote responsible for the loss of sixty turkeys and twenty-five lambs. His payment came from a variety of sources, including the customary five dollars from the county, fifteen dollars from three angry sheepmen, and one dollar contributed by the owner of the turkeys. Indeed, *Scientific American* observed in 1920 that the coyote, once "not worth the powder to shoot him," had "become a valuable source of revenue." One North Dakota couple thus kept "the wolf away from the door by dragging him in and making him pay the family's winter expenses." Shot from an airplane, their coyotes had taken "farmers' calves and sheep by dozens each year, not because of the food, but for the sheer lust of killing."[29] This passage demonstrates that it was not only the inconvenience of predators that accounted for the campaign against them.

Although the rejection of these animals was pervasive, a few critics of the Survey's policy emerged in the 1920s and 1930s. Such biologists as Olaus and Adolph Murie protested the extermination of predators, indi-cating their necessity to natural systems. During the summers of 1940 and 1941, Olaus studied the wolves of Mount McKinley. Contrary to their popular image, his strongest impression of the predators was their "friendliness."[30] Of more immediate consequence to the general public, however, were the efforts of a few popular writers determined to revise prevailing beliefs concerning meat-eaters.

Among the most notable was Ernest Thompson Seton. To demonstrate that wolves were worthy creatures, he humanized them. Their fierceness, he assured his readers, was rarely directed toward men. His grisly paintings *La Poursuite* and *The Triumph of the Wolves* emphasized the wildness of the animals rather than the menace that they represented to human society. Seton in fact refuted the "harrowing tales" which depicted "men, women and children" being "devoured by gruesome packs." Strangely enough, he reasoned, these "terrible" wolves were never seen. He thus lamented that the "traditional picture of the wolf presents an odious creature, a monster of cruelty and destruction" characterized "by nothing higher than a gluttonous appetite for food." In contrast, Seton, whose extensive wilderness experience included a six-month expedition to the Arctic Prairies, argued that these animals were "dainty as deer in matters of diet." Far from being the blood-lusting fiends of the popular imagination, wolves, in his estimation, were the purest, most virtuous of creatures.[31]

Not only do they practice monogamy, he pointed out in an essay concerning "animal marriage," but the male displays toward his wife "a feeling akin to chivalry." Because they pair for life, wolves suffered few incidents of disease, and their young enjoy the "advantage of two wise protectors." This clean living, he claimed, accounted for their defiance of "all attempts to exterminate them." On the other hand, such "promiscuous" animals as the northwestern rabbit were "periodically scourged by epidemic plagues." Along his journey to the Arctic, Seton noticed that these creatures had been "nearly exterminated" by disease.[32]

The good character of wolves, in Seton's stories, was enhanced by their tenderness. Lobo was capable of deep emotion: when his mate died at the hands of men, he wailed piteously and died of a broken heart. Despite his tremendous size and ferocity, this wolf, known as the "King of Currumpaw," was to him a symbol of "love-constancy." Seton's young wolves, moreover, received especially compassionate treatment from their elders. The orphaned Billy, for example, was adopted by a female wolf who was taken with "his very cubhood." Furthermore, Seton claimed to "have knowledge of one wolf at least whose chiefest binding urge in life was loving devotion to his blind and helpless old mother." Their wildness aside, his wolves were affectionate, endearing, near-human creatures. His stories were illustrated with anthropomorphic drawings of these animals eating with knives and forks, reading newspapers, and sitting in class-rooms.[33]

Indeed, Seton emphasized their intelligence. While most Americans viewed predators as "cunning" and "crafty," he favorably depicted wolves who lived by their wits. Billy's foster mother, for instance, was "a wolf of modern ideas." Because she was once caught, the old wolf was wary of men and their traps. Her fear wisely was conveyed to Billy, whom she instructed in the "rudiments of Wolf life." Caution concerning guns, traps, and poison, Seton explained, had "not yet had time to become ingrained as instinct"; therefore, young wolves had to be taught to avoid them. When it suited their purpose, however, wolves could make use of man's instruments: Seton related the case of a wolf at Fort Resolution who hauled up fishing lines from holes in the ice, helping himself "to what fish he required." In transmitting their knowledge to one another, wolves, he explained, employ an elaborate system of communication in-volving voice, example, and smell. "There is abundant proof," he claimed, "that the whole of a region inhabited by wolves is laid out in signal stations or intelligence depots." In his essays and stories, Seton referred to these as "wolf telephones."[34]

Such unusual portrayals undermined Seton's claim that his wolf sto-ries were rooted in fact and helped fuel the nature-faker controversy at the turn of the century. He answered his critics, however, by producing such nonfiction works as the two-volume *Life Histories of Northern Ani-mals* (1909) and the four-volume *Lives of Game Animals* (1928). These studies, widely cited by biologists, established his reputation as a compe-tent field naturalist. Yet Seton's writing was striking not only for its revision of wolf character but also for his unflattering portrayal of hu-mans. It was man, in his stories, who emerged as the unnatural creature of destruction—a kind of contaminant in the wilderness. The presence of people, he complained, "has always been ruinous" to wildlife. To him, the wolves were "correct" while man was "wrong." His signature, ending in a wolf paw print, attested to his veneration, as did his nickname, "Wolf Thompson."[35]

William J. Long, a contemporary of Seton, also sought to vindicate predators. In 1909 he assured readers in the *Independent* that the only bloodthirsty animals were those whose "natural instincts" have been thwarted—by humans or unfortunate circumstances. Savage weasels, for instance, were "almost invariably afflicted with tapeworms and parasites, which probably produce a continual irritation and craving for blood." Like Seton, Long was troubled by the "persistent slandering of honest wolves." Contrary to their traditional image, the wolves Long observed did not "kill weaker creatures indiscriminately." Nor did they compete with one another. The caribou kills Long witnessed hardly degenerated into a feeding frenzy; the wolf meals he witnessed were "as peaceable as a breakfast table."[36] The accuracy of these portrayals is not the point here. Clearly Seton and Long saw a need to revamp the image of the wolf— and the popularity of their stories indicates that at least some readers were receptive.

This effort to reconstruct the wolf has intensified during recent decades. In *Never Cry Wolf* (1963) Farley Mowat humanized predators, depicting them as gentle, compassionate creatures. Sent by the Canadian government to the Northwest Territories to investigate whether wolves were responsible for the diminishing number of caribou, Mowat claimed that the presence of these predators is actually essential to the health of the deer population. That they are reputed to benefit the herd by killing only the weak and sick helped make wolves acceptable to the American public. If the beast could not be "worked out" completely, then, at least his fangs and claws could be put to good use.

Although some recent studies have provided evidence that predators kill the strong as well, such behavior is not yet acceptable. Accordingly, Mowat's wolves destroyed nothing "for fun" and attacked humans only on rare occasions when under extreme provocation. Like those of Seton, his wolves paired for life, adopted orphaned cubs, educated their young, and even had a sense of humor. So great is Mowat's admiration for these animals that he dedicated his book to one of them. The success of *Never Cry Wolf*, coupled with the recent release of the Walt Disney film of the same title, attests to the continuing appeal of the "friendly" predator.[37] It is significant that this approach—which can be traced back to the nature fakers at the turn of the century—is required still. The implication here is that wolves are worthwhile animals deserving of protection *because* they are "good," compassionate, and useful. The rehabilitation of the wolf's character, then, indicates an unwillingness or an inability to accept nature on its own terms. In this sense, Seton and later Mowat did not break free of old perceptions; both writers found it necessary to impart human qualities to animals. What distinguished them was their attempt to include wolves, a despised species, with other benevolent animals who deserved protection.

Wolves were not the only animals to be recast early in the twentieth century. Coyotes—the quintessential varmints—were also sanitized. In *The Autobiography of a Tame Coyote* (1921), for instance, the "author" claimed, "I never steal anything except to eat it; I never kill anything merely to amuse myself, and a coyote never slanders its neighbor." This animal, moreover, was a teetotaler, refusing beer because "I had watched the effect of it on the men who drank it."[38] The point is that predators could not be defended on their own terms; to avoid condemnation they were required to act like well-behaved humans.

Seton, in any case, was heartened that coyotes thrived in the West. "They have learned how to prosper in a land of man-made plenty," he marveled, "in spite of the worst that man can do." In his story of Tito, it was the coyote who was "brave," while the domestic dog who pursued her was a "big-voiced coward." Similarly, the nature writer Enos Mills enjoyed the "coyotes' voices" he heard in the Rockies. To him, the sound was not "lonely or menacing," for "their shouts rang as merrily as though they were boys at play." Like humans, coyotes, he concluded, also "had enjoyments." Although his thoughts regarding this animal have remained unpublished until recently, Muir, too, praised the coyote, regretting that this "beautiful" and "graceful" animal has been persecuted for his taste for mutton.[39] Because many turn-of-the-century readers would not have approved of Muir's position, his wildlife portrayals which appeared in print featured such inoffensive animals as deer, squirrels, and nonpredatory birds.

The meat-eaters most readily made over in a human image were bears. As early as the 1860s, John Capen "Grizzly" Adams had demonstrated that even the most dangerous of animals could be made into a pet. In a sense, taming a grizzly was like conquering the wilderness. Adams admitted feeling "delight in subduing, little by little, a will so resolute, and a temper so obstinate." According to his autobiography, the public responded well to his efforts at mastery; Adams's collection of bears "excited the curiosity of thousands." By the early twentieth century Enos Mills was assuring his readers that grizzlies were "not ferocious." Unlike Roosevelt's terrifying descriptions, Mills's accounts of wildlife in the Rockies indicated that humans need not fear bears.[40]

In the early twentieth century visitors to the national parks came to relish the sight of these animals. Yosemite and Yellowstone offered opportunities to view them at close range. Both parks provided bear-feeding grounds for the amusement of tourists; these lured the bears to an arena with garbage. Owing to their humanlike features and humorous antics, bears were an especially popular attraction at the Yosemite zoo. Unlike wolves, who were perceived as being furtive, unfamiliar creatures, bears were very visible in national parks. According to *Yosemite Nature Notes*, they were among the best "animal friends" to be made. Yellowstone bears were also affectionate and neighborly; Seton's "Johnny Bear," based on his observations in this park, resembled a human boy in fur.[41] With such encouragement, tourists boldly approached these animals, sometimes feeding them by hand. Far from being "wrathful monsters," Yosemite and Yellowstone bears became delightful spectacles.

But they did not always conform to this amicable image. As late as 1933 one ranger naturalist lamented a mother deer's "piteous cries" when a brown bear seized her fawn. Recounted in *Yosemite Nature Notes*, this scene was labeled a "tragedy." To this day, visitors and National Park Service officials alike have exhibited surprise and dismay when an ill-behaved bear has failed to comply with human expectations. Troublesome bears continue to be killed in Glacier, Yellowstone, and Yosemite. During the last decade in Yosemite alone, the National Park Service has killed from two to twelve black bears annually—although not a single visitor there has died as a result of an encounter with one of these animals.[42] Such conflicts between humans and animals raise questions regarding the purpose of national parks. The fact that aggressive bears are still "disposed of" indicates that the interests of humans come first. To receive protection even in the national parks, then, animals are required to act peaceably.

During the last century very few animal lovers challenged this attitude. John Muir was an exception. Until his death in 1914, he viewed all wild creatures favorably, regardless of their actions. Like Seton and Mills, he portrayed bears as being "good-natured" animals. Yet when Muir was chased by an aggressive bear that did not meet his expectations, he did not condemn the animal. To his mind, no wild creatures were undeserving of respect. Throughout his writing he defended the glamourless animals. Rattlesnakes—traditionally regarded as dangerous and repulsive—were in his estimation "downright bashful." Lizards, too, were "gentle and guileless" creatures with "beautiful eyes, expressing the clearest innocence, so that, in spite of the prejudices brought from cool, lizardless countries, one must soon learn to like them." Moreover, Muir delighted in the company of a variety of insects, including grasshoppers and flies.[43] Although none of these animals possessed attractive, human-like features, Muir valued them.

Unlike most of his contemporaries, Muir refused to evaluate animal behavior by human standards. "It is right," he claimed, that creatures "make use of one another"; what bothered him was the spirit in which most humans used animals. Rather than viewing predators as an indication that something was amiss in the natural world, Muir assumed that something was amiss in human *perceptions*. His position, although atypical at the turn of the century, signalled the breakdown of the religious conviction, based on Genesis 1:28, that all creatures exist for man to subdue. His observations in the wilds led Muir to dismiss this view as "erroneous." What about the carnivores, he asked, who "smack their lips over raw man?" The notion that such troublesome beasts result from "unresolved difficulties connected with Eden's apple and the Devil" irritated Muir, who denied that "evil" animals require "cleansing."[44]

So strong was his rejection of anthropocentrism that he hoped, in a mischievous and somewhat disconcerting passage from his *Thousand-Mile Walk to the Gulf* (1916), that alligators would be "blessed now and then with a mouthful of terror-stricken man by way of dainty." In his original journal, these sentiments were reinforced by Muir's drawing, which did not appear in the published version, of an alligator eating a man while another saurian looked on with delight. Although the "universe would be incomplete without man," Muir concluded, "it would also be incomplete without the smallest transmicroscopic creature that dwells beyond our conceitful eyes and knowledge." Humans, then, should not value themselves "as more than a small part of the one great unit of creation."[45]

Muir thus exemplifies the essential link between approval of predators and ecological awareness. Once these animals had become acceptable—albeit in a civilized, sanitized form—a new ethic for wildlife, more comprehensive than anything that had yet appeared, could emerge.

6

Biocentrism

A NEW ETHIC FOR WILDLIFE

The living creation is not exclusively man-centered: it is biocentric.
LIBERTY HYDE BAILEY, *The Holy Earth*

We reached the old wolf in time to watch a fierce green fire dying in her eyes. . . . I was young then, and full of trigger-itch; I thought that because fewer wolves meant more deer, that no wolves would mean hunter's paradise. But after seeing the green fire die, I sensed that neither the wolf nor the mountain agreed with such a view.

ALDO LEOPOLD, "THINKING LIKE A MOUNTAIN"

No decade was more significant to American conservation than the 1930s. Environmental disasters, the most dramatic of which was the Dust Bowl, had forced the nation to establish new policies regarding soil, timber, and water. Never before had the consequences of human destructiveness been so keenly felt. This awareness was extended to wildlife, for attempts to "manage" game and "control" predators had resulted in ruinous imbalances in animal populations. It was during the 1930s, too, that habitat became an important issue in the protection of wildlife.

Previously, few defenders of animals had looked beyond the creatures themselves to the land they inhabited. Although national parks functioned in part as wildlife sanctuaries, their boundaries were arranged according to political rather than topographical considerations; Yellowstone, for instance, could not provide year-round protection for the elk herds which had to move to lower elevations during the winter.[1] Traditional justifications for preserving wildlife focused on individual animals or species. Humanitarians, of course, were concerned with the suffering of single creatures. Nor did hunters—preoccupied with the game necessary to their sport—look at the larger picture. Such organizations as Ducks Unlimited, for instance, were devoted to the protection of a single species. Most animal lovers focused on "innocent" and "beautiful" creatures, and hoped to protect them through the elimination of predators.

Even when this practice was questioned, the relationship between wild creatures and their environment was not always recognized. For the most part, justifications for protecting them remained narrow. Lamenting the disappearance of the panther, grizzly, and wolf, the *New York Times* appealed to pride in the nation's heritage in 1930; one of its writers warned that "our big wild animals" were making their "last stand." These words reveal that wildlife was valued for its size and attractiveness. Earlier, an article in the *Overland Monthly* entitled "The Wake of the Wolves" predicted that Americans would one day "be as zealous for the protection and preservation" of these animals "as they are now, and have been, for their extermination." It was their rarity, the author explained, that accounted for the value of carnivores.[2] For all this appreciation of vanishing species, however, there was little understanding of the importance of diversity.

Still, a few observers protested the killing of predators because it disturbed what they called the "balance of nature." As early as 1910 John Muir pointed out the folly of the jackrabbit hunts in the San Joaquin and Sacramento Valleys. "The loss of a few chickens from hawks and a few calves and sheep from coyotes," he observed, "amounted to nothing" compared to the destruction of crops and rangelands by rabbits. To remedy the imbalance they created, the "desperate" farmers were forced to the gruesome task of herding thousands of these animals into corrals, where they were clubbed to death. Had the coyotes, snakes, and predatory birds been allowed to remain in these regions, Muir concluded, farmers would not have been plagued with an overpopulation of rodents.[3]

Similar disasters involving hordes of mice in Kern County, California, further demonstrated the damage of human interference. So dense were these rodents in 1927 that streets had become impassable. One obvious explanation for such explosions in their populations was lack of predators. "We are slowly learning," noted a contributor to *Harper's*, "that the balance of nature is something which should not be too rudely disturbed without careful investigation." Even varmints, it seemed, performed "their useful functions."[4]

For this reason public opinion began to turn against government efforts at predator control in the late twenties and early thirties. Because Kansas had "once ranked the coyote in the category of evils alongside of beer, cigarets, Wall Street and the octopus," complained one writer in the *Literary Digest*, the region had become afflicted with "plagues of long-legged rabbits." Federal and state authorities, he concluded, were responsible for this "serious menace." Similarly, the *New York Times* attacked the Biological Survey's policy of extermination for failing to comply "with sound principles of conservation." Indeed, according to H. E. Anthony of the American Museum of Natural History, the protest against the Survey had reached nationwide proportions. Due to zealous predator control, wildlife in the West, he affirmed in 1931, was "confronted with the most serious crisis in its history."[5]

Anthony and other scientists thus attempted to dissuade the Survey from its policy of extermination. In 1924 several members of the American Society of Mammalogists had confronted government biologists regarding the issue of poisoning; carnivores, they argued, were necessary to curtail the numbers of rodent "pests." In the Survey's defense, E. A. Goldman claimed that the aim of his agency was not to wipe out entire species but to eliminate predators only in specific locations, particularly where they conflicted with ranchers. At any rate, he added, these animals "no longer have a place in our advancing civilization."[6]

The strongest opposition to his views came from the Museum of Vertebrate Zoology at the University of California, Berkeley. Here, director Joseph Grinnell and his assistants condemned the Survey's extermination policy as well as its propaganda. Their work reached the public in a variety of ways. First, the Museum sponsored lectures for general audiences. At nearby Yosemite, Grinnell's students further established the first official interpretive program in a national park.[7] Still, Grinnell's initial efforts could not compete with the press that the Survey had received.

According to Anthony, this agency had "unduly blacken[ed] the character of certain species" and encouraged "the public to advocate destruction of wild life." So effective was the campaign against coyotes that even reluctant westerners felt "obliged" to shoot them. The Survey considered only ranching interests, Anthony complained, at the expense of the rest of the nation, which would not benefit from elimination of its wild creatures "to make the West a sheep man's paradise." But such objections to the work of the Survey remained unheeded. As late as 1948, Ira Gabrielson, head of the agency, announced that "the ideal of ecological balance" would not determine "the kind of, extent of, and direction of predator control." In *Science* magazine Goldman in fact had dismissed Anthony's arguments as "emotional."[8]

Current scholarship has indicated that he had a point. According to Thomas R. Dunlap, it would be a mistake to equate the "balance of nature" concept used by mammalogists in their arguments against the Survey with the modern science of ecology. Their protest, he suggests, lacked the scientific evidence needed to demonstrate exactly "how predators and prey fit into a connected system." Indeed, the idea that equilibrium in nature must be maintained was "as vague as it was appealing." Donald Worster has characterized notions concerning "nature's economy" as essentially romantic; a hundred years earlier, Transcendentalists had perceived unity in nature. For centuries, western thought held that living creatures were connected through the Great Chain of Being, a hierarchy of living things.[9] These concepts, however, remained a far cry from a modern understanding of ecosystems; until the 1930s, little was known about checks and balances in animal populations. Before environmental relationships could be clearly perceived, the methods of investigating them would have to change.

By today's standards of field biology, early studies of predation appear limited. For the most part researchers merely examined the stomach contents of carnivores. Grinnell himself was mainly a taxonomist. But by the late thirties such scientists as Adolph Murie, who worked for the National Park Service, had devised a new approach. Unlike his predecessors, he observed the habits of living predators, devoting two summers to watching wolves in the wild. Murie also examined prey and the conditions of their habitat, including plants and weather. Although his conclusions were similar to those of earlier scientists who asserted the necessity of predation, Murie's research provided the essential evidence.[10]

On one level the early debate regarding predator control indicates a conflict in values. One side responded to immediate economic interests, while the other took the long view, favoring natural rather than human-imposed checks and balances. In a sense, however, each position can be described as utilitarian, for human welfare was the ultimate concern of both. Initially, consideration for natural systems had not changed the dominant precepts of American conservation; self-interest remained the strongest motivation. To be sure, a few scientists—Adolf Murie, for one—displayed a genuine affinity for predators, apart from their usefulness to their ecosystems and, by extension, to humans. But most biologists who defended predators in the early thirties would not go so far as to claim that these creatures had rights.

Even for the National Park Service, appreciation of animals for their own sakes was hardly a concern. Although committed to preserving wildlife, this institution focused on use, albeit recreational, of the resource. Upon the inception of the Park Service in 1916, Grinnell had described wildlife as an "asset" to the reserves, "particularly where the animals to be conserved are useful for game or food." To him, wild creatures were important for scientific as well as aesthetic purposes. Predators, he advised, "should be left unmolested" so as "to retain their primitive relation to the rest of the fauna." But when they became "menaces," either to other animals or to human visitors, carnivores could be destroyed. Similarly, the first tenet of Grinnell's "Wild-Life Creed," printed in *Yosemite Nature Notes* in 1926, held that "the fullest use should be made of our country's wild life resources from the standpoint of human benefit." Conservationists applauded his creed, indicating their support of his utilitarian assumptions.[11]

Nor did Grinnell's students, in compiling the National Park Service report on fauna in 1932, devote much space to ethical questions regarding animals. Instead, from the outset of this work they emphasized that wildlife was a "vital part" of the national heritage, which provided "characteristic examples of primitive America" and contributed "so much to the enjoyment derived by visitors." In fact, the second fauna report, printed in 1934, explained that man's objective in preserving animals was "selfish." The following year, an article in *Yosemite Nature Notes* agreed that "there should be at least a few places where all forms of animal life can continue to live for the pleasure and education of the many generations which follow us."[12]

Nothing illustrated the utilitarian bent of the Park Service better than its treatment of predators. Organized destruction of these animals in the reserves had been abolished in 1931. A decade earlier the striking decimation of the deer population on the Kaibab Plateau had demonstrated that carnivores were needed to stabilize numbers of game as well as bothersome rodents. Owing to the elimination of predators, an overpopulation of deer in this region of Northern Arizona had resulted in the starvation of many animals. A similar mishap in Yosemite had convinced Park Service officials of "the value of a varmint." Not only did deer destroy the vegetation of the Valley, but they had become "so common and goat-like . . . that their interest to the visitor was greatly diminished." One ranger concluded that predators, "by keeping the deer population within the limits of the grazing capacity of the range and by eliminating the weaker individuals," serve "in a useful way that fully justifies" their "protection." But when it came to "troublesome situations," killing individual predators, as Grinnell had advised earlier, remained "an accepted solution."[13]

Of all the wild creatures in the reserves, bears were the most likely to conflict with humans. Wayward individuals, characterized by the Park Service as "criminals" of "bad character," were "disposed of." Similarly, the "proper" response to encountering rattlesnakes at "human concentration points" was to kill them. The Park Service, however, regretted such measures, for "since man is superior, . . . it would be a miserable admission of defeat if he could not find ways of solving these simple problems of animal injury to man without resorting to campaigns of destruction."[14]

The problem was that park visitors, who were mostly urban, did not know how to react to wild animals. Complaints against noisy nocturnal birds and other "annoying" creatures were so frequent that the Park Service was compelled to explain why they should not be killed. But many activities in national parks failed to encourage respect for fauna. Zoos and bear-feeding grounds, for example, featured animals in artificial settings, creating a "carnival" atmosphere. The "bear dumps" in Yellowstone and Yosemite had long been an attraction to tourists, who were thus assured a glimpse of park wildlife. As many as five hundred visitors sometimes assembled in the amphitheater to view the blacks, browns, and grizzlies feed. Moreover, it was widely known that people fed these animals by hand. Neither the Park Service nor the visitors objected much to the resulting degradation of the bears, although both worried about animals who got their paws stuck in tin cans at the garbage site.[15]

Of greater concern was the injury to humans from rambunctious creatures. Articles in *Yosemite Nature Notes* cautioned against hand-feeding; other national park publications urged that the "bear show" be phased out, having served its initial purpose of "bringing the people to an appreciation of the wonderful things to be seen and done" in the reserves. By the 1930s park officials recognized that difficulties with bears stemmed from "man's efforts to force the animal life to . . . fit his concept instead of developing his concept to fit the wild life as it really exists in a natural setting." The agency abolished the bear-feeding grounds in 1943. Even this gradual removal of artificial features conveyed a degree of utility, for now visitors were afforded the "new joy of seeking out the wild creatures where they are leading their own fascinating lives."[16]

Yet attitudes in the Park Service were in a state of transition during this period. For all its anthropocentric viewpoint, the fauna series could describe "each wild animal" as a "priceless creation." Another such passage noted that predators, provided they were not exotic, had "as much right as any other member of park fauna." No human standards of morality, moreover, "should be attached to any animal." Although these brief statements hardly affected the general tone of the work, they indicated that the Park Service was moving, albeit slowly, in a new direction. Looking back on the thirties, Olaus Murie, who had become president of the Wilderness Society, claimed that the motivations of some scientists who defended predators had not been altogether clear, even to themselves. "Deep in their hearts, if they had thought it out fully," he mused, "was concern for the coyote itself."[17] But an ethic which incorporated the burgeoning science of ecology had not been articulated. To be sure, the need for a change in conservation policy was evident. The nineteenth-century method of protecting isolated species was giving way to concern for the relationship between animals and their environment.

Still, it was difficult to set aside entire habitats. While the national parks offered large areas for wildlife, none could "provide year-round sanctuary for adequate populations of species." Originally, the reserves had been created to conserve monumental scenery; their artificial boundaries were determined by economics, not ecology. Even the establishment of Everglades National Park in 1934, which appeared to signal the waning of monumentalism, was impeded by commercial interests. It seemed inevitable, even to the Park Service, that external pressures would continue to prevent the preservation of complete animal habitats.[18]

Clearly ecological awareness in itself was insufficient motivation. Arguments which emphasized the usefulness of predators to their ecosystems, for example, were unconvincing to those who had faith that humans could manipulate the environment to suit their purposes. "Has not man survived and improved his standard of living," asked one critic, "in direct proportion to the extent he has gained control of nature?"[19] Hence, several scientists began to argue for ecological integrity on moral, rather than merely practical, grounds.

This tack was not entirely new. As early as 1915, Liberty Hyde Bailey, a Cornell professor of horticulture, suggested that abuse of the natural world was unethical. His book *The Holy Earth* portrayed man as a "trustee" of the land who must honor his "obligations." Like turn-of-the-century humanitarians, Bailey rejected the notion that the world exists only for humans. "The living creation," he wrote, "is biocentric." This term suggested not only that living things are connected but also that they have a right to function in their natural environments.[20] Biocentrism was broader and more holistic than the traditional anthropocentric view of the world. Yet it differed from humanitarianism in that it was concerned not with the suffering of individual animals but with human mistreatment of nature in general.

During the next two decades this new perspective drew from the developing science of ecology. Among the biologists affected were Adolf and Olaus Murie—the brothers who opposed predator control. Olaus, the elder of the two by ten years, was especially interested in the formulation of ethics regarding the natural world. Yet the scientist who became the best-known exponent of biocentrism was Aldo Leopold. His book *A Sand County Almanac*, published posthumously in 1949, would articulate its precepts for the general public.

How this former Gifford Pinchot devotee came to develop the "land ethic" is one of the most famous stories in American environmental history. Among conservationists today, Leopold is recognized as the prophet; his ideas concerning ecological conscience are heralded as gospel. His significance was recognized by his contemporaries as well. "When Leopold's trumpet call rang through the forests," wrote Frank A. Waugh, a professor of horticulture, "echoes came back from every quarter."[21]

Leopold's early years, however, gave little indication of his ultimate philosophy. Educated at the Yale School of Forestry, he began his career in the Southwest in 1909, where he was active in varmint control. Like many avid sportsmen, he had an interest in game protection. To him, the best way to ensure large populations of game was the elimination of predators—those "skulking marauders"—who were "getting away with our deer." Leopold thus advised "going out after the last lion scalp, and getting it."[22] During this period he edited the *Pine Cone*, a bulletin of the New Mexico Game Protective Association, and wrote a game handbook. His enthusiasm for animal conservation earned him a medal of recognition from the Permanent Wild Life Fund.

Leopold's appreciation of animals led to his desire for wilderness preservation. In the early 1920s he worked to set aside a roadless area in the Gila National Forest. As a result of his efforts, the country's first wilderness reserve was created in 1924. At this time Leopold's arguments to rally public support for his cause were largely utilitarian. In *Sunset* magazine, for example, he warned that "soft 'improvements'" were changing the character of western lands, making it impossible for Americans to experience firsthand the pioneer conditions which had shaped their culture. "Of what avail are forty freedoms," he asked, "without a blank spot on the map?"[23]

By the late twenties Leopold left the Forest Service to pursue a profession in game management, which he described as "the coordination of science and use." He published the definitive text on this subject in 1933 and secured a chair in the Department of Agricultural Economics at the University of Wisconsin. But several experiences during this period were to draw Leopold away from the utilitarian ideal of "controlling" wildlife. First, a trip to view the carefully managed forests of Germany left him feeling uneasy about "sustained yield" practices; this intensely regulated landscape repulsed him. That same year, he acquired a shack in a pastoral area of Wisconsin, which was to become the setting for *A Sand County Almanac*. Here, he would observe formerly abused farmland revert to a wild, healthy state. A hunting trip to a remote wilderness in northern Mexico had convinced Leopold that, up to that point, he had seen "only sick land." And in the 1930s the land he observed in the Midwest was more damaged than it had ever been.[24]

Leopold began to refine his ideas at his Wisconsin retreat. Conservation, he feared, was getting nowhere. To his mind, the mere recognition that "land is a community" was not enough; it was also necessary that "land . . . be loved and respected." What was missing from conservation thought was an ethic. Thus far, Americans had viewed land and its inhabitants only as commodities which entailed "privileges but not obligations." To Leopold's mind, ethics, or "limitation[s] on freedom of action in the struggle for existence," were evolving; while the earliest in human history "dealt with the relation between individuals," later "accretions dealt with the relation between the individual and society."[25]

It was now time, he reasoned, to extend "social conscience" from humans to the natural world. His "land ethic" thus expanded "the boundaries of the community to include soils, waters, plants, and animals, or collectively the land." No longer could human actions, then, be determined by economic expediency. "A thing is right when it tends to preserve the integrity, stability, and beauty of the biotic community," Leopold wrote. "It is wrong when it tends otherwise." The point here was not to prevent use of resources. But Leopold affirmed "their right to continued existence, and at least in spots, their continued existence in a natural state."[26]

In order for this "ecological conscience" to take hold, man would have to relinquish his position as "conqueror of the land-community" to become "plain member and citizen of it." Indeed, Leopold believed the "greatest cultural advance . . . of the past century" to be "Darwinian ry," which not only revealed the unity of the natural world but also defied human dominance. Like Bailey, Leopold stressed the importance of a biocentric—rather than anthropocentric—outlook. As its title indicates, his essay "Thinking Like a Mountain" assumed a viewpoint broader than the merely human. This piece dramatized Leopold's eventual rejection of predator control. Although he once believed that "no wolves would mean hunter's paradise," Leopold came to realize "that neither the wolf nor the mountain agreed with such a view."[27] Humanitarians earlier had attempted to view the world from the perspective of animals. Now this approach could be supported by ecological principles.

Leopold's gradual conversion from wolf-hater to biocentrist reflected larger changes in conservation thought. As the environmental movement developed in the 1960s and 1970s, *A Sand County Almanac* became one of its most revered books. As Leopold pointed out, nineteenth-century science had provided the foundation for biocentrism. The notion that the world was not made only for humans was essential for the development of this new perspective. By the 1920s and 1930s human-made disasters such as the Dust Bowl convinced some Americans that people could not continue to view the natural world as a commodity. Disasters such as the ravaging of the Kaibab Plateau by deer also demonstrated that even predators—inconvenient and menacing as they might be to humans—were essential to their ecosystems.

Leopold was not the only nature writer to bring these themes before the American public. Sally Carrighar, too, conveyed the biocentric perspective in her popular books, *One Day on Beetle Rock* (1944) and *One Day at Teton Marsh* (1945). These told the same story from the perspectives of a variety of animals. Each chapter was devoted to a different wild creature, including a coyote, a deer mouse, a mosquito, and a frog. Uniting these disparate subjects was their relationship to each other and to their environment. What further distinguished Carrighar's books from the nature writing of previous eras was the absence of moralizing. There were no "villains" at Beetle Rock or Teton Marsh; nor were the animals characterized as being noble, heroic, or humanlike. Although the animal world she described had order, it was not guided by human standards of right and wrong. Carrighar's wild creatures simply functioned in their ecosystems—and she conveyed the vitality and the beauty of natural processes without interjecting or intruding on her subjects.[28]

Rachel Carson refined this technique a decade later. In the 1950s she produced several best-selling books, including *The Sea Around Us* and *The Edge of the Sea*. Like Carrighar, Carson kept herself out of her narrative. Instead, she focused on ecological relationships. Owing to Carson's vivid detail and her sense of wonder regarding the natural world, her writing appealed to the general public. Her most famous work, *Silent*

Spring, published in 1962, prompted national concern about the hazards of DDT to birds and other wildlife. Shortly after this book appeared, Carson, who embraced the concept of "reverence for life," received the Albert Schweitzer Medal of the Animal Welfare Institute.[29] But *Silent Spring* did more than deplore cruelty to animals; it also created a general awareness of ecology which fueled the environmental movement. While most early conservationists focused on the protection of individual animals or single species, writers such as Carson demonstrated the need to consider entire natural systems.

Perhaps the most unlikely nature writer to adopt the biocentric perspective was Joseph Wood Krutch. The early career of this celebrated drama critic gave little indication that he would one day celebrate the processes of nature. His book *The Modern Temper*, published in 1929, conveyed a disturbing sense of futility and alienation. At first Krutch was bothered by the notion derived from modern science, that the natural world is devoid of human values. After his move from the East to the remote Southwest, however, Krutch's writings became increasingly upbeat. He attributed this change in tone to intense nature study. Like Ernest Thompson Seton and William J. Long, Krutch looked to the wilds for solace from the bleaker implications of science. But unlike his predecessors, he did not find human values there. What he found instead was an understanding of the natural world on its own terms. Encounters with wildlife in the desert taught Krutch to accept that the "lion and the lamb will not—they simply cannot—lie down together." Yet he also discovered that "they are essential to one another nonetheless. And the lesson to be learned is applicable far outside the field of conservation." Late in his life, Krutch found comfort in the idea that humans are citizens of "the community of living things."[30]

Far from lamenting this revelation, Krutch extolled the value of belonging to something greater than ourselves. Whereas he once condemned mechanistic science, Krutch embraced the science of ecology. No longer did he view humans as being isolated in the universe; much of Krutch's later writing was in fact devoted to his observations of animal life. Published in the 1950s, his books *The Desert Year* and *The Voice of the Desert* encouraged readers to abandon their anthropocentric notions and view the wildlife of the Southwest from the perspective of the desert.

The impact of biocentric thinking thus reached far beyond the scientific community. The conviction that creatures other than humans have rights—advanced by nineteenth-century humanitarians—and the new understanding of the interdependence of living things (publicized by writers such as Leopold and Carson) provided the foundation for the environmental movement. By the 1960s, conservationists who accepted the concepts of ecological conscience and the land ethic assumed the label "environmentalists." Although new to the Western world, this modern development in conservation thought paralleled Native American philosophies. Traditionally, most Indian cultures had rejected the notion that land and animals were commodities or property to be owned. Their religious ceremonies encouraged reverence for wildlife as well as a holistic approach to the natural world. Accordingly, environmentalists drew inspiration not only from modern nature writers but also from the ancient traditions of Native Americans.

This shift from the human-centered tenets of nineteenth-century conservation culminated in the passage of the Rare and Endangered Species Act of 1973. Unlike previous legislation to protect wildlife, the Endangered Species Act was not motivated by economic or purely human concerns; it required the protection of habitats as well as animals. It also prompted legal action on behalf of wildlife. Using the Endangered Species Act, environmentalists filed suit in 1975 to stop construction of the Tellico Dam on the Little Tennessee River. This project, they charged, would destroy the endangered snail darter, a small minnow found only in the Little Tennessee River. Owing to a surprise ammendment in 1979, the Tellico Project was exempted from the Endangered Species Act— and the dam was built. Despite the apparent failure for environmentalists, this controversy is significant in the history of conservation thought. Centering on a tiny fish, it demonstrated that some Americans had come to value a species that is neither spectacular nor of immediate use to humans.

7

New Directions
for Protection

The animal shall not be measured by man. In a world older and more complete than ours they move finished and complete. . . . They are not brethren, they are not underlings; they are other nations, caught with ourselves in the net of life and time, fellow prisoners of the splendour and travail of the earth. HENRY BESTON, *The Outermost House*

We do not know very much at all about animals. We cannot understand them except in terms of our own needs and experiences. And to approach them solely in terms of the Western imagination is, really, to deny the animal. BARRY LOPEZ, *Of Wolves and Men*

Not all Americans who value wildlife have embraced the principles of ecology. Although biocentrism has been a dominant tenet of the environmental movement, many conservationists have retained their anthropomorphic, if not anthropocentric, approach to the animal world. Because kinship has long been an important basis for protection, solicitude remains for the most part limited to creatures closely resembling humans. Certainly the general public exhibits little sympathy for "unattractive" creatures. From an objective standpoint, there is little reason to value a squirrel more than a rat. Yet squirrels—with their large, dark eyes and small noses—are considered to be cute, desirable animals, while rats—with their beady, red eyes and long noses—are considered to be repulsive.

This tendency to project human standards of attractiveness on other creatures has intrigued some scholars. According to Stephen R. Kellert, a behavioral scientist at Yale, insects, spiders, snakes, and other animals lacking "phylogenetic relatedness" are not appreciated by the general public, whereas large mammals receive much attention. Elliot Norse of the Ecological Society also laments that "squishy" or "crawly" creatures receive little support. Furthermore, surveys of attitudes have demonstrated that most Americans still worry more about individual suffering than the maintenance of animal populations.[1] Their continued emphasis on sentience—which requires the ability to empathize—is related to their preference for humanlike animals.

Among animal lovers, a schism has resulted, for this humanitarian bent conflicts with biocentric concern for the diversity of species. During the 1980s membership in animal rights organizations increased dramatically. By 1989 the largest of these, People for the Ethical Treatment of Animals (PETA), had attracted 280,000 people. In the tradition of Henry S. Salt, PETA goes far beyond the early humane movement's general interest in kindness and mercy to "inferior" animals to a belief that other creatures have rights. Although the implications of this point—ethically and legally—are vague, PETA's position is that animals do not belong to humans. To date, this organization has protested the use of animals not only in biomedical research but also in zoos and circuses.

Animal rights advocates believe that sentient creatures should be "liberated," just as oppressed groups of humans have gained freedom. Drawing from the rhetoric of the civil rights movement of the 1960s, they predict that the cruel treatment of animals which today might seem acceptable will one day be condemned as intolerable behavior. Biocentrists, on the other hand, are more interested in the rights of the natural world in general than in those of individual creatures. Their arguments derive from the principles of ecology. Both positions are represented in such organizations as the Sierra Club and Earth First!, which sometimes creates friction between members.

The first animal rights advocates—who emerged from the humane movement of the nineteenth century—perceived other creatures in human terms. To be sure, they denied that animals exist for human use; they were in fact the first conservationists to reject the anthropocentrism of Western civilization. Yet Salt himself, who vigorously defended the autonomy of animals, could not avoid humanizing the natural world. His rejection of predators further demonstrated the limitations of the humane position. While the attribution of human characteristics to animals helped muster support for their protection during the last century, the popular naturalist John Burroughs had warned of the pitfalls of this tendency. "I would only help my reader to see things as they are," he explained, "and stimulate him to love the animals as animals, and not as men." Burroughs was careful to distinguish "the animal on the animal plane" from "the animal on the human plane." Similarly, the *New York Times* complained in 1905 that, "the dog, as we know him, is a human manufacture, rather than an animal."[2]

From the turn of the century, such anthropomorphism has led to a preoccupation with feeling which has persisted to this day. Peter Singer, a spokesman for modern animal rights advocates, continues to argue that sentient creatures have the right to live free from suffering; in his estimation, the capacity to suffer, as outlined by Jeremy Bentham in eighteenth-century England, remains the best criterion for moral standing. "If a being is not capable of suffering, or of experiencing enjoyment or happiness," he maintains, "there is nothing to be taken into account."[3] The arguments in Singer's book *Animal Liberation* are based on the ability of other creatures to feel.

Biocentrists, on the other hand, insist that humanizing animals is no longer an appropriate approach to protection. At the very least, the humane perspective is "sentimental"; at worst, it obscures what is to them the central concern of modern protection—the integrity of ecosystems. J. Baird Callicot, for instance, dismisses the moral system of the "neo-Benthamites" as biologically unsound. He in fact claims that the "idea that pain is evil and ought to be . . . eliminated" is "preposterous."[4]

Certainly humane condemnation of animal suffering has been difficult to extend to wildlife. Although ecological awareness has required humanitarians to revise their initial response to predators, hunting and meat-eating remain controversial topics. Feeling threatened, modern sportsmen have complained about the humane "hang-up about death," as well as the pervasive ignorance about conditions in the wild. Even now, humanitarians do not completely accept the naturalness of predation. Yet Aldo Leopold did not find hunting to be inconsistent with his land ethic. To his mind, shooting animals was an acceptable activity so long as it was carried out in a spirit of respect for the natural world. In any case, numerous biocentrists have noted the impossibility of protecting wild animals not only from humans but also from each other.[5]

Nor are biocentrists concerned with the claims of domestic creatures.

Callicot characterizes them as the stupid and docile creations of man. Refuting Singer, he writes that chickens and cows are incapable of "natural behavior" and therefore cannot experience frustration in factory farms. "It would make almost as much sense to speak of the natural behavior of tables and chairs," he sneers; hence, domestic animals cannot "be liberated," as Singer wishes. More importantly, the presence of domestic creatures can disrupt the ecosystem, thereby violating the land ethic.[6] Clearly, Leopold's philosophy accorded rights to soils, waters, and plants as well as to animals.

In defense, humanitarians argue that their movement does not preclude respect for natural systems. Because "habitat is so important to animals," Mary Midgley has pointed out, it too must be protected. To her, however, the ability to feel remains the most significant issue, owing to "the very dramatic difference it makes in the kind of needs which creatures have, and the kind of harm which can be done them." Singer also distinguishes between protection of sentient animals and respect for the land which supports them. Still, both philosophers downplay the clash between these two rationales for protection. Although he regrets that "environmentalists have been more concerned with wildlife and endangered species than with animals in general," Singer in fact believes that "it is not too big a jump from the thought that it is wrong to treat whales as giant vessels filled with oil and blubber to the thought that it is wrong to treat pigs as machines for converting grains to flesh."[7]

In contrast, many biocentrists see their position as "incompatible" with that of modern humanitarians. Alastair S. Gunn, for example, places the "neo-Benthamites" in the context of the "'Western' obsession with individualism." Their "atomistic, competitive notion of rights," he explains, can never be incorporated into an environmental ethic based on the primacy of the biotic community. He views the humane criterion of pain as dangerously narrow, for it excludes animals without complex nervous systems. Taking this objection one step further, Callicot associates humanitarianism with the anthropocentrism it supposedly refutes, for both perspectives "draw a firm distinction between those beings worthy of moral consideration and those not." The ideas of this movement, he regrets, have distracted ethical philosophers from the "much deeper challenge" of biocentrism, keeping them "firmly anchored to familiar modern paradigms."[8]

Recently, the humane emphasis on kinship and sentience has drawn criticism from "deep ecologists." This term indicates a rejection of the "shallow" ecology which reveals the relationships between living things only for the benefit of humans. Drawing from biocentrism, deep ecology emerged during the 1970s. Its proponents argue that all the components of the natural world—including plants and rocks—have an inherent value. Deep ecology, then, is egalitarian in assigning worth. Humanitarian arguments for animal rights, on the other hand, have resulted in "a pecking order" in the "moral barnyard."[9]

The debate between humanitarianism and biocentrism has not been confined to the realm of moral philosophy. When it comes to policy, these two perspectives are similarly difficult to reconcile. The burro controversy of the last two decades provides a notable example. Brought into desert regions by nineteenth-century prospectors, these "bothersome little beasts," as one critic has tagged them, are considerably destructive to the landscape. Because feral burros have few natural enemies and live up to twenty-five years, they multiply quickly. So great did their numbers become in China Lake, California, that they obstructed naval roads, presenting a safety hazard. Worse, in Death Valley, Bandelier, and the Grand Canyon—all protected by the National Park Service—burros compact the soil, causing erosion. Moreover, their consumption of vegetation competes with that of native wildlife, including bighorn sheep. In the Grand Canyon alone, 45,000 acres of parkland have been "severely disturbed by burro activity." As a result of their presence, Death Valley has sustained over one million dollars in damage.[10]

Initially, the Park Service solution was to shoot the burros. Since 1963, this agency officially has been concerned with preserving and re-creating "the ecological scene as viewed by the first European visitors." According to policy, exotics are no longer appropriate in the national parks. Conservation groups, such as the National Wildlife Federation, the National Audubon Society, and Sierra Club, agreed that destructive burros should be destroyed. In China Lake the Navy in fact had killed over 600 of them without issuing advance notice. But such measures immediately prompted "strong" opposition from the public. According to the *New York Times*, this issue pitted the "popular image of the burro" against the Park Service's regard for natural systems.[11]

To disgusted biocentrists, it seemed that many Americans defended the burros only because they are "cute" and "engaging." Throughout popular literature, this animal has been portrayed as an endearing creature, as Marguerite Henry's book *Brighty of the Grand Canyon* demonstrates. But Brighty's "real-life cousins," the Park Service complained, disturb features that must be protected. For this reason the agency replaced the park's bronze statue of Brighty with a plaque explaining the need to remove the burros.[12]

Humanitarian groups were quick to take action. Airlifts and adoption programs for burros were organized by the Humane Society and the Fund for Animals. This alternative, however, was as cumbersome as it was expensive, drawing criticism from biocentrists. Even so, there were those who protested the removal of burros by any methods. Joan Blue of the American Horse Protection Association, for instance, asserted that these animals "have a right to be there." Humanitarians, desperate to rescue burros from the charge that they are "non-native pests," argued that their presence in Bandelier and the Grand Canyon represents the restoration of a horselike species that vanished more than 11,000 years ago. The Park Service, of course, countered that ecosystems have changed considerably since that date. Answering humane objections, a frustrated James Watt, then secretary of the Interior, noted that "we must manage wild horses and burros as we manage other game out there." But Cleveland Amory, head of the Fund for Animals, remained undaunted, retorting that "Jim Watt should be treated like a game animal."[13]

That this discord appears throughout the pages of *Earth First!*—by far the most radical of environmentalist publications—attests to its intensity. While some members dismiss feral animals as "nothing more than long-limbed rats" responsible for "ecological imbalance," others stress the need for a stronger "compassion movement." Recently, one contributor complained that humanitarians "are counterproductive to conservation," for "they distract attention . . . from critical issues like habitat destruction, vanishing wilderness, and species extinction."[14] For the moment, resolution of this rift seems unlikely.

As the arguments on both sides indicate, each position remains limited. The humane emphasis on kinship has resulted in the continued projection of man's traits on animals. Biocentrism, on the other hand, has not altogether shed the regard for utility. To be sure, Leopold did not root his land ethic in human concerns. To his mind, human "obligations" to the environment go "over and above self-interest"; he warned that an ethic based on selfish motives can never work in the long run. Still, according to the historian Donald Worster, Leopold's ideas are "too firmly tied to the science of ecology to escape an economic bias." The land ethic thus could be reduced to an "enlightened, long-range prudence."[15]

Philosophers also have noted this drawback. Some argue that a purely biocentric outlook is impossible to obtain because humankind cannot break entirely free of its own point of view. Although Leopold indicated that people are uniquely capable of moving beyond this boundary, W. H. Murdy has suggested that it is not unnatural for them to be anthropocentric, for spiders similarly are "arachnocentric."[16] All species are preoccupied with their own survival. Moreover, biocentrism in the extreme can be interpreted as misanthropic; faced with sticky questions regarding overpopulation of humans, the true ecologist would consider only the needs of the biotic community. To this point, Leopold might have responded that strict adherence to an "ecological conscience" would have prevented such environmental crises in the first place.

Despite their limitations, both humanitarianism and biocentrism stem from traditions that have shaped conservation thought. In the nineteenth century, humanitarianism added a new dimension to protection of animals by extending rights to creatures other than humans. Modern followers see their movement as the wave of the future. Animal rights, one recent advocate predicts, "will emerge as *the* civil rights movement of the twenty-first century."[17] Today's humanitarians liken "speciesism"—the wrongful limitation of rights to humans—to racism, sexism, and other forms of discrimination. Similarly, biocentrism, supported by ecological precepts, has extended rights to all forms of wildlife. For all their differences, both philosophies approach the animal world in a spirit of humility, thereby defying centuries of Western tradition.

During the last hundred years, humanitarians have challenged what they believe to be human arrogance. According to Singer, even the concept of stewardship—invoked throughout conservation history—smacks of human conceit. He denies that animals are inferior creatures who need to be overseen by benevolent and patronizing lords. In this light, solicitude appears as nothing more than the need to restrain people from abusing other creatures. According to Singer, it is not enough merely to be kind to animals out of a sense of duty; he wishes humans to recognize the autonomy of animals. And as Judeo-Christian premises recede, he contends, assertions of man's superiority will become insupportable.[18] Following Darwin's lead, biocentrists, too, helped remove humans from the center of the universe, placing them alongside other creatures in the biotic community.

Of course, not all conservationists fall neatly into either camp. Far-sighted individuals with an ability to combine the various ideas of the movement have emerged throughout conservation history. John Muir was such a person. His recognition of the interconnection of living things, based on careful observation in the wild, has earned him an association with biocentrism; he in fact anticipated Leopold's ideas by forty years. Yet Muir was also concerned with singular creatures. Despite the seeming contradiction, he had no difficulty accepting both the individualism of humanitarians and the holism of biocentrists; to his mind, each was essential. Any creature, he wrote, "is made first for itself, then more and more remotely for all the world and worlds."[19] Of all Muir's ideas, this might prove to be the most far-reaching.

Edward Abbey was a particularly vocal exponent of both positions. Until his death in 1989, this nature writer argued for a stronger recognition of the separateness of the animal world from human concerns than even Leopold had envisioned. His books revealed concern not only for the suffering of animals but also for the rights of nonsentient creatures. Yet like Muir, Abbey went far beyond his contemporaries. In his writing he attempted to avoid the anthropomorphism which obscures "real" animals, by acknowledging their separateness from humans. Birds, he noted, have "serious concerns of their own."[20] To him, these creatures had an intrinsic value which transcends their usefulness not only to humans but also to ecosystems.

In Abbey's writing the natural world thus existed apart from humans and their perceptions. Published in 1968, his best-known work, *Desert Solitaire*, warned against the tendency to confuse "the thing observed with the mind of the observer, of constructing not a picture of external reality but simply a mirror of the thinker." To Abbey, the desert was the place most alien to people—and most appealing to him. Because it is "a realm beyond the human," this was the best landscape in which "to confront, immediately and directly . . . the bare bones of existence." Here Abbey hoped to see the vulture or the spider as "it is in itself, devoid of all humanly ascribed qualities, anti-Kantian." Like Robinson Jeffers, the California poet who described himself as an "inhumanist," Abbey rejected anything that smacked of "human solipsism."[21]

The problem, he explained, is that the human need to impose order has clouded our view of the natural world. Most people attempt to discover a "purpose" to other creatures. In contrast, Abbey urged his readers to "let being be." He argues that it is their "unconscious fear" which compels men "to reduce the wild and prehuman to human dimensions." So determined was Abbey to accept the natural world on its own terms that he could appear misanthropic: echoing a poem of Jeffers, he claimed, "I'd rather kill a *man* than a snake." At times he defied the human perspective with seeming perversity. Acknowledging that coyotes do eat lambs, he asked, "but do they eat enough? I mean, enough lambs to keep the coyotes sleek, healthy and well-fed. That is my concern." Abbey, then, reveled in nature as the "other world," indifferent to humans and their interests.[22]

It was partly for this reason that Abbey had such an affinity for predators. "It ain't wilderness," quipped a friend in *Beyond the Wall*, "unless there's a critter out there that can kill you and eat you." Abbey enjoyed the element of danger that meat-eaters brought to wild country. He suggested that the chase and the kill brought "fulfillment" to predators and "consummation" to prey.[23] He also took a particular liking to the turkey vulture—an animal which many people would find difficult to appreciate. Abbey was attracted to meat-eaters because they were the animals least amenable to people. Through his extravagant statements, he hoped to shock readers out of the notion that the natural world should conform to human expectations.

Although he was one of the most outspoken advocates of this theme, Abbey was not the first nature writer to note the separateness of other creatures. Earlier in the century, Henry Beston similarly had portrayed animals as "other nations" who could not be "measured by man." In *The Outermost House*, published in 1928, he suggested that other creatures are "not brethren," for unlike humans they are "finished and complete." His words suggest the human inability to comprehend animals as well as the futility of forcing them to conform to our values. Given this point, he wrote, "we need another and a wiser . . . concept of animals."[24] During the last three decades, environmentalists have rediscovered Beston's writing.

Recently, Barry Lopez also has complained that humans view animals only "in terms of our own needs and experiences. And to approach them solely in terms of the Western imagination is, really, to deny the animal." People, he observes, wrongly "assume that the animal is entirely comprehensible." While he sees wildlife study as worthwhile, Lopez suspects that there is no "ultimate [animal] reality to be divined" by "microscope and radio collar." Even scientists, he points out, impose human social structure on wildlife.[25]

The image of the benevolent wolf, introduced nearly a century ago by Ernest Thompson Seton, has been gaining credibility among popular natural history writers. Although the animals themselves have not changed, modern depictions endow wolves with characteristics resembling those of admirable humans: loyalty, compassion, courage, and continence. Instead of traveling in menacing, formidable packs, wolves now cooperate in "teams." Far from the bloodthirsty beasts of previous eras, today's wolves are essentially peaceful creatures who kill mostly the sick and weak. If they cannot, as prophesied in Isaiah 11:6, dwell in peace with the lamb or deer, at least they can help keep the herd and its ecosystem healthy. Organizations such as Defenders of Wildlife use this point to argue in favor of saving predators from destruction.[26] Such efforts are not limited to warm-blooded predators. Recently Greenpeace, dedicated to the protection of marine animals, launched a campaign to counter our negative image of sharks. According to the new view, sharks are not cold fish or merciless killers. Instead, they are playful animals who serve as important scavengers, ridding the oceans of weak, unhealthy creatures. The problem here is that if those concerned with animal protection base their arguments on the "friendly" nature of wild creatures, evidence to the contrary could weaken their cause.

The image of the benevolent predator, accepted even by some wildlife biologists, is in fact misleading. According to Lopez, wolves do not kill only the sick and weak; nor are they always led by the male hunter. Unfortunately, such traits—which help make wolves acceptable and appealing—have been created by humans. Americans have continued to insist that their animals act like well-behaved people. Recently, seemingly unprovoked wolves in Isle Royale National Park killed an alpha male. Puzzled scientists in this region immediately set about to find explanations. A century ago, most Americans would have viewed such behavior as typical of the rapacious wolf. Now, however, those who have come to expect peaceable wolves are shocked when these animals act otherwise. As Lopez has pointed out, "we know little about the wolf. What we know a good deal more about is what we imagine the wolf to be." So strongly do our perceptions obscure the actual animal that he has concluded that other creatures are not discovered but created. As a nature writer, Lopez recognizes the difficulty of shedding our cultural baggage; so far, most animal lovers have not been able to regard other creatures apart from humans.[27]

For all our persistent anthropomorphism, Lopez claims that animals are appealing precisely because they are not like humans. In his estimation, there is something attractive about the singularity of other creatures. "We do sense that they are somehow correct in the universe," he writes, while "we are somehow still at odds with it." To him, recognition of the "separate realities" of wildlife "is not only no threat to our own reality, but the root of a fundamental joy." Abbey, too, found the "indifference" of desert animals to be their "finest quality." He believed the "otherness" of the animal world to be a source of wonder and comfort.[28]

Nature writers are taking up this theme with increasing frequency. Bill McKibben's recent book *The End of Nature* argues that humans need to perceive the natural world as separate: "Nature's independence *is* its meaning; without it there is nothing but us." To his mind, wild animals are comforting "messengers" from another world whose presence assures us that we are part of something larger than ourselves. But the tone of McKibben's book is bleak. Grimly, he notes that through polluting the atmosphere with carbon dioxide and chlorofluorocarbons (CFCs), humans have changed the weather and rendered every spot on the planet artificial. As a result, all animals now live in a world that is human-made. As its title suggests, McKibben's book claims that we have destroyed nature and now must face the physical and spiritual consequences. According to him, the solution is to adopt a humble attitude toward the natural world—to accept its separateness and rejoice in it.

Although such writers as Abbey, Lopez, and McKibben speak for a growing number of Americans who believe that an animal does not have to be attractive, useful, or humanlike to be worthy of moral consideration, this belief remains a minority position in American society. Despite the formation of new rationales for protecting animals, current studies reveal that utilitarianism is still the strongest of incentives.[29] Yet until we abandon human-centered motives, animal protection will never be completely successful. Nor can we continue to expect animals to share our values—which by definition are a human construct. When we can accept animals for what they are rather than for what we would like them to be, we will be well on our way to developing a strong ethic to guide our actions in the natural world.

EPILOGUE

Animal lovers are becoming more aggressive. During the 1970s and 1980s organizations concerned with the protection of wild creatures acted with unprecedented boldness. The efforts of Greenpeace, which sends its members to the wild to impede whaling and sealing, are well publicized. Lesser-known groups employ similar tactics. The militant crew of the *Sea Shepherd* destroys wasteful, thirty-mile-wide drift nets that trap marine life; they also sabotage whaling vessels. The Fund for Animals confronts sport hunters in the field, hoping to dissuade them from killing wild creatures. Opposition to the use of animals for fur is just as pronounced. An animal rights organization called Trans-Species Unlimited has targeted New York City, responsible for one-third of the fur sales in the United States, for harassment. There, salon owners have found their doors glued shut, while their fur-wearing customers are splattered with red paint.

Other animal rights advocates use the legal system to protect wild creatures. The Progressive Animal Welfare Society (PAWS) recently asked courts to force the Point Defiance Zoo in Tacoma, Washington to release two beluga whales to the wild. This organization opposes the captivity of cetaceans, which are used in marine parks for amusement or ornamental purposes. Members believe that even the potential for educating humans about wildlife does not justify the confinement of animals. Additional concerns of wildlife enthusiasts include the reintroduction of wolves into Yellowstone National Park and grizzlies into the North Cascade Mountains. These developments suggest that conservationists are changing their strategy, for they are beginning to assume the offensive rather than the defensive position regarding wildlife issues.

Currently, the most dramatic cause to attract the interest of conservationists involves the northern spotted owl. Classified as a "threatened" species by the Fish and Wildlife Service, this bird is dependent on diminishing stands of old-growth trees in the Pacific Northwest. As an "indicator species," the spotted owl provides a gauge to measure the health of the old-growth ecosystem. Both the National Audubon Society—an established, mainstream organization—and Earth First!—the most militant of environmentalist organizations—have rallied to protect spotted owls and their habitat. The Audubon Society was one of twenty-five organizations which filed a lawsuit against the Fish and Wildlife Service in May 1988 for its initial failure to designate the bird as threatened.

The Endangered Species Act requires suspension of logging on public lands known to harbor the threatened owls. Because thousands of loggers will lose their jobs, this issue has pitted environmentalists against timber communities in the Pacific Northwest. Clearly many conservationists are using protection of the bird as a vehicle to save old-growth forests. Still, the spotted owl has become a focal point in the debate. In the late nineteenth and early twentieth centuries, some prominent spokesmen for the early conservation movement believed that owls—predatory birds—should be shot on sight. Now protection of owls has become an issue of national significance. A similar debate is raging in southern Arizona, where conservationists are employing an endangered red squirrel in a fight against the construction of an observatory.

Not all conservationists and animal rights advocates agree on the issues regarding wildlife protection. Sport hunting in particular remains a topic of dispute. Nor do all agree on the best methods to influence and guide humans in their approach to the natural world. Animal lovers have debated these points since the nineteenth century, when activism first emerged. However, most of the actions described here go far beyond anything attempted by early conservationists. Clearly the desire to save individual animals and animal species is gaining in force and intensity.

Still, the obstacles to protection are formidable. Ranching interests continue to oppose the presence of wolves in sections of the West; the livestock industry is fighting the restoration of these animals to Yellowstone. Similarly, hikers have formed a group called Residents Against Grizzlies in our Environment (RAGE), demonstrating the belief that even the wilderness of the North Cascade Mountains exists primarily for the benefit of people. The resistance of timber interests to habitat-conservation areas for the spotted owl further indicates an attitude which is not only human-centered but also shortsighted; old-growth forests, characterized by a diversity of species and trees at least two hundred years old, cannot be replaced. Extinction is the ultimate cruelty—and the fate of numerous species will be determined by humans during the next decades. Yet, considering how much ideas regarding other creatures have changed merely in the space of a hundred years, it would seem that Americans have come a long way. Those who complain of the "inconsistencies" of animal lovers understand neither the complexity of attitudes nor how rapidly they have developed. At the rate at which animal species are disappearing, however, one would hope that it will not take another century for Americans to appreciate and accept all forms of wildlife.

NOTES

PROLOGUE

1. "Man's Brother Beasts," *Harper's Weekly* 52 (August 22, 1908): 31; Francis Harold Rowley, *The Humane Idea: A Brief History of Man's Attitude toward the Other Animals, and the Development of the Humane Spirit into Organized Societies* (Boston: Humane Education Society, 1912), 66; Albert Leffingwell, "An Ethical Basis for Humanity to Animals," *Arena* 10 (September 1894): 478–79.
2. Thomas Stanley, "The New Humanitarianism," *Westminster Review* 155 (April 1901): 414–23; John Howard Moore, *The New Ethics* (Chicago: Samuel A. Bloch, 1909); Henry S. Salt, ed., *The New Charter: A Discussion of the Rights of Men and the Rights of Animals* (London: George Bell and Sons, 1896).
3. Mary Sayre Haverstock, *An American Bestiary* (New York: Harry N. Abrams, 1979), 11.
4. Roderick Nash, *Wilderness and the American Mind*, 3d ed. (New Haven: Yale University Press, 1982), 23–36. See also Peter N. Carroll, *Puritanism in the Wilderness: The Intellectual Significance of the New England Frontier, 1629–1700* (New York: Columbia University Press, 1969).
5. Keith Thomas, "The Beast in Man," *New York Review of Books*, April 30, 1981, 48. Although Thomas uses this quote to argue against the novelty of the late nineteenth century, the phrase "kept for the use of man" weakens his point. See also Keith Thomas, *Man and the Natural World: A History of the Modern Sensibility* (New York: Pantheon Books, 1983).
6. Nash, *Wilderness and the American Mind*, 47.
7. Ibid., 74–83.
8. Odell Shepard, ed., *The Heart of Thoreau's Journals* (Boston: Houghton Mifflin, 1927), 4; Joseph Wood Krutch, ed., *The World of Animals: A Treasury of Lore, Legend and Literature by Great Writers and Naturalists from the Fifth Century B.C. to the Present* (New York: Simon and Schuster, 1961), 296.
9. Peter J. Schmitt, *Back to Nature: The Acadian Myth in Urban America* (New York: Oxford University Press, 1969); Leo Marx, *The Machine in the Garden: Technology and the Pastoral Ideal in America* (New York: Oxford University Press, 1961). Anxieties concerning industrialization and urbanization are also discussed throughout the last half of Stephen Fox's *John Muir and His Legacy: The American Conservation Movement* (Boston: Little, Brown and Company, 1981).

10. John Muir, *Our National Parks* (Boston: Houghton Mifflin, 1901), 1. See also Roderick Nash, "Conservation as Anxiety," in Roderick Nash, ed., *The American Environment: Readings in the History of Conservation*, 2d ed. (Menlo Park, California: Addison-Wesley Publishing Company, 1976), 85–93.

11. Frank Luther Mott, *A History of American Magazines, 1885–1905*, vol. 4 (Cambridge: Harvard University Press, 1957), 13–20.

12. John F. Reiger, *American Sportsmen and the Origin of Conservation*, rev. ed. (Norman: University of Oklahoma Press, 1986).

13. Krutch, *World of Animals*, 24; Lynton Keith Caldwell, *International Environmental Policy: Emergence and Dimensions* (Durham, N.C.: Duke University Press, 1984), 4.

14. Stephen R. Kellert, *Public Attitudes Toward Critical Wildlife and Natural Habitat Issues* (Washington, D.C.: Fish and Wildlife Service, 1979); idem, "Historical Trends in Perceptions and Uses of Animals in Twentieth-Century America," *Environmental Review* 9 (Spring 1985): 19–33.

15. Mary Midgley, *Animals and Why They Matter* (Athens: University of Georgia Press, 1983), 78.

16. John Hamer, "Some Animals Are More Equal than Others," *Seattle Times*, July 8, 1984, A18.

17. Ernest Bell, "The Performing Animal," *Contemporary Review* 113 (January 1918): 93.

18. Hamer, "Some Animals are More Equal than Others," A18.

19. Rupert Hughes, "Animal and Vegetable Rights," *Harper's New Monthly Magazine* 103 (November 1901): 852–53.

20. Peter Singer, *Animal Liberation: A New Ethics for our Treatment of Animals* (New York: New York Review Books, 1975), 188. For a different perspective regarding the issue of pain among humanitarians, see Tom Regan, "The Case for Animal Rights," in Peter Singer, ed., *In Defense of Animals*, 14.

21. David Gelman, "Of Mice and Men—and Morality: Something in a Name," *Newsweek*, July 18, 1988, 65.

CHAPTER I. SCIENCE AND SENTIMENT

1. This chapter is derived from my essay, "Science, Sentiment, and Anxiety: American Nature Writing at the Turn of the Century," *Pacific Historical Review* 54 (February 1985): 33–50. John Russell, Viscount Amberley, Letter, November 10, 1874, Frances Power Cobbe Papers, Box 4, Huntington Library; Frederic Harrison, "The Ethical View: The Duties of Man to the Lower Animals," in Henry S. Salt, ed., *The New Charter*, 103; Emma Darwin, Letter, undated (ca. 1875), Frances Power Cobbe Papers, Box 4, Huntington Library; Herbert Ernest Cushman, "Professor August Weismann," *Outlook* 55 (January 16, 1897): 253; Ouida (Marie Louise de la Ramée), "The Quality of Mercy," *Nineteenth Century* 40 (August 1896): 305.

2. E. A. Ross, "Turning Towards Nirvana," *Arena* 4 (November 1891): 739, 742. For a discussion of anxiety concerning scientific theories, see: Robert C. Bannister, *Social Darwinism: Science and Myth in Anglo-American Social Thought* (Philadelphia: Temple University Press, 1979); Cynthia Eagle Russett, *Darwin in America: The Intellectual Response, 1865–1912* (San Francisco: W. H. Freeman and Company, 1976); and George Daniels, ed., *Darwinism Comes to America* (Waltham, Mass.: Blaisdell, 1968). Victorian reactions to science are examined by Gertrude Himmelfarb, *Darwin and the Darwinian Revolution* (New York: Anchor Books, 1959); James Turner, *Reckoning with the Beast: Animals, Pain, and Humanity in the Victorian Mind* (Baltimore: Johns Hopkins University Press, 1980); and Richard French, *Anti-Vivisection and Medical Science in Victorian Society* (Princeton: Princeton University Press, 1975). The latter two works argue that the emergence of animal protection societies in late-nineteenth-century England relate in part to the reaction against scientific materialism.

3. Alfred, Lord Tennyson, "In Memoriam," sec. 56.

4. Maximilian Foster, *In the Forest: Tales of Wood-life* (New York: Doubleday, 1901), 5, 50, 77.

5. John B. Jeffery, "Animal Life on the Pacific Coast Some Fifty Years Ago," *Overland Monthly* 51 (June 1908): 535.

6. Jennette Barbour Perry, "Wild Animals I Do Not Want to Know," *Critic* 40 (June 1902): 518; Caspar Whitney, "The View-Point of Caspar Whitney," *Outing* 50 (September 1907): 748, 750; George S. Hellman, "Animals in Literature," *Atlantic Monthly* 87 (March 1901): 391; Ernest Thompson Seton, *Animal Heroes* (New York: Charles Scribner's Sons, 1905), 9. Additional turn-of-the-century observers of this trend in nature writing include John Burroughs, "Animal Behavior and the New Psychology," *McClure's* 35 (July 1910): 262–70. See also Margaret Blount, *Animal Land: The Creatures of Children's Fiction* (New York: William Morrow, 1975), 323.

7. This chapter draws heavily from popular journals such as *Century*, *Atlantic Monthly*, and *Dial*, which, according to Frank Luther Mott, had circulations upwards of two hundred thousand and sometimes up to one million (*A History of American Magazines, 1885–1905*, 4:13–20).

8. Dallas Lore Sharp, "The Nature-Writer," *The Face of the Fields* (New York: Houghton Mifflin, 1911); Henry Fairfield Osborn, *Impressions of Great Naturalists: Reminiscences of Darwin, Huxley, Balfour, Cope and Others* (New York: Charles Scribner's Sons, 1925), 190; Edward Hyatt, *Two California Neighbors: A Suggestion for the English Class* (California: State of California, Superintendent of Public Instruction, n.d.), 4; "The Advent of Animals in Fiction," *Independent* 52 (April 26, 1900): 1026.

9. Ernest Thompson Seton, *Wild Animals I Have Known* (New York: Charles Scribner's Sons, 1898), 7; Betty Keller, *Black Wolf: The Life of Ernest*

Thompson Seton (Vancouver: Douglas and McIntyre, 1984), 143. The "nature faker" controversy is described in Peter J. Schmitt, *Back to Nature*, and Paul Brooks, *Speaking for Nature: How Literary Naturalists from Henry Thoreau to Rachel Carson Have Shaped America* (Boston: Houghton Mifflin, 1980). Neither of these authors, however, analyzes the relationship between "nature faking" and attitudes toward science. See also John Henry Wadland's *Ernest Thompson Seton: Man and Nature in the Progressive Era, 1880–1915* (New York: Arno, 1978). Favorably portraying Seton, Wadland defends the naturalist against charges of nature faking; he does not, however, discuss popular reactions to science. Robert H. McDonald, "The Revolt Against Instinct: The Animal Stories of Seton and Roberts," *Canadian Literature* 84 (Spring 1980): 18–29, does relate science to nature writing. Nevertheless, as its title suggests, his article addresses only the instinct versus intelligence issue and is limited, for the most part, to two writers. His conclusion emphasizes the emergence of the Boy Scouts of America, an organization in which Seton had a hand. A more recent study of the nature faker controversy is Ralph H. Lutts, *The Nature Fakers: Wildlife, Science and Sentiment* (Golden, Colo.: Fulcrum Publishing Company, 1990).

10. H. W. Boynton, "Books New and Old: Nature and Human Nature," *Atlantic Monthly* 89 (January 1902): 135.
11. Seton, *Wild Animals I Have Known*, 180, 222.
12. H. Allen Anderson, *The Chief: Ernest Thompson Seton and the Changing West* (College Station: Texas A&M University Press, 1986), 126.
13. Woods Hutchinson, "Animal Chivalry," *Contemporary Review* 76 (December 1899): 878–88; idem, "Animal Marriage," *Contemporary Review* 86 (October 1904): 485–96; Charles G. D. Roberts, *They Who Walk in the Wilds* (New York: Macmillan, 1925), 123, 153.
14. W. C. Barrett, "Character in Animals," *Science* 21 (June 9, 1893): 312.
    15. Olive Thorne Miller, "Whimsical Ways in Bird Land," *Atlantic Monthly* 77 (May 1896): 671; idem, "Beautiful and Brave was He," *Atlantic Monthly* 76 (July 1895): 60.
16. William J. Long, *Mother Nature* (New York: Harper and Brothers, 1923), 227. See also the preface to his *Ways of Wood Folk* (Boston: Ginn and Company, 1899), v-vii, and "Getting Acquainted with Wild Animals," *Independent* 72 (June 6, 1912): 1235. Ellen Velvin, too, wrote of animal uniqueness in "Animals with Histories: Individualities of the Zoo," *New York Times*, April 8, 1906, pt. 3, p. 4.
17. Seton, *Wild Animals I Have Known*, 264; idem, *Lives of the Hunted* (New York: Charles Scribner's Sons, 1901), 63.
18. Seton, *Wild Animals I Have Known*, 49.; Sara A. Hubbard, "A Quartette of Bird-Books," *Dial* 34 (June 1, 1903): 363; Ernest Ingersoll, "Our Gray Squirrels: A Study," *Harper's New Monthly Magazine* 84 (March 1892): 546; Olive

Thorne Miller, "Little Boy Blue," *Atlantic Monthly* 72 (August 1893): 176; Gene Stratton Porter, "The Birds' Kindergarten," *Outing* 40 (April 1902): 70–74.

19. John Burroughs, "Horse Sense," *Independent* 71 (November 30, 1911): 1198–1201; Jack London, *Michael—Brother of Jerry* (New York: Macmillan, 1917), 35; idem, *Jerry of the Islands* (1916; New York: Macmillan, 1927), 265–66. Articles concerning the intelligence of horses include "Other Worlds Than Ours," *Nation* 98 (May 14, 1914): 563–64; M. V. O'Shea, "The Abilities of an 'Educated' Horse," *Popular Science Monthly* 82 (February 1913): 168–76; J. Arthur Thomson, "The 'Thinking' Horses of Elberfeld," *Contemporary Review* 104 (December 1913): 799–805. For a sampling of the discussion concerning intelligent dogs, see Carton Moore-Park, "Thinking Dogs," *Outlook* 99 (December 23, 1911): 979–87, and "Don, the 'Talking' Dog," *Scientific American* 108 (May 31, 1913): 502–3.

20. John Muir, *The Story of My Boyhood and Youth* (1912; Madison: University of Wisconsin Press, 1965), 75.

21. E. E. Harriman quoted in column, "Do Animals Think?" *Literary Digest* 55 (December 8, 1917): 81.

22. Muir, *The Story of My Boyhood and Youth*, 75; Bannister, *Social Darwinism*, 138–39.

23. William J. Long, *School of the Woods: Some Life Studies of Animal Instincts and Animal Training* (Boston: Ginn and Company, 1902), 5.

24. William J. Long, "Animal Surgery," *Outlook* 75 (September 12, 1903): 126.

25. William Morton Wheeler, "Woodcock Surgery," *Science* 19 (February 26, 1904): 350.

26. S. M. Reese, "Science, Nature, and Criticism," *Science* 19 (May 13, 1904): 761.

27. John Burroughs, "Real and Sham Natural History," *Atlantic Monthly* 91 (March 1903): 298–301. See also John Burroughs, "Do Animals Think?" *Harper's New Monthly Magazine* 110 (February 1905): 354–58, and William J. Long's answer, Peter Rabbit [pseud.], "Do Animals Think?" *Harper's New Monthly Magazine* 111 (June 1905): 59–62. Also offering comment on this issue was George Gladden, "Fur, Feathers and Intellect," *Bookman* 23 (March 1906): 89–91.

28. Stephen Fox, *John Muir and his Legacy: The American Conservation Movement* (Boston: Little, Brown and Company, 1981), 119.

29. Dallas Lore Sharp, "Out-of-Doors from Labrador to Africa," *Critic* 48 (February 1906): 122.

30. Theodore Roosevelt, "Nature Fakers," *Everybody's Magazine* 17 (September 1907): 427–30. Roosevelt also lambasted the nature fakers in the lengthy dedication to his book, *Outdoor Pastimes of an American Hunter* (New York: Charles Scribner's Sons, 1905).

31. William J. Long, letter, *New York Times*, May 23, 1907, 6.

32. See, for example, Charles A. Kofoid, "Nature-Books for Summer Outings," *Dial* 27 (July 1, 1899): 14.

33. Frank M. Chapman, "The Case of William J. Long," *Science* 19 (February 26, 1904): 388; Ellen Hayes, "The Writings of William J. Long," *Science* 19 (May 13, 1904): 626; Charles Trueheart, "Upward Bound: The Great Book Bazaar," *Washington Post*, May 22, 1987.

34. Charles A. Kofoid, "The Innings of the Animals," *Dial* 31 (December 1, 1901): 440; William T. Hornaday, "Thompson's Animal Stories," *Overland Monthly* 33 (March 1899): 288. For Hornaday's views regarding the nature faker controversy, see "Animals Disprove Both Burroughs and Long," *New York Times*, June 16, 1907, pt. 5, p. 2.

35. John Burroughs, *Accepting the Universe* (Boston: Houghton Mifflin, 1921), 5; Edward Payson Evans, "The Nearness of Animals to Man," *Atlantic Monthly* 69 (February 1892): 181. See also M. Topinard quoted in "The Altruism of Animals: Are They Better Christians Than Men?" *Review of Reviews* 15 (March 1897): 346–47; Long, *Mother Nature*, 85.

36. Peter Kropotkin, *Mutual Aid: A Factor of Evolution*, ed. Paul Avrich (New York: New York University Press, 1972), 7–10; Linnie Marsh Wolfe, ed., *John of the Mountains: The Unpublished Journals of John Muir* (Cambridge: Riverside Press, 1938), 82; Liberty Hyde Bailey, *The Holy Earth* (New York: Charles Scribner's Sons, 1915), 76.

37. Lisa Mighetto, ed., *Muir Among the Animals: The Wildlife Writings of John Muir* (San Francisco: Sierra Club Books, 1986), 181; Olive Thorne Miller, "The Spinning Sisterhood," *Popular Science Monthly* 39 (October 1891): 829–30.

38. Mabel Osgood Wright, *Birdcraft: A Field Book of Two Hundred Song, Game and Water Birds* (New York: Macmillan, 1897), 216; idem, *Citizen Bird: Scenes from Bird-Life in Plain English for Beginners* (New York: Macmillan, 1897), 419.

39. Wolfe, *John of the Mountains*, 93, 165; Mighetto, *Muir Among the Animals*, 25.

40. Long, *Mother Nature*, 308. See also William J. Long, "Stories From the Trail," *Independent* 64 (June 4, 1908): 1279–80; John Burroughs, "Is Nature Cruel?" *North American Review* 208 (October 1891): 562; idem, *Accepting the Universe*, 5. This theme was similarly considered by Lucy Rider Meyer, "Is Nature Red?" *Outlook* 104 (May 24, 1913): 191–98.

41. Mighetto, *Muir Among the Animals*, 111–13; Evans, "The Nearness of Animals to Man," 184.

42. Thomas Henry Huxley, *Evolution and Ethics, 1893–1943* (London: Pilot Press, 1947), 67–68, 82; Holmes Rolston III, *Philosophy Gone Wild: Essays in Environmental Ethics* (New York: Prometheus Books, 1986), 40.

43. Ernest Thompson Seton, "The Natural History of the Ten Commandments," *Century* 73 (November 1907): 24–33; idem, *Animal Heroes*, 92.

44. Evans, "The Nearness of Animals to Man," 174–75. See also Royal Dixon, *The Human Side of Birds* (New York: Halcyon House, 1917), 152, and Richard Meade Bache, "Animal Mind and Morality," *Putnam's* 2 (April 1907): 64–69.

45. Ernest Thompson Seton, "Fable and Woodmyth," *Century* 67 (November 1903): 35; Peter Rabbit [William J. Long], "Animal Immortality," *Harper's New Monthly Magazine* 111 (November 1905): 873–78; J. G. Wood, *Man and Beast: Here and Hereafter* (New York: George Routledge and Sons, 1917); E. P. Evans, "The Aesthetic Sense and Religious Sentiment in Animals," *Popular Science Monthly* 42 (February 1893): 472–81.

46. John Burroughs, "A Critical Glance into Darwin," *Atlantic Monthly* 126 (August 1920): 241; John Muir, Letter, Bidwell Papers, March 28, 1878, Bancroft Library; Fox, *John Muir and His Legacy*, 82.

47. Seton, *Wild Animals I Have Known*, 12.

48. Mighetto, *Muir Among the Animals*, 93; Wolfe, *John of the Mountains*, 277.

49. Seton, *Wild Animals*, 12; Seton, *Lives of the Hunted*, 12; James Oliver Curwood, "Why I Write Nature Stories," *Good Housekeeping* 67 (July 1918): 149.

50. Muir, *The Story of My Boyhood and Youth*, 145; B. O. Flower, "Books of the Day," *Arena* 30 (August 1903): 215.

51. William J. Long, "Nature and Books," *Dial* 34 (June 1, 1903): 358; Gene Stratton Porter, *The Song of the Cardinal* (Indianapolis: Bobbs-Merrill Company, 1903), 143; John Burroughs, "Science and Sentiment," *Independent* 72 (February 15, 1912): 360.

52. Clifford Howard, "Love Stories of the Zoo," *Ladies' Home Journal* 18 (June 1901): 8.

CHAPTER 2. WILDERNESS HUNTERS AND BIRD LOVERS

1. Alan Devoe, "Robins for Sale: Five Cents," *Audubon* 49 (March/April 1947): 111.

2. James A. Tober, *Who Owns the Wildlife? The Political Economy of Conservation in Nineteenth-Century America* (Westport, Conn.: Greenwood Press, 1981), 17; David and Jim Kimball, *The Market Hunter* (Minneapolis: Dillon Press, 1969), 86; Mighetto, *Muir Among the Animals,* 71–72.

3. Morgan Sherwood, *Big Game in Alaska: A History of Wildlife and People* (New Haven: Yale University Press, 1981), 78; James B. Trefethen, *An American Crusade for Wildlife* (New York: Winchester Press, 1975), 31.

4. Trefethen, *An American Crusade for Wildlife,* 64.

5. Mighetto, *Muir Among the Animals,* 77.

6. Trefethen, *An American Crusade for Wildlife,* 16.

7. Kimball, *The Market Hunter,* i.

8. Tober, *Who Owns the Wildlife?* 76.

9. Ibid., 76–78.

10. John F. Reiger, ed., *The Passing of the Great West: Selected Papers of George Bird Grinnell* (New York: Winchester Press, 1972), 119.

11. William T. Hornaday, *Our Vanishing Wildlife: Its Extermination and Preservation* (New York: Zoological Society, 1913), 63; idem, *Wild Life Conservation in Theory and Practice* (New Haven: Yale University Press, 1914), 61, 211, 194.

12. Henry William Herbert, *Frank Forester's Field Sports of the United States and British Provinces of North America,* 2 vols. (1848; New York: A. Townsend and Company, 1860); John F. Reiger, *American Sportsmen and the Origins of Conservation*, 25–49. See also General Rush C. Hawkins, "Brutality and Avarice Triumphant," *North American Review* 152 (June 1891): 662–63.

13. Tober, *Who Owns the Wildlife?* 55.

14. Reiger, *American Sportsmen and the Origins of Conservation*, 44–49.

15. Trefethen, *An American Crusade for Wildlife*, 89; Alfred Runte, *National Parks: The American Experience* (Lincoln: University of Nebraska Press, 1979), 109.

16. Alfred Runte, review of Reiger's *American Sportsmen and the Origins of Conservation* (1st ed.), *Journal of Forest History* 20 (April 1976): 100–101; Thomas R. Dunlap, "Sport Hunting and Conservation, 1880–1920," *Environmental Review* 12 (Spring 1988): 51–60. For Reiger's response, see *Journal of Forest History* 20 (October 1976): 221, and *Environmental Review* 12 (Fall 1988): 94–96.

17. Brooks, *Speaking for Nature*, 105–9. See also Paul Russell Cutright, *Theodore Roosevelt: The Naturalist* (New York: Harper and Brothers, 1956).

18. John Burroughs, *Camping and Tramping With Roosevelt* (Boston: Houghton Mifflin, 1906), 80. See also Paul Russell Cutright, *Theodore Roosevelt: The Making of a Conservationist* (Urbana: University of Illinois Press, 1985).

19. Robert Underwood Johnson, *Remembered Yesterdays* (Boston: Little, Brown and Company, 1923), 388; Theodore Roosevelt, *Works of Theodore Roosevelt*, vol. 1, ed. George Bird Grinnell (New York: Charles Scribner's Sons, 1923), xvi; idem, *Outdoor Pastimes of an American Hunter* (New York: Charles Scribner's Sons, 1905), 272.

20. Theodore Roosevelt, *The Wilderness Hunter* (New York: P.F. Collier and Son, 1893), 7–8, 29; G. Edward White, *The Eastern Establishment and the Western Experience: The West of Frederic Remington, Theodore Roosevelt, and Owen Wister* (New Haven: Yale University Press, 1968), 79–93.

21. Cecil B. Hartley, *Hunting Sports of the West* (Philadelphia: John E. Potter, 1885), 8; C. H. Simpson, *Wild Life in the Far West* (Chicago: Rhodes and McClure, 1896), 15; D. K. Thomas, *Wild Life in the Rocky Mountains* (C. E. Thomas, 1917), title page.

22. Roosevelt, *The Wilderness Hunter*, 270–73.

23. Krutch, *The World of Animals*, 167; Cutright, *Theodore Roosevelt: The Naturalist*, 44.

24. Theodore Roosevelt, *Hunting the Grisly* (New York: P.F. Collier and Son, 1893), 99, 109.

25. Ibid., 175, 228, 232; idem, *Works of Theodore Roosevelt*, 376.

26. Seton, *Wild Animals I Have Known*, 13–44.

27. Roosevelt, *Hunting the Grisly*, 213; idem, *Outdoor Pastimes of an American Hunter*, 17, 21, 89, 130.

28. Brooks, *Speaking for Nature*, 111–14.

29. Frank M. Chapman, *Autobiography of a Bird-Lover* (New York: D. Appleton-Century, 1935), vii; Schmitt, *Back to Nature,* 33.

30. DeVoe, "Robins for Sale: Five Cents," 110.

31. Trefethen, *An American Crusade for Wildlife*, 129.

32. Roswell C. McCrea, *The Humane Movement: A Descriptive Survey* (New York: Columbia University Press, 1910), 247.

33. Robin W. Doughty, *Feather Fashions and Bird Preservation: A Study in Nature Protection* (Berkeley and Los Angeles: University of California Press, 1975), 101.

34. Paul Russell Cutright, *Elliot Coues: Naturalist and Frontier Historian* (Urbana: University of Illinois Press, 1981); see also Robert Henry Welker, *Birds and Men: American Birds in Science, Art, Literature, and Conservation, 1800–1900*(Cambridge: Harvard University Press, 1955), 173.

35. Thomas Gilbert Pearson, *Adventures in Bird Protection* (New York: D. Appleton-Century, 1937), title page; George Bird Grinnell, "American Game Protection: A Sketch," in George Bird Grinnell and Charles Sheldon, ed., *Hunting and Conservation* (New Haven: Yale University Press, 1925), 201.

36. Grinnell, "American Game Protection," 252; Pearson, *Adventures in Bird Protection*, 151; Hornaday, *Our Vanishing Wildlife*, 213–33, 376.

37. Grinnell, "American Game Protection," 224; Edward B. Clark, "Roosevelt on the Nature Fakirs," *Everybody's Magazine* 16 (June 1907): 774; Reiger, *American Sportsmen and the Origins of Conservation*, 34.

CHAPTER 3. THE NEW HUMANITARIANISM

1. Theodore Roosevelt, "Our Vanishing Wildlife," *Outlook* 103 (January 25, 1913): 161.

2. Richard D. French's *Anti-Vivisection and Medical Science in Victorian Society* (Princeton: Princeton University Press, 1975) and James Turner's *Reckoning with the Beast* emphasize the protection of domestic animals in England. A more recent treatment of the humane movement can be found in Roderick Frazier Nash, *The Rights of Nature: A History of Environmental Ethics* (Madison: University of Wisconsin Press, 1989).

3. Roderick Nash, ed., *The American Environment: Readings in the History of Conservation*, 2d ed. (Menlo Park, Cal.: Addison-Wesley, 1976), xii.

4. William J. Shultz, *The Humane Movement in the United States, 1910–1922* (New York: Columbia University Press, 1924), 20.

5. Peter Singer, *Animal Liberation*, 222.

6. Mary Midgley, *Animals and Why They Matter*, 89; Turner, *Reckoning with the Beast*, 80–82.

7. John Howard Moore, *Better-World Philosophy: A Sociological Synthesis* (Chicago: Charles H. Kerr, 1899; 1906), 82; Henry Childs Merwin, "Vivisection," *Atlantic Monthly* 89 (1902): 323.

8. Thomas Stanley, "The New Humanitarianism," *Westminster Review* 155 (April 1901): 414; Francis Harold Rowley, *The Humane Idea*, 32.

9. Stephen Coleridge, "Cruelty to Animals and the RSPCA," *Fortnightly Review* 101 (April 1914): 682; Wesley Mills, "The Cultivation of Humane Ideas and Feelings," *Popular Science Monthly* 43 (May 1893): 48; John Howard Moore, *Better-World Philosophy*, 232, 242, 275; idem, *The Universal Kinship* (Chicago: Charles H. Kerr, 1908), 323–24, 328–29; idem, *The New Ethics*; and Henry S. Salt, ed., *The New Charter*.

10. Ernest Bell, "The Performing Animal," *Contemporary Review* 113 (January 1918): 93.

11. William J. Shultz, *The Humane Movement in the United States*, 122; George T. Angell, *Autobiographical Sketches and Personal Recollections* (Boston: Humane Education Society, 1892), 94; *New York Times*, October 8, 1922, 21.

12. Angell, *Autobiographical Sketches and Personal Recollections*, 14.

13. Francis Harold Rowley, *The Humane Idea*, ix.

14. Roswell C. McCrea, *The Humane Movement: A Descriptive Survey* (New York: Columbia University Press, 1910), 14; *Animal World* 12 (1881): 44.

15. Roswell C. McCrea, *The Humane Movement*, 94–95; William J. Shultz, *The Humane Movement in the United States*, 130; *New York Times*, March 18, 1906, pt. 3, p. 5; Shultz, *The Humane Movement in the United States*, 25.

16. "Form First Church for Animal Rights," *New York Times*, March 14, 1921, 11; Royal Dixon, *The Human Side of Animals* (New York: Frederick A. Stokes Company, 1918), 246.

17. Henry S. Salt, *Animals' Rights Considered in Relation to Social Progress* (New York: Macmillan, 1892), 22.

18. Clara Morris, "Riddle of the Nineteenth Century: Mr. Henry Bergh," *McClure's* 18 (March 1902): 422; Letter, Henry Bergh to Loring Moody, March 5, 1872, Rare Books and Manuscripts Collection, Boston Public Library.

19. McCrea, *The Humane Movement*, 97; "Points Way to End Slaughter of Birds," *New York Times*, January 2, 1911, 20.

20. James A. Tober, *Who Owns the Wildlife? The Political Economy of Conservation in Nineteenth-Century America* (Westport, Conn.: Greenwood Press, 1981), 211.

21. Sydney H. Coleman, *Humane Society Leaders in America* (New York: American Humane Association, 1924), 41, 55. See also McCrea, *The Humane Movement*, 147, 155.

22. Coleman, *Humane Society Leaders in America*, 57, 60.

23. Clara Morris, "Riddle of the Nineteenth Century: Mr. Henry Bergh," 422; Zulma Steele, *Angel in Top Hat*, 94.

24. Frances Power Cobbe, *Life of Frances Power Cobbe by Herself*, vol. 2 (Boston: Houghton Mifflin, 1894), 556; Samuel H. Drury, "Man and Beast," *Atlantic Monthly* 97 (March 1906): 420.

25. John Howard Moore, *The Universal Kinship*, 107, 234; Ouida, "The Quality of Mercy," 302; Richard D. French *Anti-Vivisection and Medical Science in Victorian Society*, 390.

26. Stephen Winsten, *Salt and His Circle* (New York: Hutchinson, 1951), 64, 67.

27. Steele, *Angel in Top Hat*, 45.

28. Albert Leffingwell, "An Ethical Basis for Humanity to Animals," *Arena* 10 (September 1894): 478–79.

29. Coleman, *Humane Society Leaders in America*, 178; "Woman's Influence in our Work," *Our Dumb Animals* 3 (May 1871): 95.

30. Frances Power Cobbe, "The Rights of Man and the Claims of Brutes," in *Studies New and Old of Ethical and Social Subjects* (London: Trubner and Company, 1865), 220.

31. "In the Interpreter's House," *American Magazine* 69 (November 1909): 141; John Henry Barrows, "The Spirit of Humanity," *Independent* 51 (December 28, 1899): 3468; Clara Morris, "The Riddle of the Nineteenth Century: Mr. Henry Bergh," 414.

32. Thomas Stanley, "The New Humanitarianism," 414; Ouida, "The Quality of Mercy," 305. See also Brian Harrison, *Peaceable Kingdom: Stability and Change in Modern Britain* (Oxford: Clarendon Press, 1982), 82–122.

33. Frances Power Cobbe, "The Rights of Man and the Claims of Brutes," 226.

34. James Turner, *Reckoning with the Beast*, 54; George T. Angell, *Autobiographical Sketches and Personal Recollections*, Appendix, 5–14; Henry S. Salt, ed., *The Cruelties of Civilization: A Program of Humane Reform* (London: William Reeves, 1897), vii; idem, *Seventy Years among Savages* (New York: Thomas Seltzer, 1921), 132. For criticism of Turner's ideas, see Keith Thomas, "The Beast in Man," 48.

35. John Henry Barrows, "The Spirit of Humanity," 3468.

CHAPTER 4. THE BARBARISMS OF CIVILIZATION

1. George T. Angell, *Autobiographical Sketches and Personal Recollections*, 94.

2. Thomas A. Bailey and David M. Kennedy, *The American Spirit: United States History as Seen by Contemporaries*, 6th ed., vol. 1 (Lexington, Mass.: D. C. Heath, 1987), 368. See also Roderick Frazier Nash, *The Rights of Nature*, 199–213, and Lisa Mighetto, Wild Animals in American Thought and Culture, 1870s–1930s, Ph.D. diss., University of Washington, 1986, ch. 3.

3. Zulma Steele, *Angel in Top Hat*, 290.

4. Dix Harwood, *Love for Animals and How It Developed in Great Britain* (New York: Privately printed, 1928), 66.

5. Henry David Thoreau, *Walden*, ed. Sherman Paul (1854; Boston: Houghton Mifflin, 1960), 146.

6. Henry S. Salt, *Animals' Rights Considered in Relation to Social Progress*, 62; John Howard Moore, *The Universal Kinship*, 132; Janey Sevilla Campbell, "Our Brothers, the Beasts," *Nineteenth Century* 61 (May 1907): 815–16.

7. Edwin Way Teale, ed., *The Wilderness World of John Muir* (Boston: Houghton Mifflin, 1954), 314; William Frederic Bade, ed., *Steep Trails* (Boston: Houghton Mifflin, 1918), 45, 50.

8. Joseph Wood Krutch, ed., *The World of Animals*, 165; Ernest Thompson Seton, *The Trail of the Sandhill Stag and other Lives of the Hunted* (New York: E. P. Dutton, 1899; 1966), 15.

9. Harriet Beecher Stowe, "The Village Do-Nothing," *Oldtown Folks* (1869; Harvard University Press, 1966), 74; John Muir, *My First Summer in the Sierra* (Boston: Houghton Mifflin, 1911; 1916), 190.

10. G. Searing Smith, "Cruelty in Hunting," letter, *New York Times*, January 30, 1910, pt. 2, p. 10; George Brunswick, "Big and Little Game Hunters," letter, *New York Times*, January 31, 1910, 6; Lurana W. Sheldon, "The Hunter's Cruelty," letter, *New York Times*, January 2, 1910, 12; "Picture of the Chase—Cruelty to Animals," *The Animal's Friend* 2 (March 1874): 3.

11. Stephen Coleridge, "Cruelty to Animals and the RSPCA," 682; John F. Reiger, *American Sportsmen and the Origins of Conservation*, 11.

12. Henry S. Salt, *Animals' Rights*, Table of Contents; John Howard Moore, *Better-World Philosophy*, 129; American Society for the Prevention of Cruelty to Animals, Fiftieth Annual Report, 1915, 73.

13. "Girl Dyed Cat Blue to Match Her Gown," *New York Times*, February 7, 1922, 13.

14. Francis J. Dickie, "The Cruelty of the Trap," *Our Dumb Animals* 47 (May 1915): 179–80.

15. Lucy Furman, "The Price of Furs," *Atlantic Monthly* 141 (February 1928): 206–9; Thomas R. Dunlap, *Saving America's Wildlife* (Princeton: Princeton University Press, 1988), 93.

16. James Turner, *Reckoning with the Beast*, 84; "In the Interpreter's House," *American Magazine* 69 (November 1909): 141; Stephen Paget, Review of *Experiments on Animals*, *Nation* 77 (August 6, 1903): 120.

17. *Fifth Annual Report of the American Anti-Vivisection Society* (Philadelphia, 1888), 4.

18. Henry Childs Merwin, "Vivisection," *Atlantic Monthly* 89 (March 1902): 324; James Turner, *Reckoning with the Beast*, 88.

19. Stephen Winsten, *Salt and His Circle*, 64; George Orwell, *The Road to Wigan Pier* (1937; New York: Harcourt Brace Jovanich, 1958), 175.

20. Peter Singer, *Animal Liberation*, 227; "Society's Ban on Meat," *New York Times*, June 28, 1909, 5; James Turner, *Reckoning with the Beast*, 17.

21. "Evening Session," *American Vegetarian and Health Journal* 2 (October 1852): 154; "Vegetarianism—What is it?" *American Vegetarian and Health Journal* 1 (February 1851): 37; Henry S. Salt, *The Creed of Kinship* (New York: E. P. Dutton, 1935), 69; John Muir, *The Story of My Boyhood and Youth*, 181. So far, few scholars have examined the history of vegetarianism from the moral standpoint. George Dombrowski's *The Philosophy of Vegetarianism* (Amherst: University of Massachusetts Press, 1984) focuses on the ancients, though he provides some discussion of the movement in the twentieth century. Peter Singer's chapter "Man's Dominion" in *Animal Liberation* offers a brief history of speciesism, which touches on vegetarianism. While Gerald Carson's *Cornflake Crusade* (New York: Rinehart, 1957) and James C. Whorton's *Crusaders for Fitness: The History of American Health Reformers* (New Jersey: Princeton University Press, 1982) provide chapters concerning nineteenth-century vegetarianism, both authors emphasize considerations of health. Janet Barkas, *The Vegetable Passion* (New York: Charles Scribner's Sons, 1975), 79–98, includes a brief chapter on such British vegetarians as George Bernard Shaw.

22. Charles W. Forward, *Fifty Years of Food Reform: A History of the Vegetarian Movement in England, 1847–97* (London: Ideal Publishing Union, 1898), 1; E.C.B., "The Joys of Vegetarianism," letter, *Outlook* 49 (March 31, 1894): 600; Howard Williams, *The Ethics of Diet: A Biographical History of the Literature of Humane Dietetics, from the Earliest Period to the Present Day* (London: Swan Sonnenschein, 1896), iii, vii.

23. William Metcalfe, "Objects of the Convention," *American Vegetarian and Health Journal* 1 (November 1850): 5; Alfred Fellows, "The Vegetarian Guest," *Living Age* 250 (11 August 1906): 346–53. See also Charles W. Forward, *Fifty Years of Food Reform*, 15.

24. Horace Greeley, *Recollections of a Busy Life* (New York: J. B. Ford and Company, 1869), 105. See also James Turner, *Reckoning with the Beast*, 14, 17; Whorton, *Crusaders for Fitness*, 63; Carson, *Cornflake Crusade*, 30.

25. Henry S. Salt, "The Humanities of Diet" (1892), in *Animal Rights and Human Obligations*, ed. Tom Regan and Peter Singer, (Englewood Cliffs, N.J.: Prentice-Hall, 1976), 140; Charles W. Forward, *Fifty Years of Food Reform*, 22; J. E. Fries and Glen Ridge, letter, *New York Times*, June 7, 1909.

26. John Howard Moore, *Better-World Philosophy*, 131; Gerald Carson, *Cornflake Crusade*, 50.

27. Henry S. Salt, "The Humanities of Diet," 139; Lady Walb. Paget, "A Vegetable Diet," *Popular Science Monthly* 44 (November 1893): 94, 114; Hereward Carrington, *The Natural Food of Man* (London: C. W. Daniel, 1912), 160; Henry S. Salt, "The Humanities of Diet," 144.

28. Thoreau, *Walden*, 147–51.

29. Linnie Marsh Wolfe, ed., *John of the Mountains*, 97; John Muir, *My First Summer in the Sierra*, 78–79, 129–30; Michael P. Cohen, *The Pathless Way: John Muir and American Wilderness* (Madison: University of Wisconsin Press, 1984), 180; Hereward Carrington, *The Natural Food of Man*, 166.

30. Hereward Carrington, *The Natural Food of Man*, 122–23; Lady Paget, "A Vegetable Diet," 101; Howard Williams, *The Ethics of Diet*, iii; George Filer, letter, *American Vegetarian* 1 (November 1850): 11.

31. Charles W. Forward, *Fifty Years of Food Reform*, 53; A. D. Hall, "Some Aspects of Vegetarianism," *Harper's New Monthly Magazine* 123 (July 1911): 211.

32. Herman Melville, *Pierre, or, the Ambiguities* (1852; New York: Hendricks House, 1949), 353; "The Vegetarian Creed," *Living Age* 216 (8 January 1898): 127–28; "Life's Supreme Pleasure," *Atlantic Monthly* 95 (June 1905): 857.

33. Lady Paget, "A Vegetable Diet," 99; T. A. Coward, "Prevention of Cruelty to Animals," *Westminster Review* 157 (May 1902): 548; William Alcott, letter, *American Vegetarian* 1 (February 1850): 21.

34. Henry S. Salt, *Seventy Years among Savages*, 64; George Hendrick, *Henry Salt: Humanitarian Reformer and Man of Letters* (Urbana: University of Illinois Press, 1977), 52.

35. Lady Paget, "A Vegetable Diet," 98, 94; Frances Power Cobbe, "The Rights of Man and the Claims of Brutes," 226; Francis Harold Rowley, *The Humane Idea*, 64.

36. Henry S. Salt, *Animals' Rights*, 94; Stephen Winsten, *Salt and His Circle*, 203; John Howard Moore, *The New Ethics*.

37. Salt, *Animals' Rights*, 43; Muir, *The Story of My Boyhood and Youth*, 69.

38. Henry S. Salt, "The Logic of the Larder," in Regan and Singer, *Animal Rights and Human Obligations*, 186–88.

39. Salt, *Animals' Rights*, 42.

40. Leonides Hubbard, Jr., "What a Big Zoo Means to the People," *Outing* 44 (September 1904): 678; R. Jeffrey Stott, "The Historical Origins of the Zoological Park in American Thought," *Environmental Review* 5 (Fall 1981): 52–65.

41. Elizabeth Saville, "The Dew of Mercy," *Westminster Review* 173 (January 1910): 92; Ernest Bell, "The Performing Animal," *Contemporary Review* 113 (January 1918): 99; "'Living Unicorns' Get Animal Lovers Goat," *Seattle Times*, April 5, 1985, front page; R. B. Cunninghame in introduction of Charles Simpson, *El Rodeo* (London: John Lane and the Bodley Head, 1925), 3–4.

42. Jack London, *Michael—Brother of Jerry*, v–vi, 296, 161; idem, "The Madness of John Harned," in *The Bodley Head Jack London*, ed. Arthur Calder-Marshall (London: The Bodley Head, 1963), 291.

43. George L. Chindahl, *A History of the Circus in America* (Caldwell, Idaho: Caxton Printers, 1959), 209.

44. Alexander Pope, "Animal Life in a Zoo: The Modern Way of Keeping Animals," *Scientific American* 112 (April 24, 1915): 390; William T. Hornaday, *The Minds and Manners of Wild Animals: A Book of Personal Observations* (New York: Charles Scribner's Sons, 1922), 205; idem, *A Wild-Animal Round-Up: Stories and Pictures from the Passing Show* (New York: Charles Scribner's Sons, 1925), 226.

45. Thomas L. Masson, "The Truth About Wild Animals," *New York Times*, May 21, 1922, pt. 3, p. 11; William T. Hornaday, *The Minds and Manners of Wild Animals*, 52. See also Samuel A. Derieux, "Which is Your Favorite Wild Animal?" *American Magazine* 90 (July 1920): 52–55.

46. Henry Childs Merwin, "The Ethics of Horse Keeping," *Atlantic Monthly* 67 (May 1891): 631; John Howard Moore, *Better-World Philosophy*, 131.

47. Henry S. Salt, "A Lover of Animals," reprinted in George Hendrick, *Henry Salt*, 174–95; idem, *Seventy Years among Savages*, 132; Ingrid Newkirk et al., "Just Like Us? Toward a Notion of Animal Rights," *Harper's* 277 (August 1988): 50; James Turner, *Reckoning with the Beast*, 136.

48. Henry S. Salt, *Animals' Rights*, 60; idem, *Seventy Years among Savages*, 129.

49. Rupert Hughes, "Animal and Vegetable Rights," *Harper's New Monthly Magazine* 103 (November 1901): 69.

50. Newkirk et al., "Just Like Us?"; Keith Thomas, "The Beast in Man," 47; Stephen Winsten, *Salt and His Circle*, 17; Brian Harrison, "State Intervention and Moral Reform in Nineteenth-Century England," in Patricia Hollis, ed., *Pressure From Without in Early Victorian England* (London: Edward Arnold, 1974), 291.

51. Brian Harrison, *Peaceable Kingdom*, 103; Ernest Bell, "The Performing Animal," 95.

52. E. Martinengo Cesaresco, "Man and His Brother," *Living Age* 254 (August 24, 1907): 467; James Turner, *Reckoning with the Beast*, 2 and 81.

53. Ernest Bell, "The Performing Animal," 100; Ouida, "The Quality of Mercy," 295.

54. John Howard Moore, *The Universal Kinship*, 106; E. P. Evans, "Ethical Relations Between Man and Beast," *Popular Science Monthly* 45 (September 1894): 636.

55. John Muir, *A Thousand-Mile Walk to the Gulf* (Boston: Houghton Mifflin, 1915), 136–39; idem, *The Story of My Boyhood and Youth*, 89.

56. Roderick Frazier Nash, *The Rights of Nature*, 3–12.

57. Ibid., 3–12.

CHAPTER 5. WORKING OUT THE BEAST

1. Frances Backhouse, "The Coyote's No Varmint After All, Turns Out," *Canadian Geographic* 105 (August/September 1985): 42; Letter, Harold C. Bryant File, June 30, 1925, Museum of Vertebrate Zoology, University of

California, Berkeley; Barry Holstun Lopez, *Of Wolves and Men* (New York: Charles Scribner's Sons, 1978), 139.

2. A. W. Rolker, "The Rogues of a Zoo," *McClure's Magazine* 23 (May 1904): 2; Barry Lopez, *Of Wolves and Men*, 146, 165; Clifford Presnell, *National Park Service Predator Policy* (Washington, D.C.: National Park Service, March 31, 1939). See also Paul Shepard, *The Tender Carnivore and the Sacred Game* (New York: Charles Scribner's Sons, 1973), 152–53.

3. Walter S. Kerr, "A Battle of the Wild," *Sunset* 29 (September 1912): 307–8; Maximilian Foster, *In the Forest*.

4. Ernest Thompson Seton, "Billy: The Big Wolf," *The Ladies' Home Journal* 22 (September, 1905): 49.

5. Ernest Thompson Seton, *Wild Animals I Have Known*, 40–41; idem, *Trail of an Artist-Naturalist: The Autobiography of Ernest Thompson Seton* (New York: Charles Scribner's Sons, 1940), 290. See also Lisa Mighetto, "Wolves I Have Known: Ernest Thompson Seton in the Arctic," *The Alaska Journal* 15 (Winter 1985): 55–59.

6. Jack London, *The Call of the Wild* (1903; New York: New American Library, 1960), 80, 39, 14.

7. Andrew Sinclair, *Jack: A Biography of Jack London* (New York: Harper and Row, 1977), 91–92.

8. "Man's Brother Beasts," *Harper's Weekly* 52 (August 22, 1908): 31; E. Martinengo Cesaresco, "The Growth of Modern Ideas About Animals," *Contemporary Review* 91 (January 1907): 68–82; Charlotte F. Otten, ed., *A Lycanthropy Reader: Werewolves in Western Culture* (New York: Syracuse University Press, 1986), 101.

9. James H. Leuba, "Morality Among the Animals," *Harper's New Monthly Magazine* 157 (June 1928): 103; William T. Hornaday, *The Minds and Manners of Wild Animals*, 219, 223; idem, *Wild Life Conservation in Theory and Practice* (New Haven: Yale University Press, 1914), 123.

10. Willa Cather, *My Ántonia* (Boston: Houghton Mifflin, 1918), 57–58.

11. David W. Cartwright, *Natural History of Western Wild Animals and Guide for Hunters, Trappers, and Sportsmen* (Toledo, Ohio: Blade Printing and Paper Company, 1875), 96; Barry Lopez, *Of Wolves and Men*, 176–77; O. S. Whitmore, "Treed by Wolves," *Outing* 53 (March 1909): 736.

12. William T. Hornaday, *The American Natural History* (New York: Charles Scribner's Sons, 1904), 22; idem, *The Minds and Manners of Wild Animals*, 223, 269; idem, *Wild Life Conservation in Theory and Practice*, 142; idem, *Wild Animal Interviews and Wild Opinions of Us* (New York: Charles Scribner's Sons, 1929), 295; Stanley Paul Young, *The Wolf in North American History* (Caldwell, Idaho: Caxton Printers, 1946), 29; Theodore Roosevelt, *Hunting the Grisly and Other Sketches*, vol. 3 of *The Works of Theodore Roosevelt* (New York: P. F. Collier and Son, 1893), 225.

13. Edwin L. Sabin, "The Coyote," *Overland Monthly* 51 (May 1908): 474; Maximilian Foster, *In the Forest*, 58; Edwin L. Sabin, "The Coyote," 474, 478; Ernest Ingersoll, "The Hound of the Plains," *Popular Science Monthly* 30 (January 1887): 366, 364; Theodore Shoemaker, "Kiote," *Outlook* 101 (July 27, 1912): 679–82; John L. Von Blon, "Commercializing the Coyote: How a Beast That Was Not Worth Powder to Shoot Him Has Become a Valuable Source of Revenue," *Scientific American* 122 (March 6, 1920): 246; Arthur Hawthorne Carhart and Stanley Paul Young, "Senor Yip-Yap," *Sunset* 61 (December 1928): 30. See also J. Frank Dobie, Mody C. Boatright, Harry H. Ransome, eds., *Coyote Wisdom* (Austin: Texas Folklore Society, 1938), and François Leydet, *The Coyote: Defiant Songdog of the West* (Norman: University of Oklahoma Press, 1988).

14. Alexander Pope, "Animal Life in a Zoo: The Modern Way of Keeping Animals," 389–90; Theodore Roosevelt, *Hunting the Grisly and Other Sketches*, 145; William T. Hornaday, *Wild Life Conservation in Theory and Practice*, 144; idem, *Our Vanishing Wildlife: Its Extermination and Preservation* (New York: Zoological Society, 1913), 81. See also Mabel Osgood Wright, "What is a Bird Sanctuary?" *Bird-Lore* 36 (July/August 1934): 221.

15. Frances Fuller Victor, *The River of the West: Life and Adventures in the Rocky Mountains and Oregon* (San Francisco: R. J. Trumbull and Company, 1870), 90.

16. Allen L. Chickering, "Bandits, Borax and Bears: A Trip to Searles Lake in 1874," *California Historical Quarterly* 17 (June 1938): 113–14; Captain J. Hobbs, *Wild Life in the Far West* (California: Hartford, Wiley, Waterman & Eaton, 1873), 389; William T. Hornaday, *Wild Animal Round-Up: Stories and Pictures from the Passing Show* (New York: Charles Scribner's Sons, 1925), 281.

17. John Burroughs, "Glimpses of Wild Life About My Cabin," *Century* 58 (August 1899): 510; idem, *Squirrels and Other Fur-Bearers* (1875; Boston: Houghton Mifflin, 1923), 86; idem, *Camping and Tramping with Roosevelt* (Boston: Houghton Mifflin, 1906), 4; William T. Hornaday, *Wild Animal Interviews and Wild Opinions of Us*, 41, 49; idem, *Our Vanishing Wildlife*, 81.

18. John Burroughs, *Locust and Wild Honey* (Boston: Houghton Mifflin, 1879); Mary Austin, *The Land of Little Rain* (1903; New York: Natural History Library, 1961), 32; William T. Hornaday, *Our Vanishing Wildlife*, 80–81; C. H. Oneal, "Winged Death," *Yosemite Nature Notes* 9 (January 1930): 6.

19. Rob Carson, "In the Realm of the Beast," *Pacific Northwest* 18 (November 1984): 52; Alston Chase, *Playing God in Yellowstone* (Boston: Atlantic Monthly Press, 1986), 146; Gary Snyder, Afterword in Paul Shepard and Barry Sanders, *The Sacred Paw: The Bear in Nature, Myth and Literature* (New York: Viking, 1985), 208. For a related discussion on fear of wilderness, see Roderick Nash, *Wilderness and the American Mind*, 24.

20. Frances Power Cobbe, *The Life of Frances Power Cobbe by Herself*, 2:557; idem, *Studies New and Old of Ethical and Social Subjects* (London: Trubner and Company, 1865), 229; Henry S. Salt, *Animals' Rights*, 54; idem, *Seventy Years Among Savages*, 131; Howard Williams, *The Ethics of Diet*, title page; Peter Singer, *Animal Liberation*, 252. See also Zulma Steele, *Angel in Top Hat*, 189–90.

21. George T. Angell, *Autobiographical Sketches and Personal Recollections*, 78; Steele, *Angel in Top Hat*, 236–37.

22. Steele, *Angel in Top Hat*, 45.

23. William T. Hornaday, "Fighting Among Wild Animals," *Munsey's Magazine* 25 (April 1901): 132.

24. "In the Interpreter's House," *American Magazine* 69 (November 1909): 144; Ernest Bell, "The Performing Animal," *Contemporary Review* 113 (January 1918): 93; Lisa Mighetto, ed., *Muir Among the Animals*, 99.

25. Donald Worster, *Nature's Economy: The Roots of Ecology* (San Francisco: Sierra Club Books, 1977), 262, 266–67.

26. Ibid., 263; Thomas R. Dunlap, *Saving America's Wildlife*, 112–123; Mabel Osgood Wright, "Stories from Birdcraft Sanctuary," *Bird-Lore* 24 (September/October 1922): 253; idem, "The Making of Birdcraft Sanctuary," *Bird-Lore* 17 (July/August 1915): 263–73.

27. "Open Season for Utah Pests," *New York Times*, May 2, 1920, pt. 7, p. 17; R. K. Stewart, *Report to the Governor of Alaska on Cooperative Predatory-Animal Investigations and Control in the Territory for the Period July 1, 1927 to Feb 28, 1929* (Juneau: Bureau of Biological Survey), 6; Worster, *Nature's Economy*, 264.

28. "War on Wild Life Saves Vast Herds," *New York Times*, October 1, 1930, pt. 2, p. 12; Theodore Shoemaker, "Kiote," 683; "Predatory Animal Control", *New York Times*, November 27, 1921, pt. 9, p. 19. See also James A. Tober, *Who Owns the Wildlife?* 87–89.

29. R. K. Stewart, *Report to the Governor of Alaska*, 3; "Sixty Hounds in a Coyote Hunt," *Literary Digest* 84 (March 28, 1925): 70; Fred A. Hunt, "The Wake of the Wolves," *Overland Monthly* 64 (November 1914): 458, 461; John L. Von Blon, "Commercializing the Coyote," 246; W. A. Mara, "A New Way of Keeping the Wolf from the Door," *American Magazine* 114 (October 1932): 66.

30. Worster, *Nature's Economy*, 279.

31. Ernest Thompson Seton, "The Habits of Wolves," *American Magazine* 64 (October 1907): 642; idem, *The Arctic Prairies* (New York: Harper and Row, 1911), 38–39; idem, *Great Historic Animals, Mainly About Wolves* (New York: Charles Scribner's Sons, 1937), 1.

32. Seton, "The Habits of Wolves," 638; idem, "The Natural History of the Ten Commandments," *Century* 75 (November 1907): 24.

33. Seton, *Wild Animals I Have Known*, 37, 43; idem, "Billy: The Big Wolf,"

Ladies' Home Journal 22 (August 1905): 5. See also Lisa Mighetto, "Wolves I Have Known," 59.

34. Seton, "Billy: The Big Wolf," 5–6; idem, "The Habits of Wolves," 643.

35. Adolf Murie, for example, cited Seton in *The Wolves of Mount McKinley*, Fauna Series no. 5 (Washington, D.C.: National Park Service, 1944), 16, 17, 40. See also H. Allen Anderson, *The Chief*, 126–27; Lisa Mighetto, "Wolves I Have Known," 55; James MacArthur, "Wolf Thompson and his Wild Animals," *Bookman* 9 (March 1899): 71–74.

36. William J. Long, "The Sociology of a Wolf Pack," *Independent* 66 (June 3, 1909): 1179–85.

37. Farley Mowat, *Never Cry Wolf* (Boston: Little, Brown and Company, 1963), 203. For criticism of Mowat's ideas, see Jim Rearden, "Fairy Tales and Wolves," *Alaska* 51 (January 1985): 26, 74–75.

38. Madge Morris Wagner, *The Autobiography of a Tame Coyote* (San Francisco: Harr Wagner Publishing Company, 1921), 4, 29.

39. Ernest Thompson Seton, "Tito: The Story of the Coyote That Learned How," *Scribner's* 28 (August 1900): 325; Enos Mills, *Wild Life on the Rockies* (Boston: Houghton Mifflin, 1909), 77; Lisa Mighetto, ed., *Muir Among the Animals*, 176–77. See also John Muir's short paragraph, "Twenty Hill Hollow," *Overland Monthly* 9 (July 1872): 83.

40. John Capen Adams, *The Hair-breadth Escapes and Adventures of "Grizzly Adams" in Catching and Conquering the Wild Animals Included in his Menagerie* (New York: Wynkoop, Hallenbeck, and Thomas, 1860), 10; Enos Mills quoted in "Grizzly Psychology," *Literary Digest* 48 (March 21, 1914): 668. See also Enos Mills, "Rescuing Her Cub," *Atlantic Monthly* 130 (October 1922): 527–30.

41. Richard A. Bartlett, *Yellowstone: A Wilderness Besieged* (Tucson: University of Arizona Press, 1985), 387–89; Alfred Runte, *National Parks*, 168–69; C. P. Russell, "Some Animal Friends You May Make in Yosemite," *Yosemite Nature Notes* 4 (May 1925): 36–37; Ernest Thompson Seton, "Johnny Bear," *Scribner's* 28 (December 1900): 658–71. For information concerning bears in Yosemite, see "Game Bears Delight Visitors," *Yosemite Nature Notes* 1 (July 31, 1922): 2; M. E. Beatty, "Yosemite's Bear Banquet," *Yosemite Nature Notes* 12 (June 1933): 59–60; J. B. Newell, "Two Bears," *Yosemite Nature Notes* 5 (January 30, 1926): 7; "Zoo Bear Prefers Captivity," *Yosemite Nature Notes* 2 (December 31, 1923): 2–3.

42. B. A. Thaxter, "Do Bears Attack Deer?" *Yosemite Nature Notes* 12 (July 1933): 72–73; Donna E. Haupt, "Grizzly Country," *Life* 7 (August 1984): 38–46; Alfred Runte, *Yosemite: The Embattled Wilderness* (Lincoln: University of Nebraska Press, 1990), 224–25.

43. John Muir, *Our National Parks*, 204, 208; idem, *My First Summer in the Sierra*, 142.

44. Lisa Mighetto, ed., *Muir Among the Animals*, 191; John Muir, Florida and

Cuba Journal, John Muir Papers, Holt-Atherton Center for Western Studies, University of the Pacific, Stockton, California.

45. Mighetto, ed., *Muir Among the Animals*, 192.

CHAPTER 6. BIOCENTRISM

1. Alfred Runte, *National Parks*, 119–20. See also George M. Wright, Joseph S. Dixon, and Ben H. Thompson, *Fauna of the National Parks of the United States: A Preliminary Survey, Series 1* (Washington, D.C.: National Park Service, May 1932), 37.

2. "Last Stand of Our Big Wild Animals," *New York Times*, June 8, 1930, pt. 5, p. 15; Fred A. Hunt, "The Wake of the Wolves," *Overland Monthly* 64 (November 1914): 458–61.

   3.Lisa Mighetto, ed., *Muir Among the Animals*, 187–89.

4. H. E. Anthony, "The Control of Predatory Mammals," *Science* 74 (September 18, 1931): 288–90.; Walter Prichard Eaton, "Our Wild Animal Neighbors," *Harper's New Monthly Magazine* 136 (January 1918): 275.

   5."Giving the Coyote a Good Name," *Literary Digest* 92 (March 26, 1927): 61; "Defenders of 'Varmints'," *New York Times*, April 30, 1930, 24; H. E. Anthony, "Control of Predatory Mammals," 288–90.

6. Thomas R. Dunlap, *Saving America's Wildlife*, 51.

7. Alfred Runte, *Yosemite*, 100–118.

8. H. E. Anthony, "Control of Predatory Mammals," 288–90; Paul L. Lambert, "Coyotes and Their Habits," *Outlook* 115 (March 28, 1917): 570; Donald Worster, *Nature's Economy*, 281; E. A. Goldman, "The Control of Injurious Animals," *Science* 75 (March 18, 1932): 309.

9. Thomas R. Dunlap, "Values for Varmints: Predator Control and Environmental Ideas, 1920–1939," *Pacific Historical Review* 53 (May 1984): 150–51; Worster, *Nature's Economy*, 104; Arthur O. Lovejoy, *The Great Chain of Being* (Cambridge: Harvard University Press, 1936), 183–207.

10. Dunlap, *Saving America's Wildlife*, 74–76.

11. Joseph Grinnell, "Animal Life as an Asset of National Parks," *Science* 44 (September 15, 1916): 375–80; idem, "A Wild-Life Creed," *Yosemite Nature Notes* 8 (August 31, 1926): 2. An early draft of the latter document, edited by George Bird Grinnell, appears in the Joseph Grinnell file (1925), Museum of Vertebrate Zoology, University of California, Berkeley.

12. Wright et al., *Fauna of the National Parks of the United States: A Preliminary Survey*, 2; George M. Wright and Ben H. Thompson, *Fauna of the National Parks of the United States: Wildlife Management in the National Parks, Series 2*, (Washington, D.C.: National Park Service, July 1934), 15; A. E. Borell, "Wildlife Policies in Yosemite," *Yosemite Nature Notes* 12 (January 1935): 9.

13. Worster, *Nature's Economy*, 258–90; Wright et al., *Fauna of the National Parks: A Preliminary Survey*, 35; M. D. Bryant, "A Mountain Lion Kill," *Yosemite*

Nature Notes 15 (October 1936): 79; Wright and Thompson, *Fauna of the National Parks: Wildlife Management*, 22.

14. Wright et al., *Fauna of the National Parks: A Preliminary Survey*, 70; Wright and Thompson, *Fauna of the National Parks: Wildlife Management*, 22, 17, and 19.

15. Wright et al., *Fauna of the National Parks: A Preliminary Survey*, 70; Runte, *National Parks*, 168–69; G. Clarence Adams, "The Wild Animals of Yellowstone Park," *Overland Monthly* 74 (August 1919): 93–102.

16. Wright et al., *Fauna of the National Parks: A Preliminary Survey*, 84, 54.

17. Ibid., 54, 48; Dunlap, *Saving America's Wildlife*, 61.

18. Wright et al., *Fauna of the National Parks: A Preliminary Survey*, 37; Runte, *National Parks*, 144–46.

19. Worster, *Nature's Economy*, 281.

20. Liberty Hyde Bailey, *The Holy Earth*, 20, 32, and 30. For a brief discussion of Bailey's ideas and their connection to those of Leopold, see Roderick Nash, *Wilderness and the American Mind*, 194–95. See also idem, *The Rights of Nature*, 146–47.

21. Nash, *Wilderness and the American Mind*, 199; Frank A. Waugh, "Wilderness to Keep," *Review of Reviews* 81 (February 1930): 146.

22. Curt Meine, *Aldo Leopold: His Life and Work* (Madison: University of Wisconsin Press, 1988), 155; Aldo Leopold, "Varmints," *The Pine Cone* (January 1919), repr. in Susan L. Flader, *Thinking Like a Mountain: Aldo Leopold and the Evolution of an Ecological Attitude Toward Deer, Wolves, and Forests* (Columbia: University of Missouri Press, 1974).

23. Aldo Leopold, "Conserving the Covered Wagon: Shall We Save Parts of the Far Western Wilderness From Soft 'Improvements'?" *Sunset* 54 (March 1925): 21, 54; "The Green Lagoons," *American Forests* 51 (August 1945): 414.

24. Worster, *Nature's Economy*, 285; Nash, *Wilderness and the American Mind*, 192.

25. Aldo Leopold, "The Land Ethic," in *A Sand County Almanac: With Essays on Conservation from Round River* (1949; New York: Ballantine Books, 1970), 237–64.

26. Ibid.

27. Ibid., 240; Nash, *Wilderness and the American Mind*, 193; Leopold, "Thinking Like a Mountain," in *A Sand County Almanac*, 137–41.

28. Dunlap, *Saving America's Wildlife*, 88.

29. For more information regarding Rachel Carson, see Paul Brooks, *The House of Life: Rachel Carson at Work* (Boston: Houghton Mifflin, 1972) and Carol B. Gartner, *Rachel Carson* (New York: Frederick Ungar Publishing Company, 1983).

30. Joseph Wood Krutch, *The Voice of the Desert: A Naturalist's Interpretation* (New York: William Sloane Associates, 1954), 194, 198; see also idem, *More*

Lives Than One (New York: William Sloane Associates, 1962), 290–334 and idem, *The Great Chain of Life* (Boston: Houghton Mifflin Company, 1956), 162.

31. Robert Cahn, *Footprints on the Planet: A Search for an Environmental Ethic* (New York: Universe Books, 1978), 10–20.

CHAPTER 7. NEW DIRECTIONS FOR PROTECTION

1. Stephen R. Kellert, *Public Attitudes Toward Critical Wildlife and Natural Habitat Issues*, 18, 22; Elliot Norse quoted in Kathryn Holmes, "Death Among the Lowlife," *Sierra* 71 (March/April 1986): 22; Stephen R. Kellert, "Historical Trends in Perceptions and Uses of Animals in Twentieth-Century America," 19–33. For his study, Kellert quantified animal-related newspaper articles from 1900–1970 by volume and type; sources included the *Los Angeles Times*, *Hartford Courant*, *Buffalo Bulletin* (Wyoming), and the *Dawson News* (Georgia).

2. John Burroughs, *My Dog Friends*, ed. Clara Barrus (Boston: Houghton Mifflin, 1928): 103; "Animal Wit Indoors and Out," *Atlantic Monthly* 109 (February 1912): 198; "Animals as Friends," *New York Times*, April 13, 1905, 19.

3. Peter Singer, *Animal Liberation*, 316.

4. J. Baird Callicot, "Animal Liberation: A Triangular Affair," in Donald Scherer and Thomas Attig, eds., *Ethics and the Environment* (Englewood Cliffs, N.J.: Prentice-Hall, 1983), 69. See also Mary Midgley, "Brutality and Sentimentality," *Philosophy* 54 (July 1979): 385, and Paul Shepard, *Thinking Animals: Animals and the Development of Human Intelligence* (1965; New York: Viking Press, 1978), 245–46.

5. John G. Mitchell, "Bitter Harvest: Hunting in America," *Audubon* 81 (May 1979): 53, 61; Peter Singer, *Animal Liberation*, 252.

6. Callicot, "Animal Liberation: A Triangular Affair," 67. For an earlier view on domestic animals, see "Does Domestication Make Animals Stupid?" *Review of Reviews* 38 (August 1908): 245–46.

7. Mary Midgley, *Animals and Why They Matter*, 90; Singer, *Animal Liberation*, 215–16, 272.

8. Alastair S. Gunn, "Traditional Ethics and the Moral Status of Animals," *Environmental Ethics* 5 (Summer 1983): 36; Callicot, "Animal Liberation: A Triangular Affair," 60, 72.

9. Bill Devall and George Sessions, *Deep Ecology: Living as if Nature Mattered* (Salt Lake City: Peregrine Smith Books, 1985), 55.

10. Dennis A. Williams and Jeff B. Copeland, "They Shoot Burros, Don't They?" *Newsweek* 96 (July 7, 1980): 24; "Park Service May Kill Off Death Valley's Wild Burros," *New York Times*, February 28, 1977, 16.

11. A. Starker Leopold et al., "Wildlife Management in the National Parks," *National Parks Magazine* 37 (April 1963), insert, vi; "Killing of Burros is Delayed," *New York Times*, March 26, 1977, 8; "Reprieve for Burros," *New York Times*, April 2, 1977, 8. See also "Wild Burros Still Under Fire," *Newsweek* 97 (April 13, 1981): 17–18.

12. Joseph Stocker, "Battle of the Burro," *National Wildlife* 18 (August/September 1980): 14–15; Williams and Copeland, "They Shoot Burros, Don't They?" 24; Marguerite Henry, *Brighty of the Grand Canyon* (Chicago: Rand McNally, 1953).

13. Williams and Copeland, "They Shoot Burros, Don't They?" 24; "NPCA Intervenes in Burro Lawsuit," *National Parks and Conservation Magazine* 54 (November 1980): 22; "Wild Burros Still Under Fire," 18.

14. Sam Droege and Ron Baker, letters, *Earth First!* 6 (February 2, 1986): 3; Reed Noss, letter, *Earth First!* 6 (March 20, 1986): 3.

15. Aldo Leopold, "The Land Ethic," 251; Donald Worster, *Nature's Economy*, 289. See also Richard A. Watson, "A Critique of Anti-Anthropocentric Biocentrism," *Environmental Ethics* 5 (Fall 1983): 256.

16. W. H. Murdy, "Anthropocentrism: A Modern Version," in Scherer and Attig, eds., *Ethics and the Environment*, 13.

17. Gary Francione quoted in "Just Like Us? Toward A Notion of Animal Rights," *Harper's* 277 (August 1988): 44.

18. Singer, *Animal Liberation*, 235–73.

19. John Muir, "Animals," John Muir Papers, Holt-Atherton Center for Western Studies, University of the Pacific.

20. Edward Abbey, *Desert Solitaire: A Season in the Wilderness* (New York: Ballantine Books, 1968), 18–19. See also Edward Abbey, *Down the River* (New York: E. P. Dutton, 1981), 29.

21. Abbey, *Desert Solitaire*, 270, 6.

22. Edward Abbey, *Beyond the Wall: Essays from the Outside* (New York: Holt, Rinehart and Winston, 1984), 43; idem, *Desert Solitaire*, 216, 20, 35.

23. Doug Peacock quoted in Abbey, *Beyond the Wall*, 167; Abbey, *Desert Solitaire*, 113.

24. Henry Beston, *The Outermost House* (Boston: Houghton Mifflin, 1928), 19–20.

25. Barry Lopez, *Of Wolves and Men*, 248, 80, 54, 32.

26. *Wolf Facts* [pamphlet] (Washington, D.C., Defenders of Wildlife, 1987).

27. Lopez, *Of Wolves and Men*, 5–8.

28. Ibid., 249, 285; Abbey, *Desert Solitaire*, 300–301.

29. Kellert, "Historical Trends," 31.

SELECT BIBLIOGRAPHY

ARCHIVAL SOURCES

Bergh, Henry. Letters. Rare Books and Manuscripts Collection, Boston Public Library, Boston.

Burroughs, John. Papers. Huntington Library, San Marino, California.

Cobbe, Frances Power. Papers. Huntington Library, San Marino, California.

Grinnell, Joseph. Papers. Museum of Vertebrate Zoology, University of California, Berkeley.

Hornaday, William T. Papers. Library of Congress, Washington, D.C.

London, Jack. Papers. Huntington Library, San Marino, California.

Muir, John. Papers. In John Bidwell Papers and Robert Underwood Johnson Papers. Bancroft Library, Berkeley, California.

———. Papers. Holt-Atherton Center for Western Studies, University of the Pacific, Stockton, California.

———. Papers. Huntington Library, San Marino, California.

John Muir Family. Interviews. John Muir National Historic Site, Martinez, California.

Royal Society for the Prevention of Cruelty to Animals. Pamphlets. Rare Books and Manuscripts Collection, Boston Public Library, Boston.

GOVERNMENT DOCUMENTS

Bureau of Biological Survey. Reports. Alaska State Historical Library, Juneau.

———. Reports. California State Historical Library, Sacramento.

———. Reports. Washington State Historical Library, Olympia.

Yosemite National Park. Predator Policy Reports. Yosemite National Park Research Library.

———. *Yosemite Nature Notes*. Yosemite National Park Research Library.

SECONDARY SOURCES: BOOKS,
ARTICLES, PAMPHLETS

Owing to the thoroughness of the notes, many of which are annotated, secondary sources are listed here without annotation.

BOOKS

Abbey, Edward. *Desert Solitaire: A Season in the Wilderness.* New York: Ballantine Books, 1968.

———. *The Journey Home*. New York: E. P. Dutton, 1977.

———. *Down the River*. New York: E. P. Dutton, 1981.

———. *Beyond the Wall: Essays from the Outside*. New York: Holt, Rinehart and Winston, 1984.

Adams, John Capen. *The Hair-breadth Escapes and Adventures of "Grizzly Adams" in Catching and Conquering the Wild Animals Included in his Menagerie*. New York: Wynkoop, Hallenbeck, and Thomas, 1860.

Allen, Thomas B. *Guardian of the Wild: The Story of the National Wildlife Federation, 1936–1986*. Bloomington and Indianapolis: Indiana University Press, 1987.

Anderson, H. Allen. *The Chief: Ernest Thompson Seton and the Changing West*. College Station: Texas A&M University Press, 1986.

Angell, George T. *Autobiographical Sketches and Personal Recollections*. Boston: Humane Education Society, 1892.

Austin, Mary. *The Land of Little Rain*. 1903. New York: Natural History Library, 1961.

Bade, William Frederic, ed. *Steep Trails*. Boston: Houghton Mifflin, 1918.

Bailey, Liberty Hyde. *The Holy Earth*. New York: Charles Scribner's Sons, 1915.

Baker, Ron. *The American Hunting Myth*. New York: Vantage Press, 1985.

Barkas, Janet. *The Vegetable Passion*. New York: Charles Scribner's Sons, 1975.

Barnum, P. T. *Struggles and Triumphs: or, The Life of P. T. Barnum, Written by Himself*. New York: A. A. Knopf, 1927.

Bartlett, Richard A. *Yellowstone: A Wilderness Besieged*. Tucson: University of Arizona Press, 1985.

Beston, Henry. *The Outermost House*. Boston: Houghton Mifflin, 1928.

Blanchan, Neltje. *Birds Worth Knowing*. New York: Doubleday, Page and Company, 1917.

Blount, Margaret. *Animal Land: The Creatures of Children's Fiction*. New York: William Morrow, 1975.

Brooks, Paul. *The House of Life: Rachel Carson at Work*. Boston: Houghton Mifflin, 1972.

———. *Speaking for Nature: How Literary Naturalists from Henry Thoreau to Rachel Carson Have Shaped America*. Boston: Houghton Mifflin, 1980.

Burroughs, John. *Ways of Nature*. New York: William H. Wise, 1905.

———. *Camping and Tramping with Roosevelt*. Boston: Houghton Mifflin, 1906.

———. *Accepting the Universe*. Boston: Houghton Mifflin, 1921.

———. *Squirrels and other Fur Bearers*. 1875. Boston: Houghton Mifflin, 1923.

———. *My Dog Friends*. Ed. Clara Barrus. Boston: Houghton Mifflin, 1928.

Cahn, Robert. *Footprints on the Planet: A Search for an Environmental Ethic*. New York: Universe Books, 1978.

Callicot, J. Baird. *Companion to A Sand County Almanac: Interpretive and Critical Essays*. Madison: University of Wisconsin Press, 1987.

———. *In Defense of the Land Ethic: Essays in Environmental Philosophy*. Albany: State University of New York Press, 1988.

Carrighar, Sally. *One Day on Beetle Rock*. New York: Alfred Knopf, 1945.

———. *One Day at Teton Marsh*. New York: Alfred Knopf, 1947.

Carrington, Hereward. *The Natural Food of Man*. London: C. W. Daniel, 1912.

Carson, Gerald. *Cornflake Crusade*. New York: Rinehart, 1957.

———. *Men, Beasts and Gods: A History of Cruelty and Kindness to Animals*. New York: Charles Scribner's Sons, 1972.

Carson, Rachel. *Under the Sea-Wind: A Naturalist's Picture of Ocean Life*. New York: Simon and Schuster, 1941.

———. *The Sea Around Us*. New York: Oxford University Press, 1951.

———. *The Edge of the Sea*. Boston: Houghton Mifflin, 1955.

———. *Silent Spring*. Boston: Houghton Mifflin, 1962.

Cartwright, David W. *Natural History of Western Wild Animals and Guide for Hunters, Trappers, and Sportsmen*. Toledo, Ohio: Blade Printing and Paper Company, 1875.

Cather, Willa. *My Ántonia*. Boston: Houghton Mifflin, 1918.

Chapman, Frank M. *Autobiography of a Bird-Lover*. New York: D. Appleton-Century, 1935.

Chase, Alston. *Playing God in Yellowstone*. Boston: Atlantic Monthly Press, 1986.

Chindahl, George L. *A History of the Circus in America*. Caldwell, Idaho: Caxton Printers, 1959.

Clark, Kenneth. *Animals and Men: Their Relationship as Reflected in Western Art from Prehistory to the Present Day*. London: Thames and Hudson, 1977.

Clark, Stephen R. L., *The Nature of the Beast: Are Animals Moral?* New York: Oxford University Press, 1982.

Cobbe, Frances Power. *Studies New and Old of Ethical and Social Subjects*. London: Trubner and Company, 1865.

———. *Life of Frances Power Cobbe by Herself*. 2 vols. Boston: Houghton Mifflin, 1894.

Cohen, Michael P. *The Pathless Way: John Muir and American Wilderness*. Madison: University of Wisconsin Press, 1984.

Coleman, Sydney H. *Humane Society Leaders in America*. New York: American Humane Association, 1924.

Cutright, Paul Russell. *Theodore Roosevelt: The Naturalist*. New York: Harper and Brothers, 1956.

———. *Elliot Coues: Naturalist and Frontier Historian*. Urbana: University of Illinois Press, 1981.

———. *Theodore Roosevelt: The Making of a Conservationist*. Urbana: University of Illinois Press, 1985.

Devall, Bill, and George Sessions. *Deep Ecology: Living as if Nature Mattered*. Salt Lake City: Peregrine Smith Books, 1985.

Dixon, Royal. *The Human Side of Birds*. New York: Frederick A. Stokes Company, 1917.

———. *The Human Side of Animals*. New York: Frederick A. Stokes Company, 1918.

Dobie, J. Frank, Mody C. Boatright, and Harry H. Ransome, eds. *Coyote Wisdom*. Austin: Texas Folklore Society, 1938.

Dombrowski, George. *The Philosophy of Vegetarianism*. Amherst: University of Massachusetts Press, 1984.

Dorf, Philip. *Liberty Hyde Bailey: An Informal Biography*. Ithaca: Cornell University Press, 1956.

Doughty, Robin W. *Feather Fashions and Bird Preservation: A Study in Nature Protection*. Berkeley and Los Angeles: University of California Press, 1975.

Dunlap, Thomas R. *Saving America's Wildlife*. Princeton: Princeton University Press, 1988.

Ehrenfeld, David. *The Arrogance of Humanism*. New York: Oxford University Press, 1978.

Eisley, Loren. *The Immense Journey*. New York: Random House, 1957.

Evans, Edward Payson. *Evolutional Ethics and Animal Psychology*. New York: D. Appleton and Company, 1898.

Flader, Susan L. *Thinking Like a Mountain: Aldo Leopold and the Evolution of an Ecological Attitude Toward Deer, Wolves, and Forests*. Columbia: University of Missouri Press, 1974.

Forward, Charles W. *Fifty Years of Food Reform: A History of the Vegetarian Movement in England, 1847–97*. London: Ideal Publishing Company, 1898.

Foster, Maximilian. *In the Forest: Tales of Wood-life*. New York: Doubleday, 1901.

Fox, Michael W. *Returning to Eden: Animal Rights and Human Responsibility*. New York: Viking, 1980.

Fox, Stephen. *John Muir and his Legacy: The American Conservation Movement*. Boston: Little, Brown and Company, 1981.

French, Richard. *Anti-Vivisection and Medical Science*. Princeton: Princeton University Press, 1975.

Fritzell, Peter A. *Nature Writing in America: Essays upon a Cultural Type*. Ames: Iowa State University Press, 1990.

Gartner, Carol B. *Rachel Carson*. New York: Frederick Ungar Publishing Company, 1983.

Gillespie, Angus K., and Jay Mechling, eds. *American Wildlife in Symbol and Story*. Knoxville: University of Tennessee Press, 1987.

Glacken, Clarence. *Traces on the Rhodian Shore: Nature and Culture in Western Thought from Ancient Times to the End of the Eighteenth Century*. Berkeley and Los Angeles: University of California Press, 1967.

Greeley, Horace. *Recollections of a Busy Life*. New York: J. B. Ford and Company, 1869.

Grinnell, George Bird. *The Passing of the Great West: Selected Papers of George Bird Grinnell*. Ed. John F. Reiger. New York: Winchester Press, 1972.

Grinnell, George Bird, and Charles Sheldon, eds. *Hunting and Conservation*. New Haven: Yale University Press, 1925.

Harrison, Brian. *Peaceable Kingdom: Stability and Change in Modern Britain*. Oxford: Clarendon Press, 1982.

Hartley, Cecil B. *Hunting Sports of the West*. Philadelphia: John E. Potter, 1885.

Harwood, Dix. *Love for Animals and How it Developed in Great Britain*. New York: Privately printed, 1928.

Haverstock, Mary Sayre. *An American Bestiary*. New York: Harry N. Abrams, 1979.

Hawthorne, Hildegarde. *Enos Mills of the Rockies*. Boston: Houghton Mifflin, 1935.

Hendrick, George. *Henry Salt: Humanitarian Reformer and Man of Letters*. Urbana: University of Illinois Press, 1977.

Henry, Marguerite. *Brighty of the Grand Canyon*. Chicago: Rand McNally, 1953.

Herbert, Henry William. *Frank Forester's Field Sports of the United States and British Provinces of North America*. 2 vols. 1848. New York: A. Townsend and Company, 1860.

Hobbs, Captain J. *Wild Life in the Far West*. California: Hartford, Wiley, Waterman & Eaton, 1873.

Hollis, Patricia, ed. *Pressure from Without in Victorian England*. London: Edward Arnold, 1974.

Hornaday, William T. *The American Natural History*. New York: Charles Scribner's Sons, 1904.

————. *Our Vanishing Wildlife: Its Extermination and Preservation*. New York: Zoological Society, 1913.

————. *Wildlife Conservation in Theory and Practice*. New Haven: Yale University Press, 1914.

————. *The Minds and Manners of Wild Animals: A Book of Personal Observations*. New York: Charles Scribner's Sons, 1922.

————. *A Wild-Animal Round-Up: Stories and Pictures from the Passing Show*. New York: Charles Scribner's Sons, 1925.

Huth, Hans. *Nature and the American: Three Centuries of Changing Attitudes*. Berkeley and Los Angeles: University of California Press, 1957.

Ingersoll, Ernest. *Wild Neighbors: Out-Door Studies in the United States*. New York: Macmillan, 1924.

Johnson, Robert Underwood. *Remembered Yesterdays*. Boston: Little, Brown and Company, 1923.

Keller, Betty. *Black Wolf: The Life of Ernest Thompson Seton*. Vancouver, B.C.: Douglas and McIntyre, 1984.

Kellert, Stephen R. *Public Attitudes Toward Critical Wildlife and Natural Habitat Issues*. Washington, D.C.: Fish and Wildlife Service, 1979.

Kimball, David, and Jim Kimball. *The Market Hunter*. Minneapolis: Dillion Press, 1969.

Krutch, Joseph Wood. *The Voice of the Desert: A Naturalist's Interpretation*. New York: William Sloane Associates, 1954.

——. *The World of Animals: A Treasury of Lore, Legend and Literature by Great Writers and Naturalists from the Fifth Century B.C. to the Present*. New York: Simon and Schuster, 1961.

Leopold, Aldo. *A Sand County Almanac: With Essays on Conservation from Round River*. 1949. New York: Ballantine Books, 1970.

Leydet, François. *The Coyote: Defiant Songdog of the West*. Norman: University of Oklahoma Press, 1988.

London, Jack. *Michael—Brother of Jerry*. New York: Macmillan, 1917.

——. *Jerry of the Islands*. 1916. New York: Macmillan, 1927.

——. *The Call of the Wild*. New York: New American Library, 1960.

——. *The Bodley Head Jack London*. Ed. Arthur Calder-Marshall. London: The Bodley Head, 1963.

Long, William J. *Ways of Wood Folk*. Boston: Ginn and Company, 1899.

——. *School of the Woods: Some Life Studies of Animal Instincts and Animal Training*. Boston: Ginn and Company, 1902.

——. *How Animals Talk*. New York: Harper and Brothers, 1919.

——. *Mother Nature*. New York: Harper and Brothers, 1923.

Lopez, Barry Holstun. *Of Wolves and Men*. New York: Charles Scribner's Sons, 1978.

Lovejoy, Arthur O. *The Great Chain of Being: A Study of the History of An Idea*. Cambridge: Harvard University Press, 1936.

Lund, Thomas A. *American Wildlife Law*. Berkeley and Los Angeles: University of California Press, 1980.

Lutts, Ralph H. *The Nature Fakers: Wildlife, Science & Sentiment*. Golden, Colo.: Fulcrum Publishing, 1990.

McCormick, John. *Reclaiming Paradise: The Global Environmental Movement*. Bloomington and Indianapolis: Indiana University Press, 1989.

McCrea, Roswell. *The Humane Movement: A Descriptive Survey*. New York: Columbia University Press, 1910.

McKibben, Bill. *The End of Nature*. New York: Random House, 1989.

Martin, Calvin. *Keepers of the Game: Indian-Animal Relationships and the Fur Trade*. Berkeley and Los Angeles: University of California Press, 1978.

Matthiessen, Peter. *Wildlife in America*. 1959. New York: Penguin Books, 1977.

Meine, Curt. *Aldo Leopold: His Life and Work*. Madison: University of Wisconsin Press, 1988.

Melville, Herman. *Pierre, or, the Ambiguities*. 1852. New York: Hendricks House, 1949.

Merchant, Carolyn. *The Death of Nature: Women, Ecology, and the Scientific Revolution*. San Francisco: Harper and Row, 1980.

————. *Ecological Revolutions: Nature, Gender, and Science in New England*. Chapel Hill: University of North Carolina Press, 1989.

Merriam, Florence A. *A-Birding on a Bronco*. New York: Houghton Mifflin, 1896.

Midgley, Mary. *Beast and Man: The Roots of Human Nature*. New York: New American Library, 1980.

————. *Animals and Why They Matter*. Athens: University of Georgia Press, 1983.

Mighetto, Lisa, ed. *Muir Among the Animals: The Wildlife Writings of John Muir*. San Francisco: Sierra Club Books, 1986.

Miller, Olive Thorne. *Little Brothers of the Air*. New York: Houghton Mifflin, 1893.

————. *The Bird Our Brother*. New York: Houghton Mifflin, 1908.

Mills, Enos. *Wild Life on the Rockies*. Boston: Houghton Mifflin, 1909.

Mitchell, Lee Clark. *Witnesses to a Vanishing America: The Nineteenth-Century Response*. Princeton: Princeton University Press, 1981.

Moore, John Howard. *Better-World Philosophy: A Sociological Synthesis*. Chicago: Charles H. Kerr, 1906.

————. *The Universal Kinship*. Chicago: Charles H. Kerr, 1908.

————. *The New Ethics*. Chicago: S. A. Bloch, 1909.

Morris, Richard Knowles, and Michael W. Fox, eds. *On the Fifth Day: Animals Rights and Human Ethics*. Washington, D.C.: Acropolis Books, 1978.

Mowat, Farley. *Never Cry Wolf*. Boston: Little, Brown and Company, 1963.

Muir, John. *Our National Parks*. New York: Houghton Mifflin, 1901.

————. *My First Summer in the Sierra*. Boston: Houghton Mifflin, 1911.

————. *The Story of My Boyhood and Youth*. Boston: Houghton Mifflin, 1913.

————. *A Thousand-Mile Walk to the Gulf*. Boston: Houghton Mifflin, 1915.

————. *Travels in Alaska*. Boston: Houghton Mifflin, 1915.

————. *Steep Trails*. Ed. William Frederic Bade. Boston: Houghton Mifflin, 1918.

————. *John of the Mountains: The Unpublished Journals of John Muir*. Ed. Linnie Marsh Wolfe. Cambridge: Riverside Press, 1938.

————. *Muir Among the Animals: The Wildlife Writings of John Muir*. Ed. Lisa Mighetto. San Francisco: Sierra Club Books, 1986.

Murie, Adolf. *The Wolves of Mount McKinley*. Fauna Series no. 5. Washington, D.C.: National Park Service, 1944.

Nash, Roderick. *Wilderness and the American Mind*. 3d ed. New Haven: Yale University Press, 1982.

―――. *The Rights of Nature: A History of Environmental Ethics*. Madison: University of Wisconsin Press, 1989.

―――, ed. *The American Environment: Readings in the History of Conservation*. 2d ed. Menlo Park, Calif.: Addison-Wesley Publishing Company, 1976.

Orwell, George. *The Road to Wigan Pier*. 1937. New York: Harcourt Brace Jovanovich, 1958.

Osborn, Henry Fairfield. *Impressions of Great Naturalists: Reminiscences of Darwin, Huxley, Balfour, Cope and Others*. New York: Charles Scribner's Sons, 1925.

Otten, Charlotte F., ed. *A Lycanthropy Reader: Werewolves in Western Culture*. New York: Syracuse University Press, 1986.

Pearson, Thomas Gilbert. *Adventures in Bird Protection*. New York: D. Appleton-Century Company, 1937.

Peters, R. S., ed. *Nature and Conduct*. London: Macmillan, 1975.

Porter, Gene Stratton. *The Song of the Cardinal*. Indianapolis: Bobbs-Merrill Company, 1903.

Regan, Tom. *All That Dwell Therein: Animal Rights and Environmental Ethics*. Berkeley and Los Angeles: University of California Press, 1982.

―――. *The Case for Animal Rights*. Berkeley and Los Angeles: University of California Press, 1983.

―――. *Animal Sacrifices: Religious Perspectives on the Use of Animals in Science*. Philadelphia: Temple University Press, 1986.

Regan, Tom, and Peter Singer, eds. *Animal Rights and Human Obligations*. Englewood Cliffs, N.J.: Prentice-Hall, 1976.

Reiger, John F. *American Sportsmen and the Origins of Conservation*. Rev. ed. Norman: University of Oklahoma Press, 1986.

Roberts, Charles C. D. *They Who Walk in the Wilds*. New York: Macmillan, 1925.

Rolston, Holmes, III. *Philosophy Gone Wild: Essays in Environmental Ethics*. New York: Prometheus Books, 1986.

―――. *Environmental Ethics: Duties to and Values in the Natural World*. Philadelphia: Temple University Press, 1988.

Roosevelt, Theodore. *Hunting the Grisly and Other Sketches*. New York: P. F. Collier and Son, 1893.

―――. *The Wilderness Hunter*. New York: G. P. Putnam's Sons, 1900.

―――. *Outdoor Pastimes of an American Hunter*. New York: Charles Scribner's Sons, 1905.

―――. *The Works of Theodore Roosevelt*. 24 vols. Ed. George Bird Grinnell. New York: Charles Scribner's Sons, 1923.

Rowley, Francis Harold. *The Humane Idea: A Brief History of Man's Attitude Toward the Other Animals, and the Development of the Humane Spirit into Organized Societies*. Boston: Humane Education Society, 1912.

Runte, Alfred. *National Parks: The American Experience*. 2d ed. Lincoln: University of Nebraska Press, 1987.

————. *Yosemite: The Embattled Wilderness*. Lincoln: University of Nebraska Press, 1990.

Salt, Henry S. *Animals' Rights Considered in Relation to Progress*. New York: Macmillan, 1894.

————. *Seventy Years Among Savages*. New York: Thomas Seltzer, Inc., 1921.

————. *The Story of My Cousins: Brief Animal Biographies*. London: Watts & Co., 1922.

————. *The Creed of Kinship*. New York: E. P. Dutton, 1935.

————, ed. *The New Charter: A Discussion of the Rights of Men and the Rights of Animals*. London: George Bell and Sons, 1896.

————, ed. *The Cruelties of Civilization: A Program of Humane Reform*. London: William Reeves, 1897.

Scherer, Donald, and Thomas Attig, eds. *Ethics and the Environment*. Englewood Cliffs, N.J.: Prentice-Hall, 1983.

Schmitt, Peter J. *Back to Nature: The Acadian Myth in Urban America*. New York: Oxford University Press, 1969.

Serpell, James. *In the Company of Animals: A Study of Human-Animal Relationships*. New York: Basil Blackwell, 1986.

Seton, Ernest Thompson. *Wild Animals I Have Known*. New York: Charles Scribner's Sons, 1898.

————. *Lives of the Hunted*. New York: Charles Scribner's Sons, 1901.

————. *Animal Heroes*. New York: Charles Scribner's Sons, 1905.

————. *The Arctic Prairies*. New York: Harper and Row, 1911.

————. *Great Historic Animals, Mainly About Wolves*. New York: Charles Scribner's Sons, 1937.

————. *Trail of an Artist-Naturalist: The Autobiography of Ernest Thompson Seton*. New York: Charles Scribner's Sons, 1940.

————. *The Trail of the Sandhill Stag and Other Lives of the Hunted*. 1899. New York: E. P. Dutton, 1966.

Sharp, Dallas Lore. *The Face of the Fields*. New York: Houghton Mifflin, 1911.

Shepard, Odell, ed. *The Heart of Thoreau's Journals*. Boston: Houghton Mifflin, 1927.

Shepard, Paul. *The Tender Carnivore and the Sacred Game*. New York: Charles Scribner's Sons, 1973.

————. *Thinking Animals: Animals and the Development of Human Intelligence*. 1965. New York: Viking Press, 1978.

Shepard, Paul, and Barry Sanders. *The Sacred Paw: The Bear in Nature, Myth, and Literature*. New York: Viking, 1985.

Sherwood, Morgan. *Big Game in Alaska: A History of Wildlife and People*. New Haven: Yale University Press, 1981.

Shultz, William J. *The Humane Movement in the United States, 1910–1922*. New York: Columbia University Press, 1924.

Simpson, Charles. *El Rodeo*. London: John Lane and the Bodley Head, 1925.

Sinclair, Andrew. *Jack: A Biography of Jack London*. New York: Harper and Row, 1977.

Singer, Peter. *Animal Liberation: A New Ethics for Our Treatment of Animals*. New York: New York Review Books, 1975.

————, ed. *In Defense of Animals*. New York: Blackwell, 1985.

Steele, Zulma. *Angel in Top Hat*. New York: Harper and Brothers, 1942.

Sterling, Philip. *The Life of Rachel Carson*. New York: Thomas Y. Crowell, 1970.

Stowe, Harriet Beecher. *Oldtown Folks*. 1869. Cambridge, Mass.: Harvard University Press, 1966.

Strong, Douglas H. *Dreamers and Defenders: American Conservationists*. Lincoln: University of Nebraska Press, 1988.

Swigget, H. D. *James Oliver Curwood: Disciple of the Wilds*. New York: Paebar Company, 1943.

Tanner, Thomas. *Aldo Leopold: The Man and his Legacy*. Ankeny, Iowa: Soil Conservation Society of America, 1987.

Teale, Edwin Way, ed. *The Wilderness World of John Muir*. Boston: Houghton Mifflin, 1954.

Thomas, Keith. *Man and the Natural World: A History of the Modern Sensibility*. New York: Pantheon Books, 1983.

Thoreau, Henry David. *Walden*. 1854. Boston: Houghton Mifflin, 1960.

————. *The Heart of Thoreau's Journals*. Ed. Odell Shepard. Boston: Houghton Mifflin, 1927.

Tober, James A. *Who Owns the Wildlife? The Political Economy of Conservation in Nineteenth-Century America*. Westport, Conn.: Greenwood Press, 1981.

Trefethen, James B. *An American Crusade for Wildlife*. New York: Winchester Press, 1975.

Turner, E. S. *All Heaven in a Rage*. London: Michael Joseph, 1964.

Turner, Frederick. *Beyond Geography: The Western Spirit Against the Wilderness*. New York: Viking Press, 1980.

————. *Rediscovering America: John Muir in his Time and Ours*. New York: Viking, 1985.

Turner, James. *Reckoning with the Beast: Animals, Pain, and Humanity in the Victorian Mind*. Baltimore: Johns Hopkins University Press, 1980.

Victor, Frances Fuller. *The River of the West: Life and Adventures in the Rocky Mountains and Oregon*. San Francisco: R. J. Trumbull and Company, 1870.

Wadland, John Henry. *Ernest Thompson Seton: Man and Nature in the Progressive Era, 1880–1915*. New York: Arno, 1978.

Wagner, Madge Morris. *The Autobiography of a Tame Coyote*. San Francisco: Harr Wagner Publishing Company, 1921.

Welker, Robert Henry. *Birds and Men: American Birds in Science, Art, Literature, and Conservation, 1800–1900*. Cambridge, Mass.: Harvard University Press, 1955.

White, G. Edward. *The Eastern Establishment and the Western Experience: The West of Frederic Remington, Theodore Roosevelt, and Owen Wister*. New Haven: Yale University Press, 1968.

Whorton, James C. *Crusaders for Fitness: The History of American Health Reformers*. Princeton: Princeton University Press, 1982.

Wild, Peter. *Enos Mills*. Boise: Boise State University Press, 1979.

————. *Pioneering Conservationists of Western America*. Missoula: Mountain Press, 1979.

Williams, Howard. *The Ethics of Diet: A Biographical History of the Literature of Humane Dietetics, from the Earliest Period to the Present Day*. London: Swan Sonnenschein, 1896.

Winsten, Stephen. *Salt and his Circle*. New York: Hutchinson, 1951.

Wolfe, Linnie Marsh, ed. *John of the Mountains: The Unpublished Journals of John Muir*. Cambridge: Riverside Press, 1938.

Wood, J. G. *Man and Beast: Here and Hereafter*. New York: George Routledge and Sons, 1917.

Worster, Donald. *Nature's Economy: The Roots of Ecology*. San Francisco: Sierra Club Books, 1977.

Wright, George M., Joseph S. Dixon, and Ben H. Thompson. *Fauna of the National Parks of the United States: A Preliminary Survey, Series 1*. Washington, D.C.: National Park Service, May 1932.

Wright, George M., and Ben H. Thompson. *Fauna of the National Parks of the United States: Wildlife Management in the National Parks, Series 2*. Washington, D.C.: National Park Service, July 1943.

Wright, Mabel Osgood. *Birdcraft: A Field Book of Two Hundred Song, Game and Water Birds*. New York: Macmillan, 1897.

————. *Citizen Bird: Scenes from Bird-Life in Plain English for Beginners*. New York: Macmillan, 1897.

————. *Four-Footed Americans and their Kin*. New York: Macmillan, 1898.

————. *The Friendship of Nature*. New York: Macmillan, 1898.

————. *The Heart of Nature*. New York: Macmillan, 1906.

Young, Stanley Paul. *The Wolf in North American History*. Caldwell, Idaho: Caxton Printers, 1946.

ARTICLES AND PAMPHLETS

Adams, G. Clarence. "The Wild Animals of Yellowstone Park." *Overland Monthly* 74 (August 1919): 93–102.

"The Advent of Animals in Fiction." *Independent* 52 (April 26, 1900): 1026–27.

"The Altruism of Animals: Are They Better Christians Than Men?" *Review of Reviews* 15 (March, 1897): 346–47.

Anderson, H. Allen. "Ernest Thompson Seton in Yellowstone Country." *Montana: The Magazine of Western History* 34 (Spring 1984): 46–59.

"Animal Etiquette." *Living Age* 204 (March 30, 1895): 819–22.

"The Animal View of Man." *Popular Science Monthly* 41 (June 1892): 256–60.

Anthony, H. E. "The Control of Predatory Mammals." *Science* 74 (September 18, 1931): 288–90.

Bache, Richard Meade. "Animal Mind and Morality." *Putnam's* 2 (April 1907): 64–69.

Backhouse, Frances. "The Coyote's No Varmint After All, Turns Out." *Canadian Geographic* 105 (August/September 1985): 42.

Barrett, W. C. "Character in Animals." *Science* 21 (June 9, 1893): 312.

Barrows, John Henry. "The Spirit of Humanity." *Independent* 51 (December 28, 1899): 3467–70.

Beard, J. Carter. "The American Black Wolf." *Scientific American* 67 (July 16, 1892): 41.

Beatty, M. E. "Yosemite's Bear Banquet." *Yosemite Nature Notes* 12 (June 1933): 59–60.

Bell, Ernest. "The Performing Animal." *Contemporary Review* 113 (January 1918): 93–100.

Borell, A. E. "Wildlife Policies in Yosemite." *Yosemite Nature Notes* 12 (January 1935): 9.

Boynton, H. W. "Books New and Old: Nature and Human Nature." *Atlantic Monthly* 89 (January 1902): 134–41.

Bryant, M. D. "A Mountain Lion Kill." *Yosemite Nature Notes* 15 (October 1936): 78–79.

Burroughs, John. "Glimpses of Wild Life About My Cabin." *Century* 58 (August 1899): 500–511.

———. "Real and Sham Natural History." *Atlantic Monthly* 91 (March 1903): 298–301.

———. "Do Animals Think?" *Harper's New Monthly Magazine*, 110 (February 1905): 354–58.

———. "Animal Behavior and the New Psychology." *McClure's* 35 (July 1910): 262–70.

———. "Horse Sense." *Independent* 71 (November 30, 1911): 1198–1201.

———. "Animal Wit Indoors and Out." *Atlantic Monthly* 109 (February 1912): 196–205.

———. "Science and Sentiment." *Independent* 72 (February 15, 1912): 360–61.

———. "Is Nature Cruel?" *North American Review* 208 (October 1918): 558–66.

———. "A Critical Glance into Darwin." *Atlantic Monthly* 126 (August 1920): 237–47.

Campbell, Janey Sevilla. "Our Brothers, the Beasts." *Nineteenth Century* 61 (May 1907): 808–20.

Carhart, Arthur Hawthorne, and Stanley Paul Young. "Senor Yip-Yap." *Sunset* 61 (December 1928): 30.

Carson, Rob. "In the Realm of the Beast." *Pacific Northwest* 18 (November 1984): 47–55, 60–61.

Cesaresco, E. Martinengo. "The Growth of Modern Ideas About Animals." *Contemporary Review* 91 (January 1907): 68–82.

———. "Man and His Brother." *Living Age* 254 (August 24, 1907): 460–72.

Chapman, Frank M. "The Case of William J. Long." *Science* 19 (February 26, 1904): 388.

Chickering, Allen L. "Bandits, Borax and Bears: A Trip to Searles Lake in 1874." *California Historical Quarterly* 17 (June 1938): 113–14.

Clark, Edward B. "Roosevelt on the Nature Fakirs." *Everybody's Magazine* 16 (June 1907): 774.

Coleridge, Stephen. "Cruelty to Animals and the RSPCA." *Fortnightly Review* 101 (April 1914): 682–85.

Coward, T. A. "Prevention of Cruelty to Animals." *Westminster Review* 157 (May 1902): 546–51.

Curwood, James Oliver. "Why I Write Nature Stories." *Good Housekeeping* 67 (July 1918): 32–33, 149–50.

Cushman, Herbert Ernest. "Professor August Weismann." *Outlook* 55 (January 16, 1897): 252–53.

Derieux, Samuel A. "Which is Your Favorite Wild Animal?" *American Magazine* 90 (July 1920): 52–55.

Devoe, Alan. "Robins for Sale: Five Cents." *Audubon* 49 (March/April 1947): 108–12.

Dickie, Francis J. "The Cruelty of the Trap." *Our Dumb Animals* 47 (May 1915): 179–80.

"Do Animals Think?" *Literary Digest* 55 (December 8, 1917): 81.

"Does Domestication Make Animals Stupid?" *Review of Reviews* 38 (August 1908): 245–46.

"Don, the 'Talking' Dog." *Scientific American* 108 (May 31, 1913): 502–3.

Drury, Samuel H. "Man and Beast." *Atlantic Monthly* 97 (March 1906): 420–23.

Dunlap, Thomas R. "Values for Varmints: Predator Control and Environmental Ideas, 1920–1939." *Pacific Historical Review* 53 (May 1984): 150.

———. "Sport Hunting and Conservation, 1880–1920." *Environmental Review* 12 (Spring 1988): 51–60.

Eaton, Walter Prichard. "Our Wild Animal Neighbors." *Harper's New Monthly Magazine* 136 (January 1918): 263–75.

Evans, Edward Payson. "The Nearness of Animals to Men." *Atlantic Monthly* 69 (February 1892): 171–84.

————. "The Aesthetic Sense and Religious Sentiment in Animals." *Popular Science Monthly* 42 (February 1893): 472–81.

————. "Ethical Relations Between Man and Beast." *Popular Science Monthly* 45 (September 1894): 634–66.

"Evening Session." *American Vegetarian and Health Journal* 2 (October 1852): 154.

Fellows, Alfred. "The Vegetarian Guest." *Living Age* 250 (11 August 1906): 346–53.

Flower, B. O. "Books of the Day." *Arena* 30 (August 1903): 215.

Furman, Lucy. "The Price of Furs." *Atlantic Monthly* 141 (February 1928): 206–9.

"Game Bears Delight Visitors." *Yosemite Nature Notes* 1 (July 31, 1922): 2.

Gifford, John. "The Protection of Our Wild Plants and Animals." *Science* 22 (October 20, 1893): 215.

"Giving the Coyote a Good Name." *Literary Digest* 92 (March 26, 1927): 61.

Gladden, George. "Fur, Feathers and Intellect." *Bookman* 23 (March 1906): 89–91.

Goldman, E. A. "The Control of Injurious Animals." *Science* 75 (March 18, 1932): 309–11.

Grinnell, George Bird. "The Last of the Buffalo." *Scribner's* 12 (September 1892): 267–86.

Grinnell, Joseph. "Animal Life as an Asset of National Parks." *Science* 44 (September 15, 1916): 375–80.

————. "A Wild-Life Creed." *Yosemite Nature Notes* 8 (August 31, 1926): 2.

"Grizzly Psychology." *Literary Digest* 48 (March 21, 1914): 665–70.

Gunn, Alastair S. "Traditional Ethics and the Moral Status of Animals." *Environmental Ethics* 5 (Summer 1983): 36.

Hall, A. D. "Some Aspects of Vegetarianism." *Harper's New Monthly Magazine* 123 (July 1911): 208–13.

Haupt, Donna E. "Grizzly Country." *Life* 7 (August 1984): 38–46.

Hawkins, General Rush C. "Brutality and Avarice Triumphant." *North American Review* 152 (June 1891): 656–70.

Hayes, Ellen. "The Writings of William J. Long." *Science* 19 (May 13, 1904): 626.

Hellman, George S. "Animals in Literature." *Atlantic Monthly* 87 (March 1901): 391–97.

Holmes, Kathryn. "Death Among the Lowlife." *Sierra* 71 (March/April 1986): 22.

Hornaday, William T. "Thompson's Animal Stories." *Overland Monthly* 33 (March 1899): 288.

————. "Fighting Among Wild Animals." *Munsey's Magazine* 25 (April 1901): 121–32.

————. "A True Bear Story." *The Cosmopolitan* 37 (October 1904): 709–14.

————. "The Psychology of Wild Animals." *McClure's* 30 (February 1908): 469–79.

Howard, Clifford. "Love Stories of the Zoo." *Ladies' Home Journal* 18 (June 1901): 8.

Hubbard, Leonides, Jr. "What a Big Zoo Means to the People." *Outing* 44 (September 1904): 670–78.

Hubbard, Sara A. "A Quartette of Bird-Books." *Dial* 34 (June 1, 1903): 363.

Hughes, Rupert. "Animal and Vegetable Rights." *Harper's New Monthly Magazine* 103 (September 1901): 852–53.

Hunt, Fred A. "The Wake of the Wolves." *Overland Monthly* 64 (November 1914): 458–61.

Hutchinson, Woods. "Animal Chivalry." *Contemporary Review* 76 (December 1899): 878–88.

————. "Animal Marriage." *Contemporary Review* 86 (October, 1904): 485–96.

Hyatt, Edward. *Two California Neighbors: A Suggestion for the English Class.* California: State of California, Superintendent of Public Instruction, n.d. [Pamphlet, Huntington Library].

Ingersoll, Ernest. "The Hound of the Plains." *Popular Science Monthly* 30 (January 1887): 366–64.

————. "Our Gray Squirrels: A Study." *Harper's New Monthly Magazine* 84 (March 1892): 546.

"In the Interpreter's House." *American Magazine* 69 (November 1909): 141–44.

Jeffery, Major John B. "Animal Life on the Pacific Coast Some Fifty Years Ago." *Overland Monthly* 51 (June 1908): 534–36.

"The Joys of Vegetarianism." *Outlook* 49 (March 31, 1894): 600.

Keck, David. "A Battle to the Death." *Yosemite Nature Notes* 7 (January 1928): 7.

Kellert, Stephen R. "Historical Trends in Perceptions and Uses of Animals in Twentieth-Century America." *Environmental Review* 9 (Spring 1985): 19–33.

Kerr, Walter S. "A Battle of the Wild." *Sunset* 29 (September 1912): 307–8.

Kofoid, Charles Atwood. "Nature-Books for Summer Outings." *Dial* 27 (July 1, 1899): 13–14.

————. "The Innings of the Animals." *Dial* 31 (1 December 1901): 439–40.

Lambert, Paul L. "Coyotes and Their Habits." *Outlook* 115 (March 28, 1917): 570.

Leffingwell, Albert. "An Ethical Basis for Humanity to Animals." *Arena* 10 (September 1894): 474–82.

Leopold, A. Starker. "Wildlife Management in the National Parks." *National Parks Magazine* 37 (April 1963): insert, i-vi.

Leopold, Aldo. "Conserving the Covered Wagon: Shall We Save Parts of the Far Western Wilderness From Soft 'Improvements'?" *Sunset* 54 (March 1925): 21 and 56.

————. "The Green Lagoons." *American Forests* 51 (August 1945): 376–77, 414.

Leuba, James H. "Morality Among the Animals." *Harper's New Monthly Magazine* 157 (June 1928): 103.

"Life's Supreme Pleasure." *Atlantic Monthly* 95 (June 1905): 855–57.

Long, William J. "Nature and Books." *Dial* 34 (June 1, 1903): 358.

————. "Wild Animals at Home." *Outlook* 74 (June 6, 1903): 355–64.

————. "Animal Surgery." *Outlook* 75 (September 12, 1903): 126.

————. "Do Animals Think?" *Harper's New Monthly Magazine* 111 (June 1905): 59–62.

————. "Animal Immortality." *Harper's New Monthly Magazine* 111 (November 1905): 873–78.

————. "Stories From the Trail." *Independent* 64 (June 4, 1908): 1279–80.

————. "The Sociology of a Wolf Pack." *Independent* 66 (June 3, 1909): 1179–85.

————. "Getting Acquainted with Wild Animals." *Independent* 72 (June 6, 1912): 1234–35.

MacArthur, James. "Wolf Thompson and his Wild Animals." *Bookman* 9 (March 1899): 71–74.

MacDonald, Robert H. "The Revolt Against Instinct: The Animal Stories of Seton and Roberts." *Canadian Literature* 84 (Spring 1980): 18–29.

McGregor, Robert Kuhn. "Deriving a Biocentric History: Evidence from the Journal of Henry David Thoreau." *Environmental Review* 12 (Summer 1988): 117–26.

"Man's Brother Beasts." *Harper's Weekly* 52 (August 22, 1908): 31.

Mara, W. A. "A New Way of Keeping the Wolf from the Door." *American Magazine* 114 (October 1932): 66.

Merwin, Henry Childs. "The Ethics of Horse Keeping." *Atlantic Monthly* 67 (May 1891): 631–39.

————. "Vivisection." *Atlantic Monthly* 89 (March 1902): 320–25.

Metcalfe, William. "Objects of the Convention." *American Vegetarian and Health Journal* 1 (November 1850): 5.

Meyer, Lucy Rider. "Is Nature Red?" *Outlook* 104 (May 24, 1913): 191–98.

Midgley, Mary. "Brutality and Sentimentality." *Philosophy* 54 (July 1979): 385–89.

Mighetto, Lisa. "Science, Sentiment, and Anxiety: American Nature Writing at the Turn of the Century." *Pacific Historical Review* 54 (February 1985): 33–50.

————. "Muir Among the Animals." *Sierra* 70 (March/April 1985): 69–71.

————. "Wolves I Have Known: Naturalist Ernest Thompson Seton in the Arctic." *Alaska Journal* 15 (Winter 1985): 54–59.

————. "Wildlife Protection and the New Humanitarianism." *Environmental Review* 12 (Spring 1988): 37–49.

Miller, Olive Thorne [Harriet Mann]. "The Spinning Sisterhood." *Popular Science Monthly* 39 (October 1891): 822–32.

————. "Little Boy Blue." *Atlantic Monthly* 72 (August 1893): 169–77.

————. "Beautiful and Brave was He." *Atlantic Monthly* 76 (July 1895): 59–68.

————. "Whimsical Ways in Bird Land." *Atlantic Monthly* 77 (May 1896): 670–75.

Mills, Enos. "Rescuing Her Cub." *Atlantic Monthly* 130 (October 1922): 527–30.

Mills, Wesley. "The Cultivation of Humane Ideas and Feelings." *Popular Science Monthly* 43 (May 1893): 46–51.

Mitchell, John G. "Bitter Harvest: Hunting in America." *Audubon* 81 (May 1979): 50–83.

Moore, John Howard. "Evidences of Relationship." *Our Dumb Animals* 47 (August 1914): 33–34.

Moore-Park, Carton. "Thinking Dogs." *Outlook* 99 (December 23, 1911): 979–87.

Morris, Clara. "Riddle of the Nineteenth Century: Mr. Henry Bergh." *McClure's* 18 (March 1902): 414–22.

"The Mountain Weasel." *Yosemite Nature Notes* 2 (June 26, 1923): 3.

Muir, John. "Twenty Hill Hollow." *Overland Monthly* 9 (July 1872): 83.

Newell, J. B. "Two Bears." *Yosemite Nature Notes* 5 (January 30, 1926): 7.

Newkirk, Ingrid, Gary Francione, Roger Goldman, and Arthur Caplan. "Just Like Us? Toward a Notion of Animal Rights." *Harper's* 277 (August 1988): 43–52.

"Notable Vegetarians." *Literary Digest* 46 (May 24, 1913): 1196–97.

"NPCA Intervenes in Burro Lawsuit." *National Parks and Conservation Magazine* 54 (November 1980): 22.

Oneal, C. H. "Winged Death." *Yosemite Nature Notes* 9 (January 1930): 6.

O'Neal, Herbert. "Mountain Weasel Makes a Kill." *Yosemite Nature Notes* 12 (November 1933): 101.

O'Shea, M. V. "The Abilities of an 'Educated' Horse." *Popular Science Monthly* 82 (February, 1913): 168–76.

"Other Worlds Than Ours." *Nation* 98 (May 14, 1914): 563–64.

Ouida [Marie Louise de la Ramée]. "The Quality of Mercy." *Nineteenth Century* 40 (August 1896): 293–305.

"Our Dumb Animals." *Independent* 61 (August 30, 1906): 529–31.

Paget, Lady Walb. "A Vegetable Diet." *Popular Science Monthly* 44 (November 1893): 94–102.

Perry, Jeanette Barbour. "Wild Animals I Do Not Want to Know." *Critic* 40 (June 1902): 518.

"Picture of the Chase—Cruelty to Animals." *The Animal's Friend* 2 (March 1874): 3.

Pope, Alexander. "Animal Life in a Zoo: The Modern Way of Keeping Animals." *Scientific American* 112 (April 24, 1915): 390.

Porter, Gene Stratton. "The Birds' Kindergarten." *Outing* 40 (April 1902): 70–74.

Rearden, Jim. "Fairy Tales and Wolves." *Alaska* 51 (January 1985): 26, 74–75.

Reese, S. M. "Science, Nature, and Criticism." *Science* 19 (May 13, 1904): 761.

Reiger, John F. Response to Review. *Journal of Forest History* 20 (October, 1976): 221.

———. Response to Review. *Environmental Review* 12 (Fall 1988): 94–96.

Rolker, A. W. "The Rogues of a Zoo." *McClure's* 23 (May 1904): 2.

Roosevelt, Theodore. "Nature's Fakers." *Everybody's Magazine* 17 (September 1907): 427–30.

———. "Our Vanishing Wildlife." *Outlook* 103 (January 25, 1913): 161–62.

Ross, E. A. "Turning Towards Nirvana." *Arena* 4 (November 1891): 739, 742.

Runte, Alfred. Review of John F. Reiger's *American Sportsmen and the Origins of Conservation* (1st ed.). *Journal of Forest History* 20 (April 1976): 100–101.

Russell, C. P. "Some Animal Friends You May Make in Yosemite." *Yosemite Nature Notes* 4 (May 1925): 36–37, 40.

Sabin, Edwin L. "The Coyote." *Overland Monthly* 51 (May 1908): 474–78.

Samson, Jack. "Seton: America's Forgotten Naturalist." *Field and Stream* 78 (April 1974): 60, 194.

Saville, Elizabeth. "The Dew of Mercy." *Westminster Review* 173 (January 1910): 86–95.

Seton, Ernest Thompson. "Some More About Wolves." *Forest and Stream* 48 (March 6, 1897): 183–84.

———. "Tito: The Story of the Coyote that Learned How." *Scribner's* 28 (August 1900): 316–25.

———. "Johnny Bear." *Scribner's* 28 (December 1900): 658–71.

———. "Fable and Woodmyth." *Century* 67 (November 1903): 35.

———. "Billy: The Big Wolf." *The Ladies' Home Journal* 22 (August 1905): 5–6; 22 (September 1905): 10, 49.

———. "The Habits of Wolves, Including Many Facts About Animal Marriage." *American Magazine* 64 (October 1907): 636–45.

———. "The Natural History of the Ten Commandments." *Century* 73 (November 1907): 24–33.

Sharp, Dallas Lore. "Out-of-doors from Labrador to Africa." *Critic* 48 (February 1906): 122.

Shoemaker, Theodore. "Kiote." *Outlook* 101 (July 27, 1912): 679–83.

Sheldon, Charles M. "The Confessions of a Vegetarian." *Independent* 60 (June 21, 1906): 1457–58.

"Sixty Hounds in a Coyote Hunt." *Literary Digest* 84 (March 28, 1925): 70.

Stanley, Thomas. "The New Humanitarianism." *Westminster Review* 155 (April 1901): 414–23.

Stocker, Joseph. "Battle of the Burro." *National Wildlife* 18 (August/September 1980): 14–15.

Stott, R. Jeffrey. "The Historical Origins of the Zoological Park in American Thought." *Environmental Review* 5 (Fall 1981): 52–65.

Thaxter, B. A. "Do Bears Attack Deer?" *Yosemite Nature Notes* 12 (July 1933): 72–73.

Thomas, Keith. "The Beast in Man." *New York Review of Books* 28 (April 30, 1981): 47–48.

Thomson, J. Arthur. "The 'Thinking' Horses of Elberfeld." *Contemporary Review* 104 (December 1913): 799–805.

Thorndike, Edward. "Do Animals Reason?" *Popular Science Monthly* 55 (August 1899): 480–90.

"The Vegetarian Creed." *Living Age* 216 (January 8, 1898): 127–28.

"Vegetarianism—What is it?" *American Vegetarian and Health Journal* 1 (February 1851): 37.

Von Blon, John L. "Commercializing the Coyote: How a Beast That Was Not Worth the Powder to Shoot Him Has Become a Valuable Source of Revenue." *Scientific American* 122 (March 6, 1920): 246, 258.

Watson, Richard A. "A Critique of Anti-Anthropocentric Biocentrism." *Environmental Ethics* 5 (Fall 1983): 256.

Waugh, Frank A. "Wilderness to Keep." *Review of Reviews* 81 (February 1930): 146.

Wheeler, William Morton. "Woodcock Surgery." *Science* 19 (February 26, 1904): 350.

White, Lynn, Jr. "The Historical Roots of Our Ecological Crisis." *Science* 155 (10 March 1967): 1203–7.

Whitmore, O. S. "Treed by Wolves." *Outing* 53 (March 1909): 736.

Whitney, Caspar. "The View-Point of Caspar Whitney." *Outing* 50 (September 1907): 748–50.

"Wild Burros Still Under Fire." *Newsweek* 97 (April 13, 1981): 17–18.

Williams, Dennis A., and Jeff B. Copeland. "They Shoot Burros, Don't They?" *Newsweek* 96 (July 7, 1980): 24.

Wolf, Clara Holzmark. "Some Interesting Facts About Wild Animals." *Overland Monthly* 58 (November 1911): 439–44.

Wolf Facts. Pamphlet. Washington, D.C.: Defenders of Wildlife, 1987.

"Women's Influence in Our Work." *Our Dumb Animals* 3 (May 1871): 95.

Worster, Donald. "The Intrinsic Value of Nature." *Environmental Review* 4 (Spring 1980): 43–49.

Wright, Mabel Osgood. "The Making of Birdcraft Sanctuary." *Birdlore* 17 (July/August 1915): 263–73.

———. "Stories from Birdcraft Sanctuary." *Birdlore* 24 (September/October 1922): 253–55.

———. "What is a Bird Sanctuary?" *Birdlore* 36 (July/August 1934): 219–25.

"Zoo Bear Prefers Captivity." *Yosemite Nature Notes* 2 (December 31, 1923): 2–3.

A-Birding on a Bronco (Merriam), 14
Abbey, Edward, xii, 114, 115, 118
Abolitionism, xi, 53, 54
Adams, John Capen ("Grizzly"), 90, 91
Adirondack Mountains, 33
Aesop, 4, 12
Albert Schweitzer Medal, 105
Alcoholism, 64
Alcott, Bronson, 61
Alcott, William, 65
Alligator(s), 19, 34, 92
Alps, 35
American Angler, 27
American Anti-Vivisection Society, 59
American Bands of Mercy, 46, 48, 52
American Horse Protection Association, 112
American Humane Education Society, 44, 45
American Magazine, 58
American Museum of Natural History, 13, 19, 38, 39, 96
American Natural History, The (Hornaday), 75
American Ornithological Union's "model law," 39
American Revolution, 73
American Society of Mammalogists, 96
American Sportsman, 27
American Vegetarian, 61
American Vegetarian Society, 61
Amory, Cleveland, 112
Angell, George T., 45, 52, 83
Angling, 31, 32, 34, 35, 55, 56, 57
Animal Heroes (Seton), 15
Animal Kingdom, The, 45
Animal liberation, 7, 60, 108, 110

Animal Liberation (Singer), 109
Animal psychology, 73
Animal rights, 24, 45, 56, 66, 67, 74, 83, 98, 100, 119, 120; *cf* biocentrism, 108–14; defined, 47; *cf* kindness to animals, 70, 71, 108; and First Church for Animal Rights, 46, 47, 73; skepticism toward, xi, 6, 7, 71. *See also* Humanitarianism
Animals; feral, 111–12; importance of labels for, 7, 70, 76; intelligence of (domestic), 15, 16; morality of, 76, 78, 79–92; spirituality of, 23, 46, 47, 73, 78; treatment of (domestic), 2, 42–67, 70–74, 107–14, 123 n. 5. *See also* Conservation, Wildlife, and names of specific animals
Animal's Friend, 57
Animals' Rights (Salt), 45, 55, 72
Animal Welfare Institute, 105
Animal World, 46
Antelope, 29, 30
Anthony, H. E., 96, 97
Anthropocentrism, 76, 93, 107, 121; biblical origins of, 43, 92; biocentrists' challenge of, 101–06; humanitarians' challenge of, 41, 42, 46, 47, 70, 72, 73, 74; in national parks, 99, 100; among sportsmen and bird lovers, 40, 41; in Western civilization, xi, 5, 6, 26, 43, 101, 108, 110, 113, 114, 118
Anthropomorphism, 4, 23–26, 87, 107–09, 114, 117
Anti-Steel Trap League, 58
Antivivisection, 46, 47, 50, 52, 58, 59, 61, 68, 82
Aquinas, Thomas, 43

Arctic, 11, 87
Arena, 1, 50
Arizona, 99, 120
Atlantic Monthly, 19, 22, 23, 44, 49, 58
Audubon, John James, 13, 28
Audubon Society, 25, 48, 111; in Connecticut, 20; and spotted owl, 120; founding of, 39; and humanitarianism, 5; and rejection of predators, 85; and sportsmen, 27; and arguments for bird protection, 40, 42, 43
Austin, Mary, 81
Autobiography of a Tame Coyote, The, 90

"Back to Nature" movement, 3, 4, 9, 38
Bailey, Liberty Hyde, 20, 94, 101, 103
Balance of nature, 95, 97
Band of Mercy, 46, 48, 52
Bandelier National Monument, 111, 112
Barnum, P. T., 83
Barnum and Bailey Circus, 68, 69
Bear, The (Columbia Pictures), 24
Bear(s), 24, 25, 30, 34, 37, 75, 119; aggression of, 19, 36, 80, 81; gentleness of, 20, 82, 90–92; intelligence of, 17; in national parks, 85, 91, 99, 100; in zoos, 69. *See also* photo essays "Wildlife in the National Parks" and "Illustrations of Predators"
Beaver, 29, 30, 58
Bell, Ernest, 68, 72
Bentham, Jeremy, 43, 44, 109
Bergh, Henry, 51, 59, 71; background of, 48–49; and Society for the Prevention of Cruelty to Animals, 45; and Society for the Prevention of Cruelty to Children, 46; and pigeon shoots, 48; and slaughter of buffalo, 47; and rejection of predators, 83; satirized, 48, 50; as vice-president of Audubon Society, 48
Beston, Henry, 107, 115, 116

Bide-a-Wee Home, 46
Bignall, Effie, 15
Biocentrism, 93–107 passim; and acceptance of predators, 5, 6; *cf* humanitarianism, 7, 101, 108–14; and misanthropy, 113; resistance to, 6. *See also* Ethics
Birdcraft (Wright), 20
Bird-Lore, 39
Bird Our Brother, The (Miller), 24
Bird(s), 21, 24, 25, 33, 40, 46, 80, 83, 90; abundance of, 28; altruism of, 19; conservation of, 27, 37–41, 48; destruction of, 28–31, 38, 39, 57; individuality of, 14; intelligence of, 15, 17, 18; intrinsic value of, 114; in national parks, 99; as predators, 19, 20, 81, 82, 85, 95, 120; in zoos, 69. *See also* Audubon Society and names of specific birds
Birds of the Colorado Valley (Coues), 40
Birds of the Northwest (Coues), 40
Bison. *See* Buffalo
Black Beauty, 45, 53
Blanchan, Neltje, 38
Blue, Joan, 112
Boone, Daniel, 35
Boone and Crockett Club, 31–33
Boynton, H. W., 9, 13
Boy Scouts of America, 126 n. 9
Brighty of the Grand Canyon (Henry), 112
British Vegetarian Society, 61, 62
Bryant, William Cullen, 3
Buffalo, 28, 29, 30, 32, 47, 82
Bull fighting, 69
Bureau of Biological Survey, 40, 85, 86, 96, 97
Burros, 111, 112
Burroughs, John, 12, 16, 25, 38; and benevolence of nature, 19, 20; and nature fakers, 17, 18, 20, 108, 109; and opposition to hunting, 56; and order in nature, 23; and Theodore Roosevelt, 33; and rejection of predators, 81; *Wake-Robin,* 38
Byrd, William, II, 2

California, 30, 80, 86, 95, 111
California Museum of Sciences, 85
Callicot, J. Baird, 109, 110
Call of the Wild, The (London), 77
Canada, 11, 13, 77, 89
Caribou, 30, 89
Carrighar, Sally, 104
Carrington, Hereward, 64
Carson, Rachel, 104–06
Catesby, Mark, 2
Cather, Willa, 79
Cat(s), 57, 70, 80, 83. *See also* Cougars
Cattle, 16, 29, 46, 49, 65, 66, 85, 86, 95, 110
Century, 23
Cetaceans, 119
Chapman, Frank M., 13, 19, 37, 38
Chlorofluorocarbons, 117
Christianity, 43, 44, 46, 66, 83, 114
Cincinnati Zoo, 29
Circuses, 67, 68, 83, 108. *See also* Zoos and photo essay "Humanitarians and the Treatment of Animals"
Citizen Bird (Wright), 20, 24
Civil War, 53, 54
Clever Hans (horse), 16
Clubb, Henry, 61
Cobbe, Frances Power, 49, 51, 82, 83
Cole, Thomas, 3
Coleman, Sydney H., 50
Coleridge, Samuel Taylor, 67
Coleridge, Stephen, 44
Conservation, 96, 98, 100, 103, 105–07, 112–14; American Ornithological Union's "model law," 39; changes in strategy for, 119; defined, xi, xii; and the Endangered Species Act, 75, 106, 120; factions in, 7, 42, 47; and the Lacey Act of 1894, 32; and the Lacey Act of 1900, 32; motivations for, xi, xii, 23–26, 47; and rejection of predators, 79; and species diversity, 7, 108; utilitarian, xi, 2, 5, 27–32, 37–42, 57, 84, 98, 102, 118; and the Weeks-McLean Act of 1913, 39;

and zoos, 67. *See also* names of specific individuals, organizations, and agencies
Coues, Elliot, 40
Cougar(s), 19, 30, 76, 80, 85, 95. *See also* Lions
Coyote(s), 75, 80, 85, 86, 90, 95, 96, 100, 104, 115
Crane, Stephen, 10
Crockett, Davy, 35
Curwood, James Oliver, 24, 25

Darwin, Charles, 1, 9, 10, 19, 20, 44, 73, 114
Darwin, Emma, 9
Darwinism, 1, 4, 5, 103; implications of, 9–11, 19–22, 26; as survival of the fittest, 11, 15. *See also* Evolution
DDT, 105
Death Valley National Monument, 111
Declaration of Independence, xi
Deep Ecology, 111. *See also* Biocentrism
Deer, 11, 29, 31, 37, 80, 83, 87, 89, 90, 91, 99, 102, 104, 116
Defenders of Wildlife, 58, 116
Desert Solitaire (Abbey), 114
Desert Year, The (Krutch), 105
Dial, 19
Dixon, Royal, 46, 47
Dog(s), 9, 13, 15, 16, 24, 31, 36, 49, 77, 78, 83, 109
Dreiser, Theodore, 10
Drift nets, 119
Ducks Unlimited, 94
Dunlap, Thomas R., 97
Dust Bowl, 94, 104

Eagle(s), 19, 82
Earth First!, 27, 108, 120
Earth First!, 112
Ecological Society, 107
Ecology, 6, 7, 74, 93, 97, 100–13 passim
Ecosystems. *See* Habitat

Edge of the Sea, The (Carson), 104
Elberfeld horses, 15–16
Elephants, 69. *See also* photo essay "Humanitarians and the Treatment of Animals"
Elk, 29, 30, 32, 80, 94
Emerson, Ralph Waldo, 3
End of Nature, The (McKibben), 117
Endangered Species Act, 75, 106, 120
England; and Darwinism, 9, 10, 20, 21, 22; humanitarianism in, 1, 5, 44–46, 49–53, 55, 58, 59, 61, 62, 64–66, 72, 82, 83, 109, 125 n. 2, 135 n. 21; hunting etiquette in, 31; intelligent horses in, 16
Enlightenment, 2
Environmentalism, xi, 27, 41, 42, 75, 101, 104–07, 110, 112, 116, 120
Ethics, xii, 21–23, 54, 62, 74, 78, 79, 84, 92, 108; and biocentrism, 5, 6, 93–106 passim; and Deep Ecology, 111; and empathy, 72, 76; evolution of, 1, 5, 6, 66, 73, 103, 118; and intrinsic worth, 114–18; kinship as a basis for, 1, 5, 23–26, 52, 56, 61, 66, 68, 72, 73, 107, 108, 111, 112; and land ethic, 101–04, 106, 109, 110, 113; and rejection of kinship, 114–18; sentience as basis for, 5, 7, 42–45, 47, 48, 57, 70, 82, 108–12; and stewardship, 101, 113. *See also* Humanitarianism and Animal rights
Europe, 79. *See also* names of specific countries
Evans, Edward Payson, 19, 21, 22, 73
Everglades National Park, 101
Evermann, Barton Warren, 85
Evolution, 1, 9, 23, 73, 78. *See also* Darwinism

Factory farms, 110
Farming, 29, 86, 95, 102
Field and Stream, 27
Field Sports (Herbert), 31
First Church for Animal Rights, 46, 47, 73

Fish, 56, 65, 106
Fish and Wildlife Service, 40, 119, 120
Fishing. *See* Angling
Florida, 39
Food, Home, and Garden, 61
Forest and Stream, 27, 30, 39
Forest Reserve Act, 32, 39
Fortnightly Review, 57
Foster, Maximilian, 4, 11, 76
Four-Footed Americans and their Kin (Wright), 24
Fox, 13
France, 38, 59
"Frank Forester." *See* Henry William Herbert
Friendship of Nature, The (Wright), 21
Frogs, 104
Fund for Animals, The, 27, 112, 119
Furman, Lucy, 58
Fur wearing, 7, 119

Gabrielson, Ira, 97
Game management, 84, 94, 102, 112
Gandhi, Mohandas Karamchand, 72
Garrison, William Lloyd, 54
Geese, 14
Germany, 59, 102
Gila National Forest, 102
Glacier National Park, 91
Goat(s), 30, 99
Goldman, E. A., 96, 97
Good Housekeeping, 24
Gophers, 82
Gorillas, 15
Graham, Sylvester, 62
Grand Canyon National Park, 111, 112
Grand Pacific Hotel, 30
Great Chain of Being, 97
Great Historic Animals (Seton), 75
Great Northern Railway, 29
Greeks, 61, 62
Greeley, Horace, 62
Greenpeace, 116, 119
Grinnell, George Bird, 30–33, 39–41
Grinnell, Joseph, 96–99

Grizzlies, 24, 25, 36, 37, 75, 80, 81, 90, 91, 95, 99, 119. *See also* photo essay "Illustrations of Predators"
Grizzly King, The (Curwood), 24
Gunn, Alastair S., 110

Habitat, 7, 33, 94, 97, 98, 100, 101, 103–06, 109, 110, 112–14, 116, 120
Harper's, 64, 71, 95
Harper's Weekly, 1
Harrison, Brian, 72
Hartley, Cecil B., 34
Hawk(s), 20, 82, 83, 95
Henry, Marguerite, 112
Herbert, Henry William ("Frank Forester"), 31
Hobbs, Captain J., 81
Holy Earth, The (Bailey), 20, 94, 101
Hornaday, William T.; *The American Natural History,* 75; and New York Zoological Park, 19, 30, 69, 79; and bird protection, 40, 41; and hunting, 30, 31; *Our Vanishing Wildlife,* 30; and Ernest Thompson Seton, 19; and rejection of predators, 78–82, 84; and zoos, 69, 70. *See also* photo essays "Humanitarians and the Treatment of Animals," and "Predator Control"
Horse(s), 13, 15, 16, 31, 46, 49, 59, 72, 79, 112
How Animals Talk (Long), 17
Hughes, Rupert, 71
Humane Review, The, 45
Humane Society, 57, 112
Humanitarian, The, 45
Humanitarian League, 45, 53
Humanitarianism, 42–74 passim, 76, 124 n. 20; and abolitionism, 53, 54; and benevolence of nature, 59; and biocentrism, 7, 101, 104, 106, 108–14; and blood sports, 7, 48, 52–57, 61; and buffalo, 47; and circuses, 67–69; and cock fighting, 46; and confinement of wild animals, 7, 52, 53; and conservationists, 5, 41–43, 47, 48, 57; defined, 1, 5, 7, 43, 44,

47, 48; and environmental movement, xi; and fur wearing, 7, 119; and the importance of women, 50, 51; and meat-eating, 47, 52, 53, 59–67, 83, 109, 135 n. 21; and misanthropy, 49–50; opposition to, 6, 7, 48–50, 60, 71–73; organizations for, 45–47; origins of, 5; promotional literature of, 6, 45, 55, 57, 83; as recent development, 1, 44, 50; rejection of predators, 5, 82–84; and slaughter, 62–63, 65–67; and trapping, 57, 58, 119; and vivisection, 46, 47, 52, 53, 58, 59, 61; and wildlife habitats, 7; and zoos, 67–70. *See also* Animal rights, names of specific individuals and organizations, and photo essay "Humanitarianism and the Treatment of Animals"
Human Side of Animals, The (Dixon), 46
Human Side of Birds, The (Dixon), 46
Hunting, 27–41 passim, 75, 85, 94; as market hunting, 28–32, 38, 39; opposition to, 7, 24, 25, 27, 33, 34, 52, 54–57, 61, 109; as pot hunting, 31. *See also* Sportsmen and photo essay "Hunters":
Hunting Sports of the West (Hartley), 34
Hunting Trips of a Ranchman (Roosevelt), 33, 37
Huxley, Thomas Henry, 20–22
Hyndman, H. M., 60

Independent, 12, 52, 88
Indians, 80, 106
Industrialization, 3, 34, 43, 51, 72
Ingersoll, Ernest, 15
Insect(s), 14, 21, 82, 83, 92, 104, 107
Isle Royale National Park, 117

Jack London Club, 68, 69
Javelina, 36. *See also* Pigs
Jeffers, Robinson, 115
John Burroughs Medal, 13
Josselyn, John, 28

Kaibab Plateau, 99, 104
Kansas, 96
Kant, Immanuel, 43, 115
Kellert, Stephen R., 107, 144 n. 1
Kerr, Walter S., 76
Kingsford, Anna, 50
Kipling, Rudyard, 12
Koko (talking gorilla), 15
Kropotkin, Peter, 20
Krutch, Joseph Wood, 105

Labor, 52, 65, 66
Lacey, John F., 32
Lacey Act of 1894, 32
Lacey Act of 1900, 32, 39
Ladies' Home Journal, The, 38
Lamarck, de Chevalier, 16
Land of Little Rain, The (Austin), 81
Leonardo da Vinci, 1
Leopold, A. Starker, photo essay
    "Wildlife in the National Parks"
Leopold, Aldo, 94, 101–04, 106, 109,
    110, 112–14
Leuba, James H., 78
Liberalism, 66, 67, 70, 73, 108, 110
Liberator, The, 54
Life-Histories of Northern Animals
    (Seton), 13, 88
Lincoln, Abraham, 54
Lion(s), 68, 76, 84, 102, 105. See also
    Cougars
Literary Digest, 16, 86, 96
Literary naturalism, 10, 78
Little Brothers of the Air (Miller), 24
Little Red Riding Hood, 79
Little Tennessee River, 106
Lives of Game Animals (Seton), 13, 88
Lives of the Hunted (Seton), 24
Lizards, 92
Lodge, Henry Cabot, 31, 32
Logging, 29, 120
London, Jack, 36, 79; The Call of the
    Wild, 77, 78; and humanitaria-
    nism, 68, 69; and intelligent dogs,
    16; Michael—Brother of Jerry, 68;
    and savagery of animals, 4, 11

Long, William J., 36; and benevolence
    of nature, 19–21, 105; and excep-
    tional animals, 15; How Animals
    Talk, 17; and individuality of ani-
    mals, 14; and intelligence of ani-
    mals, 15–17; and nature faker
    controversy, 17–19; and nature
    writing, 25; Northern Trails, 19;
    and order in nature, 23; School of
    the Woods, 15, 16; on Theodore
    Roosevelt, 18, 33; and wolves, 18,
    20, 21, 88, 89
Lopez, Barry, 76, 107, 116–18
Lover of Animals, A (Salt), 70
Lyell, Charles, 10

McClure's, 49, 76
McKibben, Bill, 117, 118
Martha (last passenger pigeon), 29
Massachusetts, 39, 59, 83
Melville, Herman, 65
Merriam, C. Hart, 85
Merriam, Florence A., 14, 38
Merwin, Henry Childs, 44, 59
Metcalfe, William, 61, 62, 64
Mexico, 103
Mice, 7, 82, 83, 95, 104
Michael—Brother of Jerry (London),
    68
Michigan, 79
Midgley, Mary, 110
Miller, Olive, 14, 15, 18, 20, 24, 38
Mills, Enos, 14, 90, 91
Mining, 29
Minnesota, 75
Moby Dick (Melville), 65
Modern Temper, The (Krutch), 105
Moles, 82
Montaigne, de Michel Eyquem, 1
Montana, 86
Moore, John Howard, 42, 44, 45, 49,
    55, 57, 62, 66, 73
Moose, 82
Morris, Clara, 49, 51
Mountaineering, 35
Mount McKinley, 86

Mowat, Farley, 89, 90
Muhamed, 16
Muir, John; and angling, 56; and an-
    thropocentrism, 73, 92, 93; and
    "Back to Nature" movement, 3, 4;
    and benevolence of nature, 11, 20,
    21; as biocentrist, 114; and hunt-
    ing, 55, 56; and intelligence of ani-
    mals, 16, 18; and meat-eating, 60,
    61, 63, 64, 66; *My First Summer in
    the Sierra,* 63; and order in nature,
    23; *Our National Parks,* 3; and pas-
    senger pigeons, 28, 29; as popular
    writer, 6, 11, 12, 38; and predators,
    40–43, 95; and protection of wild-
    life, 25, 33, 84; *The Story of My
    Boyhood and Youth,* 16, 25; and
    Theodore Roosevelt, 33, 34; and
    wilderness experience, 11, 12
Murdy, W. H., 113
Murie, Adolph, 86, 97, 98, 101
Murie, Olaus, 86, 100, 101
Museum of Vertebrate Zoology, 96
Muskrat(s), 17, 58
Mutual Aid (Kropotkin), 20
My Ántonia (Cather), 79
My First Summer in the Sierra (Muir),
    63

Nash, Roderick, 42
Nation, 59
National Association of Audubon So-
    cieties. *See* Audubon Society
National Forests, 32, 33, 85. *See also*
    names of specific forests
National Forest Service, 84, 102
National Parks, 32, 33, 91, 94, 96, 100,
    111. *See also* names of specific
    parks and photo essay "Wildlife in
    the National Parks"
National Park Service, 76, 85, 91, 97–
    101, 111, 112
National Wildlife Federation, 111
Native Americans, 80, 106
Natural Food of Man, The (Car-
    rington), 64

Nature fakers controversy, 12, 13, 17–
    19, 21, 26, 88, 89, 125 n. 9
Nature writing, 9–26 passim, 76, 78;
    and benevolence of nature, 9, 11,
    19–21; and biocentrism, 104, 105;
    and calls for protection of animals,
    23–25; and hunting stories, 27, 31–
    37, 79; and importance of animals'
    perspective, 12; increases in vol-
    ume of, 4, 11; and intrinsic worth
    of animals, 114–18; as introduction
    to wildlife, 9; and morality in na-
    ture, 22, 23; as a new genre, 4, 11–
    13; and portrayals of predators,
    76–82, 86–93. *See also* names of
    specific writers and photo essay
    "Nature Writers"
Navy, 111
Neo-Lamarckianism, 16
Never Cry Wolf (Mowat), 89
New Jersey, 83
Newsweek, 7
New York, 39, 45, 46, 50, 58, 67, 83
New York Herald, 48
New York Times, 18, 56, 60, 62, 85, 95,
    96, 109, 111
New York Zoological Park, 19, 30, 69,
    79
Nineteenth Century, 10, 55
Norris, Frank, 10
Norse, Elliot, 107
North Cascade Mountains, 119, 120
North Dakota, 86
Northern Trails (Long), 19
Northwest Territories, 89
Nutall Ornithological Club of Cam-
    bridge, 33, 39

Of Wolves and Men (Lopez), 107
Oldtown Folks (Stowe), 56
One Day at Teton Marsh (Carrighar),
    104
One Day on Beetle Rock (Carrighar),
    104
Opossum, 30
Origin of Species, The (Darwin), 1

Orwell, George, 60
Otter, 30
Ouida. *See* Ramée, Marie Louise de la
Our Dumb Animals, 45, 50, 57, 59, 68
Our National Parks (Muir), 3
Outermost House, The (Beston), 107, 115
Outing, 68
Outlook, 10, 61, 85
Overland Monthly, 86, 95
Owl(s), 82, 119–21

Panthers. *See* Cougars
Passenger pigeons, 28, 29
Pearson, T. Gilbert, 40
Pelican Island, 39
Pennsylvania, 39
People for the Ethical Treatment of Animals (PETA), 108
Permanent Wild Life Fund, 102
Pets, 70
Philosophy, 109–18. *See also* Ethics and names of specific philosophers
Pierre (Melville), 65
Pig(s), 34, 36, 66, 67, 110
Pinchot, Gifford, 84, 101
Pine Cone, 102
Point Defiance Zoo, 119
Political economy, 52
Popular Science Monthly, 44, 64, 65, 73
Porcupine, 30
Porter, Gene Stratton, 15, 18, 25
Poultry, 80, 86, 95, 110
Predators, 74–93 passim; appreciation of, 86–104, 115–17; and biocentrism, 5, 6; colonial attitudes toward, 2; control of, 84–86, 94–99, 101–03; fear of, 6, 82; humanitarians' rejection of, 5, 82–84; hunters' rejection of, 5. *See also* photo essays "Predator Control" and "Illustrations of Predators"
Principles of Geology (Lyell), 10
Progressive Animal Welfare Society (PAWS), 119
Progressivism, 84

Puritanism, 2, 6, 54
Pythagoras, 1, 62, 65

Rabbit(s), 30, 49, 80, 83, 87, 95, 96
Raccoon, 30
Ramée, Marie Louise de la [pseud. Ouida], 49, 50
Ranch Life on the Hunting Trail (Roosevelt), 33
Ranching, 84, 96, 120
Rat(s), 19, 82, 107, 112
Reagan, Ronald, 19
Reiger, John F., 32, 41, 57
Remington, Frederic, 4
Reptiles, 83. *See also* names of specific reptiles
Residents Against Grizzlies in our Environment (RAGE), 120
Ringling, Charles, 69
Ringling Brothers Circus, 69
Roberts, Charles, 13, 14
Rocky Mountains, 14, 29, 91
Rodents, 80, 95, 96, 99. *See also* names of specific rodents
Rodeos, 68
Rolston, Holmes, III, 22
Romans, 61, 62
Romanticism, 2–4
Roosevelt, Theodore, 55, 84, 91; and Boone and Crockett Club, 31; and factions of conservation movement, 42; and hunting stories, 33–37; *Hunting Trips of a Ranchman,* 33, 37; and Ingersoll, Ernest, 15; interest in natural history of, 33; and nature faker controversy, 18, 19, 21; and Pelican Island, 39; and predators, 35–37, 79, 80; *Ranch Life on the Hunting Trail,* 33; as sportsman and bird lover, 40; and strenuous life, 34–36; and teddy bear, 37; as utilitarian conservationist, 27, 33, 37, 39, 41; *The Wilderness Hunter,* 34
Ross, E. A., 10
Russia, 20, 49, 79

Salt, Henry S., 47, 50, 52, 57, 68; and animal rights v. kindness to animals, 70, 71, 108; *Animals' Rights*, 45, 55, 72; and Humanitarian League, 45; *A Lover of Animals*, 70; pets, 70; and rejection of predators, 83, 108; and socialism, 65, 66; and Henry David Thoreau, 55; and vegetarianism, 60, 62, 63, 66, 67

Sand County Almanac, A (Leopold), 101, 102, 103, 104

School of the Woods (Long), 15, 16

Schurz, Carl, 32

Science, 1, 4, 5, 6, 9–12, 16, 17, 23, 25, 44, 52, 53, 61, 73, 78, 96–98, 100–02, 104–08, 116, 117, 125 n. 2, 126 n. 9. *See also* Darwinism and Ecology

Science, 14, 17, 43, 44, 61, 97

Scientific American, 69, 80

Sea Around Us, The (Carson), 104

Seals, 119

Sea Shepherd, 119

Seattle Times, 6

Seton, Ernest Thompson; *Animal Heroes*, 15; and animal rights, 24; anthropomorphism of, 23, 87, 88, 91; as artist, 4, 77, 87; and benevolence of nature, 11, 20, 105; and Boy Scouts of America, 126 n. 9; and exceptional animals, 14, 15; *Great Historic Animals, Mainly About Wolves*, 75; and intelligence of animals, 15, 88; *Life-Histories of Northern Animals*, 13, 88; *Lives of Game Animals*, 13, 88; *Lives of the Hunted*, 24, 56; and morality in nature, 22, 23; and nature faker controversy, 18, 19; and "new school" of nature writing, 11–13; and nobility of animals, 13, 14; as popular writer, 11; recipient of John Burroughs Medal, 13; *Wild Animals I Have Known*, 13, 24, 76; and wilderness experience, 11, 12, 87; and

wolves, 20, 36, 77, 79, 86–90, 116. *See also* photo essays "Nature Writers" and "Illustrations of Predators"

Sharks, 116

Sharp, Dallas Lore, 12, 18, 23

Shaw, George Bernard, 61

Sheep, 14, 15, 30, 80, 84–86, 95, 96, 105, 115, 116

Shultz, William J., 43

Sierra Club, 27, 108, 111

Silent Spring (Carson), 104, 105

Sinclair, Upton, 61

Singer, Peter, 7, 60, 109, 110, 113, 114

Skunk(s), 30, 58

Snail darter, 106

Snake(s), 20, 81, 83, 92, 95, 99, 107, 115

Socialism, 65, 66, 68

Society for the Prevention of Cruelty to Animals (SPCA), 45, 46, 49–51, 59, 83; and animal acts, 62; and interest in wild birds, 48, 57; and interest in wildlife conservation, 47; *Our Dumb Animals*, 45, 50, 57, 59, 68; and zoos, 68. *See also* Humanitarianism and names of specific leaders

Society for the Prevention of Cruelty to Children, 46

Song of the Cardinal, The (Porter), 25

Speciesism, 113, 135 n. 21

Spider(s), 20, 107, 113, 115

Sportsmen, 27–41 passim, 42, 75, 94, 120; and etiquette in the field, 31, 34; v. humanitarians, 48; opposition to, 7, 24–27, 33, 34, 52, 54–57, 61, 109, 119; and plume trade, 42; stories for, 27, 31–37; and utilitarian conservation, 5, 27, 28, 30–33, 37, 39, 41. *See also* Boone and Crockett Club, Hunting, names of specific sportsmen, and photo essay "Hunters"

Squirrel(s), 14, 15, 21, 30, 90, 107, 120

Stevenson, Robert Louis, 10

Story of My Boyhood and Youth, The
    (Muir), 16, 25
Stowe, Harriet Beecher, 53, 54, 56
Strange Case of Dr. Jekyll and Mr.
    Hyde, The (Stevenson), 10
Sunday Mercury, 83
Sunset, 102

Teddy bear, 37
Tellico Dam, 106
Temperance, 60, 66, 68
Tennyson, Alfred, 10, 83
Texas, 79, 86
Thomas, Keith, 72, 123 n. 5
Thoreau, Henry David, 3, 33, 54, 55,
    63
Thousand-Mile Walk to the Gulf, A
    (Muir), 92
Tiger(s), 55, 83
Transcendentalism, 3, 63, 97
Trans-Species Unlimited, 119
Trapping, 57, 58, 85, 86, 88
Turner, James, 43, 52, 58, 60
Turtle, 50

Uncle Tom's Cabin (Stowe), 53
Universal Kinship, The (Moore), 73

Vegetarianism, 47, 49, 52, 59–67, 83,
    109, 135 n. 21
Victor, Frances Fuller, 81
Vivisection, 58, 59. See also Anti-
    vivisection
Vogue, 38
Voice of the Desert, The (Krutch), 105
Vulture(s), 81, 82, 115

Wake-Robin (Burroughs), 38
Walden (Thoreau), 3, 55, 63
Waldorf-Astoria, 46
Walton, Izaak, 31
Washington (state), 59
Watt, James, 112
Waugh, Frank A., 102
Weasel(s), 81, 89
Weeks-McLean Act of 1913, 39

Weismann, August, 10, 16
Westminster Review, 68
Whale(s), 110, 119
Wheeler, William Morton, 17
Whitmore, O. S., 75
Wild Animals I Have Known (Seton),
    13, 19, 24
Wilderness, 2–4, 11–13, 21, 34, 35, 69,
    82, 90, 102, 103, 105, 109, 120
Wilderness Hunter, The (Roosevelt), 34
Wilderness Society, 100
Wildlife, xi–121 passim; colonial atti-
    tudes toward, 2, 67; and conflicts
    with feral animals, 111; cruelty to-
    ward, 7, 24–27, 45–48, 50–52, 54–
    57, 60–64, 66–70, 72–75; destruc-
    tion of, 28–30, 37–39, 84–86, 94–
    99, 101–03, 105; economic value
    of, 28, 29, 86, 113; and endangered
    species, 106, 110, 119–21; and exo-
    tics, 29, 100, 111; extinction of, 28,
    29, 121; medieval attitudes toward,
    78; modern attitudes toward, 6, 7;
    Native American attitudes toward,
    80, 106; and perceptions of abun-
    dance, 28; and poaching, 32. See
    also Animals and names of specific
    animals
Wild Life in the Far West (Hobbs), 81
Wild Life in the Far West (Simpson),
    35
Wild Life in the Rocky Mountains
    (Thomas), 35
Williams, Howard, 61
Wilson, Alexander, 28
Wisconsin, 55, 102, 103
Woodchuck, 30
Wolves, 21, 78, 83, 85, 94, 95, 97; ag-
    gression of, 36, 77, 79, 80, 81; ap-
    preciation of, 75, 86–90, 103, 104,
    116, 117; fear of, 6, 75, 82, 87;
    feeding habits of, 18, 75, 87; and
    reintroduction into the wild, 119,
    120. See also photo essay "Illustra-
    tions of Predators"
Women's rights, 60

Worster, Donald, 84, 97, 113
Wright, Mabel Osgood, 20, 21, 24, 38

Yellowstone National Park, 32, 82, 91, 94, 99, 119, 120
Yosemite National Park, 33, 91, 96, 99, 100
Yosemite Natural History Association, 82

Yosemite Nature Notes, 91, 98, 100
Yosemite Zoo, 91, 99

Zoos, 19, 29, 30, 69, 79, 91, 99, 119; opposition to, 7, 52, 67, 68, 108, 119. *See also* names of specific zoos and photo essay "Humanitarians and the Treatment of Animals"

ABOUT THE AUTHOR

LISA MIGHETTO received her Ph.D. from the University of Washington in 1986. Currently, she teaches environmental and western history at the University of Puget Sound. Her publications have appeared in *Harper's*, *Environmental Review*, *Pacific Historical Review*, *Pacific Historian*, *Sierra*, *Columbia*, and *The Alaska Journal*. She also edited *Muir Among the Animals: The Wildlife Writings of John Muir*. Her most recent work concerns the environment of the Pacific Northwest— and she is now writing a book on that topic.